EXPLORING CHURCH HISTORY

EXPLORING
CHURCH
HISTORY

A Guide to History, World Religions, and Ethics

Three Books in One

JAMES P. ECKMAN

CROSSWAY BOOKS
WHEATON, ILLINOIS

Exploring Church History: A Guide to History, World Religions, and Ethics

Copyright © 2002, 2004 by Evangelical Training Association

Previously published as separate books:
Exploring Church History © 2002
The Truth About Worldviews © 2004
Biblical Ethics © 2004

Three-in-one edition first published 2008.

Published by Crossway Books
        a publishing ministry of Good News Publishers
        1300 Crescent Street
        Wheaton, Illinois 60187

Cover design: Jon McGrath

Cover illustration: Jessie McGrath

First printing 2008

Printed in the United States of America

Exploring Church History: unless noted otherwise, Scripture quotations are taken from *The New American Standard Bible.* Copyright © 1960, 1962, 1963, 1968, 1971, 1972, 1973, 1975, 1977, and 1995 by The Lockman Foundation. Used by permission.

Scripture references marked ASV are from the *American Standard Version of the Bible.*

The Truth About Worldviews: Scripture quotations are taken from *The New American Standard Bible.* Copyright © 1960, 1962, 1963, 1968, 1971, 1972, 1973, 1975, 1977, and 1995 by The Lockman Foundation. Used by permission.

Biblical Ethics: Unless noted otherwise, Scripture quotations are taken from *The New American Standard Bible.* Copyright © 1960, 1962, 1963, 1968, 1971, 1972, 1973, 1975, 1977, and 1995 by The Lockman Foundation. Used by permission.

Scripture references marked NIV are from *The Holy Bible: New International Version.* Copyright © 1973, 1978, 1984 by International Bible Society. Used by permission of Zondervan Publishing House. All rights reserved. The "NIV" and "New International Version" trademarks are registered in the United States Patent and Trademark Office by International Bible Society. Use of either trademark requires the permission of International Bible Society.

Library of Congress Cataloging-in-Publication Data

Eckman, James P. (James Paul)

Exploring church history : a guide to history, world religions, and ethics / James P. Eckman.

    p. cm.

   "Three books in one."

   First published as: Exploring church history. Wheaton, IL. : Crossway, c2002. 2nd published as: The truth about worldviews. Wheaton Il. : Crossway Books, c2004. 3rd published as: Biblical ethics. Wheaton IL. : Crossway Books, c2004.

   Includes bibliographical references.

   ISBN 978-1-58134-977-1 (tpb)

   1. Church history. 2. Religions. 3.Apologetics. 4. Christianity—Philosophy. 5. Christian ethics. 6. Postmodernism—Religious aspects—Christianity. I. Title.

BR145.3.E25   2008

230—dc22   2007039500

VP		18	17	16	15	14	13	12	11	10	09	08
15	14	13	12	11	10	9	8	7	6	5	4	3	2	1

CONTENTS

BOOK ONE:
EXPLORING CHURCH HISTORY

INTRODUCTION

IN GENERAL MOST CHRISTIANS are abysmally ignorant of their Christian heritage. Yet an awareness of the history of God's church can help us serve the Lord more effectively. First, knowledge of church history brings a sense of perspective. Many of the cultural and doctrinal battles currently being fought are not really that new. We can gain much from studying the past. Second, church history gives an accurate understanding of the complexities and richness of Christianity. As we realize this diversity and the contributions many individuals and groups have made to the church, it produces a tolerance and appreciation of groups with which we may personally disagree. Finally, church history reinforces the Christian conviction that the church will triumph! Jesus' words, "I will build My church," take on a richer meaning.

As the chapter titles indicate, this book takes a chronological approach to church history—The Ancient Church, The Medieval Church, The Reformation Church, and The Modern Church. Each chapter emphasizes the theological progress and developing consensus within the church on what the Scriptures taught, as well as the institutional development of the church. The chapters on the Reformation (6 and 7) stress the restructuring and fragmentation of the church during the sixteenth and seventeenth centuries. One cannot understand the church today without this background.

Finally, the last five chapters of the book give consideration to the church's struggle with the modern world. Darwinism, Marxism, industrial capitalism, antisupernaturalism, and the challenge of poverty have pressured the church in multiple ways. To a great extent these struggles continue today. Yet through the modern missions movement and revivals, God continues to accomplish His redemptive purposes.

You are about to begin an exciting study. It is my prayer that this book will change your life. I trust that when you are finished, you will have a deeper appreciation for your splendid heritage and a profound conviction that Christ's church will triumph.

ABOUT THE AUTHOR

Dr. James P. Eckman is the Academic Vice-President, Dean, and Professor of Bible and History at Grace University in Omaha, Nebraska. He holds a B.S. from Millersville University of Pennsylvania, an M.A. from Lehigh University, a Th.M. from Dallas Theological Seminary, and a Ph.D. from the University of Nebraska. While at Dallas Theological Seminary, he received the Charles A. Nash Award in Historical Theology. An ordained minister, Dr. Eckman's specialty is in historical theology, with an emphasis on the American church and revivalism. In addition to hosting a weekly radio program, *Issues in Perspective*, he also performs dramatic monologues on figures from church history such as Augustine, Martin Luther, John Calvin, and Jonathan Edwards. He is married and is the father of two children.

Chapter One

FOUNDATION OF THE CHURCH: THE APOSTOLIC AGE

But when the fullness of the time came,
God sent forth His Son . . .

IN GALATIANS 4:4 the apostle Paul wrote, "But when the fullness of the time came, God sent forth His Son." Paul realized that the first century was a unique period of history, the precise time for God's Son to enter human history.

Unlike any previous period, the Mediterranean world was united. Throughout this world, the imperial armies of Rome maintained a forced peace—the famous *Pax Romana* (30 B.C.–A.D. 180). As the army guarded the empire from robbers and pirates, trade flourished on both land and sea. Prosperity and wealth followed. Rome brought stability and order to its cities, with free food and public games at the taxpayers' expense.

The Roman roads provided an infrastructure that knit the empire together. As a result, the army could be anywhere in the realm within two weeks. Communications from the emperor traveled with a speed unheard of in previous empires. In God's providence, the early church also utilized this communications network to spread the Gospel.

As the imperial army moved with ease through its domain, it carried out the orders of the Caesar with efficiency and discipline. But the Gospel also penetrated the army. For example, Paul speaks of believers in the Praetorian guard, an elite force closest to the emperor (Phil. 1:13). Also, Christianity first came to Britain through Roman soldiers. So significant was the impact of Christianity on the army that one historian called the Roman army the "mouthpiece of the gospel" (Cairns, 37).

The Roman world was also a Greek world. Rome conquered the Greeks militarily, but in many ways the Greeks conquered Rome intellectually. The common language of the day was *koine* Greek, the language spread throughout the empire by Alexander the Great. In God's sovereignty, this was the language of His revelation, the New Testament. In addition, Greek philosophy heavily influenced the way the Roman world thought. Greek philosophers wanted to know truth and the place of human beings in the universe. Despite the variations within Greek philosophy, most of its philosophers shared the belief that there was a realm beyond the physical world, the domain of the transcendent. Christianity took advantage of this hunger for truth and for transcendent reality. Witness Paul's argument with the philosophers in Acts 17, his presentation of Jesus in Colossians 1, and John's philosophical argument in his Gospel and First Epistle. The Greco-Roman world was intellectually "set up" for the Gospel.

The Roman world also pulsated with religious exhilaration and anticipation. Josephus, a first-century Jewish historian, told of the Eastern cults, false messiahs, and religious fervor that permeated the empire. Many in Israel envisioned the Messiah coming at any moment. The Zealots wanted a revolution against Rome. The Essenes wanted a prophet of light who would expel the darkness of evil. The Pharisees wanted a nationalist leader who would restore the law and free Israel from Rome's oppression.

Furthermore, after the Jewish exile of earlier centuries and the subsequent Diaspora (the migration of Jews throughout the Roman Empire), the synagogue system represented a Jewish presence in every major city. Each time Paul entered a city, he first took the gospel message to the Jews in the synagogue. Only after that did he move on to the Gentiles.

THE LEADERS OF THE APOSTOLIC CHURCH
Peter

Pentecost (fifty days after the crucifixion and ten days after the ascension of Christ) marks the birth of the church. As the Spirit filled the 120 believers who were waiting and praying, the miracle of tongues caused a sensation. Some observers accused the Christians of drunkenness. At this point, Peter emerged as the spokesperson for the early church.

Peter dominates the first fifteen chapters of Acts. As the first among the Twelve to see the resurrected Christ, he emerged as the leader of the small community of believers before Pentecost (Acts 1:15). He even insisted that Judas Iscariot be replaced.

At Pentecost he preached the Spirit-inspired sermon that produced three thousand converts. He cut through the fog of exclusive Judaism by declaring of Jesus that "there is salvation in no one else; for there is no other name under heaven that has been given among men by which we must be saved" (Acts 4:12). He performed miracles, defied the Jerusalem authorities, disciplined Ananias and Sapphira, and set up deacons as helpers so the apostles could study and preach. Despite his slip at Antioch when he withdrew from fellowship with Gentile converts (Gal. 2:14), he championed the Gospel's penetration into the Gentile world.

As the decisive speaker at the Jerusalem Council (A.D. 49) in Acts 15, he brilliantly defended Gentile church membership. After the council, the book of Acts is silent concerning Peter; his activities simply cannot be pinpointed with any certainty. We can, however, be definite about his authorship of 1 and 2 Peter.

Was Peter the founder of the Roman church, its first bishop, and hence its first pope? Incomplete evidence shows he did do missionary work in Antioch and later in Rome, but there is no evidence that he was Rome's bishop or that he stayed long in Rome. In fact, recent scholarship has shown that the church had a presbyterian structure into the second century and was rather decentralized into the fourth. It is difficult to argue that Rome was the ecclesiastical, let alone theological, center of the early Christian church. At best, it was merely a place of honor.

The end of Peter's life is wrapped in tradition. The best evidence establishes that Peter died a martyr's death during Nero's persecutions, about A.D. 68. The apocryphal *Acts of Peter* contends that he died crucified upside down on a Roman cross. That he was crucified would fit Christ's words of John 21:18-19. Of the rest of the tradition, we simply cannot be sure.

John

As one of the "pillars" of the Jerusalem church (Gal. 2:9), John, brother of James and son of Zebedee, was Peter's coworker (Acts 1:13; 3:1–4:23; 8:14-25). Together they healed and preached in the name of Jesus the Messiah. When ordered to stop, they obeyed God rather than men. By laying hands on the new Samaritan converts, Peter and John exercised general supervision over the burgeoning church in Samaria. Although he was probably at the Jerusalem Council of Acts 15, his name does not appear in Acts after his brother James was martyred (Acts 12:1-2). We do not know when he left Jerusalem.

The book of Revelation reveals that John was exiled, probably in the early nineties by Roman Emperor Domitian, to Patmos for preaching the Word of God and for his "testimony of Jesus" (1:9). There John recorded the visions he "saw," which constitute the framework for understanding events surrounding the second coming of Christ. Emperor Nerva apparently released John from exile sometime between A.D. 96 and 98.

After his exile the most reliable evidence places John in Ephesus, where, after living to an old age, he died a natural death. In Ephesus he trained such disciples as Polycarp, Papias, and Ignatius—all strategic leaders of the second-century church. Indeed, this mentoring role may give meaning to his self-described title, "the elder," in 2 and 3 John.

John's most significant contribution to the church was his writing. His Gospel is unique. Only 8 percent of it is related in the synoptic Gospels of Matthew, Mark, and Luke; the remaining 92 percent is original with John. Most exceptional is his instruction regarding the deity of Christ. Jesus is the eternal *Logos* (1:1-18), the great "I am" (8:58).

John likewise gives emphasis to the Spirit, especially in the Upper Room Discourse (14–16). There Jesus asked the Father to send another Helper who will indwell believers, teach them truth and enable them to recall it, and convict the world of its sin, righteousness, and judgment. It is the Spirit who regenerates (3:6), and it is He who brings satisfaction and fulfillment to those who believe in Jesus (7:37-39).

Paul

The other decisive leader of the apostolic church was Paul, in whose life three great ancient traditions intersected. Religiously, he was a Jew, culturally a Greek, and politically a Roman. He was born in Tarsus, a major university town and the principal city of the province of Cilicia. Paul understood his Jewish heritage in terms of the Abrahamic covenant (Phil. 3:5-6). His parents may have named him Saul after Israel's first king, who was also of the tribe of Benjamin. Paul was trained in Pharisaism at the rabbinic school in Jerusalem headed by Gamaliel (Acts 22:3; Phil. 3:5). His familiarity with Greek authors (Acts 17:28; 1 Cor. 15:33; Titus 1:12) and his use of Greek argumentation (Rom. 2:1–3:20; Col. 1:15-20) suggests a Greco-Roman influence.

The Pharisees were not particularly tolerant of new religious movements. So when the "people of the Way" spread to Damascus (Acts 9:1-

2), Rabbi Saul had no problem receiving a commission from the high priest to extradite Jewish Christians to Jerusalem. On the road to that city, Saul met his resurrected Messiah.

Approximately thirteen years separated Paul's conversion and his first missionary journey (A.D. 48). Paul claimed to be *the* missionary to the Gentiles. The missionary journeys that Luke documented in Acts bear this out. The first of these probably provoked the most controversy.

During that trip (Acts 13–14), Paul and Barnabas evangelized Cyprus and the southern part of Galatia. As Gentile churches flourished, two fundamental questions surfaced: What was the relationship between Christianity and Judaism? How is a person justified? A Judaistic group from Judea insisted that circumcision was necessary for salvation— something that contradicted Paul's free-grace Gospel. Hence the Jerusalem Council of Acts 15.

The council affirmed Paul's doctrine of free grace, adding only that Gentile converts abstain from certain practices. Thus the mother church affirmed Paul's ministry of justification by faith plus nothing! Following the council, Paul embarked on two additional missionary journeys that are recorded in Acts 15:26–21:16.

After these journeys he went to Jerusalem to report to James and the elders about his activities in the Gentile churches. There, as a result of trumped-up charges, Roman authorities arrested him. Over the next two years, Paul was imprisoned in Caesarea and stood trial before the Roman procurator Felix, his successor Porcius Festus, and Herod Agrippa II, the titular king of the Jews. Asserting his Roman citizenship, he appealed to Caesar and headed for Rome where officials placed him under house arrest.

Because of the difficulty of determining the exact chronology and place names that appear in the Pastoral Epistles (1 and 2 Timothy and Titus), it seems best to assume that Paul was subsequently released and ministered for six more years (A.D. 62–67). Some scholars even suggest that Paul not only ministered to Asia Minor and Greece but also reached Spain before he was arrested at the height of Nero's persecutions. He was most likely executed by decapitation in the spring of A.D. 68.

SIGNIFICANT WOMEN OF THE NEW TESTAMENT

The Scriptures affirm the equality of men and women, both created in the image of God (Gen. 1:26-27) and in their position in Christ (Gal. 3:28). While the Bible proclaims equality of the sexes, it also argues for functional differences (role differences) within the home (Eph. 5:22-33; Col. 3:18-19) and within the church (1 Cor. 11:2-16; 14:33-36; 1 Tim. 2:8-15; 3:1-13; 5:1-25; Titus 1:6-9). Whatever the precise meanings and applications of these crucial Pauline passages may be, church history bears witness to an extraordinary number of women in the early church.

The Gospel was a liberating force in the ancient world, challenging old and established traditions rooted in human prejudice. These gradually died. Contempt, discrimination, and demeaning references often characterized rabbinic teachings about women. Rabbis, for instance, were encouraged not to teach women or even speak to them. According to Jewish tradition, women could never be a part of the count needed to establish a synagogue. But Luke cited both men and women who were baptized and persecuted and who contributed to the growth of the church (Acts 5:14; 8:12; 9:2; 17:4, 12).

Women in Jesus' Day

The challenge to ancient traditions began with Jesus' earthly ministry, in which women played a most significant role. Many women financially supported the ministry of Jesus and His disciples and ministered to Him personally (Matt. 27:55-56; Mark 15:40-41; Luke 8:3). The Gospels usually depict Mary, sister of Martha, as seated at Jesus' feet—an honor normally given to men. Several women had the immensely important distinction of bearing the news of Christ's resurrection—a quite remarkable honor in light of strict Jewish teachings on valid testimony.

Not only were women involved in the ministry of Jesus, but they participated in the events at Pentecost (Acts 1:14). Since the narrative of events in the Upper Room continues into Acts 2, we must assume that the women present were likewise filled with the Holy Spirit at Pentecost (2:1-4).

Women in the Early Church

The book of Acts also gives accounts of women who played active roles in ministry in the early church. Dorcas (Tabitha) was the only woman in the New Testament to be called a "disciple" (9:36). Her death caused a major stir in Joppa, prompting the believers to urge Peter to travel from nearby Lydda. Peter prayed, and Dorcas was raised from the dead! Mary of Jerusalem, John Mark's mother (12:12), was a wealthy widow whose house became the vital hub of the Jerusalem church. There the young church found refuge and security during the intense persecutions of Herod Agrippa. Lydia, a wealthy woman of commerce and apparently Paul's first convert in Europe, opened her home to Paul and Silas (16:14-15).

But the early church did not limit women to nonverbal ministry. One of the more remarkable women of the New Testament was Priscilla (Prisca). She and her husband, Aquila, early converts to the faith, were banished from Rome. They became intimate friends with Paul, with whom they shared hospitality and the craft of tent-making (Acts 18:1-3). In some way they had risked their lives for Paul (Rom. 16:3-5), perhaps at the same time heightening his awareness of the growing church in Rome. Most significantly, both Priscilla and Aquila took Apollos, the eloquent preacher from Alexandria, "and explained to him the way of God more accurately" (Acts 18:26). Obviously Priscilla knew biblical truth and could explain it with clarity. That the ministry of this couple was well known and widespread is evidenced by the frequent references to them in Paul's writings (Rom. 16:3; 1 Cor. 16:19; 2 Tim. 4:19). Tradition has it that Priscilla was martyred in Rome.

Another woman of New Testament significance was Phoebe (Rom. 16:1-2). Because she was probably the bearer of Paul's letter to the Romans, Paul commends her to the Roman church, asking that they "receive her in the Lord in a manner worthy of the saints," and "help her in whatever matter she may have need of you." He also says of her that she was a "helper," which clearly implies active and important functions in the church. Was she, therefore, representing Paul in some official capacity, as perhaps a "deaconess" ("servant" of v. 1), as some have argued? From these two verses, we simply cannot be certain she held an authoritative office in the church at Cenchrea. However, it is clear that Phoebe was significant enough for Paul to go out of his way to single her out and ask the Roman church to take care of her.

Two passages indicate that women functioned as prophets in the early church. Acts 21:9 introduces Philip the evangelist as having four daughters who were "prophetesses." From Paul's instruction in 1 Corinthians 11:5, it would seem that Philip's daughters were not exceptions, for Paul's instructions about women's head coverings occurs in the context of women "praying or prophesying" in the worship service. Whatever the nature of these ministries, women gifted by the Holy Spirit exercised notable responsibilities in the early church.

Other women of the New Testament fulfilled pivotal ministry roles. Euodias and Syntyche (Phil. 4:2-3) were identified as "fellow workers" with Paul, a remarkable designation when one remembers that Paul also labeled Titus and Timothy "fellow workers." Paul classified Andronicus and Junias [Junia] (Rom. 16:7)—probably a husband and wife—as "outstanding among the apostles," most likely a reference to their role as ones commissioned by the Roman church for special duties, not the New Testament office of apostle. Finally, in the list of "fellow workers" in Romans 16, ten of the twenty-nine people commended by Paul were women.

Women thus played a decisive role in the beginning of Christianity. Their work both complemented the duties of men and involved some leadership responsibilities. Although there are no recorded examples of women evangelists, elders, or formal teachers of biblical truth, their function was both vibrant and vital in the ongoing progress of the Gospel—a clear testimony to the liberating power of Jesus Christ.

With the deaths of Peter, Paul, and John, the mantle of leadership passed to a new generation, the Apostolic Fathers. The Fathers stood on the shoulders of giants, but their theology was often undeveloped. We take up their story in the next chapter.

FOR FURTHER DISCUSSION

1. What was the Pax Romana, and what were some of its characteristics?
2. How did the great Roman road system aid the spread of the Gospel?
3. What were some of the important contributions that Greek philosophy made to the setting of the Roman world?
4. Who were some of the groups of first-century Judaism, and what were their expectations?
5. List some of the decisive contributions that Peter, Paul, and John each made to the apostolic church.
6. In what roles were women involved in the early church, according to the New Testament?

Chapter Two

THE APOSTOLIC FATHERS

The test of one's doctrine is following the bishop.
The Episcopal office comes from God, not from man.
Christians are to respect him as they respect
God the Father.

IGNATIUS OF ANTIOCH, EPISTLE TO THE EPHESIANS

BY THE END OF THE FIRST CENTURY, the death of the apostles produced a leadership vacuum in the church. Who had the authority to
lead the believers? Who would guide and guard this flourishing new
Christian faith? A group generally called the Church Fathers filled the
gap.

As a term of affection and esteem, "father" was generally given to
spiritual leaders of the church (known as elders or bishops). The Fathers
can be divided into three groups: the Apostolic Fathers (A.D. 95–150),
the Apologists (A.D. 150–300), and the Theologians (A.D. 300–600).
The Apostolic Fathers wrote what was generally devotional and edifying in nature; the Apologists produced literature that defended the faith
and countered error; the Theologians began doing systematic theology.
The next several chapters cover each of these groups.

This chapter concentrates on the Apostolic Fathers, individuals who
wrote Christian literature and gave leadership to the church from A.D.
95 to 150. Their writings reflected a deep commitment to the Old
Testament and an understanding that the new faith of Christianity fulfilled the Old Testament. There is, therefore, little theological reflection
or doctrinal analysis from the Apostolic Fathers. Their desire was to edify
and exhort the saints and give them the hope they needed to persevere.
We can best describe their work as devotional, pietistic (encouraging
holy living), and pastoral.

The Apostolic Fathers served and led a church exploding with growth and zeal. Such realities demanded counsel, advice, and practical guidelines for spiritual growth and action for both individual Christians and local church bodies. Thus the writings of the Apostolic Fathers often glorified martyrdom and celibacy and stressed the importance of baptism in ways that make modern evangelicals quite uncomfortable. But the time in which they wrote, the first fifty years of the second century, marked a church struggling with how to live obediently and how to structure the church in a vastly pagan culture.

Clement of Rome

As the bishop, or elder, of Rome, Clement (A.D. 30–100) shouldered the responsibility for dealing with a major disturbance in Corinth. As when Paul wrote to the church forty years earlier, the Corinthian church suffered from factionalism and bitterness. Therefore, Clement exhorted the Corinthians to exercise love, patience, and humility as the key to develop sound Christian interpersonal relationships. He also underscored obedience to church leadership as essential for church harmony and desperately needed unity.

Because it is the earliest example of Christian literature outside the New Testament, Clement's letter to the Corinthians is profoundly important. He quoted the Old Testament so frequently that we can readily see how dependent the early church was on its authority. His many allusions to Paul's writings and life also show how widespread Paul's influence was. Finally, as Clement called for obedience to the church leadership, he argued that church elders received their authority from the apostles, who received their authority from Christ. Over the next several centuries, the church decisively expanded this idea of succession.

Ignatius

Because of his martyrdom, Ignatius is considered a giant among the early Church Fathers. The bishop of Antioch in Syria, he was arrested by Roman authorities for his Christian testimony. As he made his way to Rome for execution, he visited several cities along the way. His subsequent letters to these seven churches, written about A.D. 110, stressed the twin themes of heresy and unity. The heresy he addressed was an early form of Gnostic teaching (see the next chapter), which denied the full humanity of Jesus. Thus Ignatius argued that the best defense against such heresy and the foremost guarantee of unity was the bishop.

When Ignatius called for submission to the bishop, he revealed a subtle change developing in the early church. The New Testament documents show a plurality of church leadership in the first century, principally elders and deacons. However, the growth of the church in the empire demanded a greater degree of authority and superintendence over the local churches. That is apparently why Ignatius stressed to the elders and deacons of the seven churches that they submit to a bishop who would coordinate and rule over their local churches. This, he claimed, was necessary to deal with false teaching and to foster unity among the churches. Subsequent generations of church leaders expanded the office of bishop.

The Shepherd of Hermas

Written about A.D. 150 by a freed slave, *The Shepherd of Hermas* is a rather bizarre work of five visions patterned somewhat after John's book of the Revelation. In graphic detail, Hermas, drawing on personal experiences of himself and his family, depicted the evils of a decadent civilization very much in decline. Repentance and the call to holy living dominate the work.

Polycarp

As a disciple of the apostle John and as bishop of Smyrna, Polycarp wrote a most significant letter to the church at Philippi about A.D. 110. The value of this letter with its copious Old Testament quotations is its dependence on many of the circulating books of the New Testament, especially those written by Paul. This letter shows that the early second-century church regarded the New Testament books as authoritative in calling Christians to holy living.

Polycarp's martyrdom at age eighty-six in A.D. 155 remains one of the great narratives of the early church. At his trial he did nothing to provoke his accusers but passionately defended Jesus Christ as his Lord. He died at the fiery stake, giving praise to his Lord. Venerated for centuries as a model martyr, Polycarp illustrates the truth stated by the apologist Tertullian later that "the blood of martyrs is the seed of the church."

Didache

One of the most significant of the early church writings is the *Didache*, or *The Teaching of the Twelve*. Probably written during the first decade of the second century as a church manual, the *Didache* presents a remarkable picture of early church life. The manual gives counsel on how to do baptisms, how to conduct worship services and the Lord's Table, and how to exercise church discipline. The book likewise furnishes valuable advice on how to detect false teaching in the church. The final part of the manual exhorts Christians to holy living in light of the second coming of Jesus.

Other writings of the Apostolic Fathers survive, and each reflects the themes summarized in this chapter. However, in about A.D. 150 a significant change occurs in the writings of the church leaders. One notes a more apologetic style as the leaders combat theological error creeping into the church. This shift marks the beginning of the second group of Church Fathers known as the Apologists, the subject of the next chapter.

FOR FURTHER DISCUSSION

1. Summarize the reasons why the church used the term "father" when referring to their early leaders.
2. What are the three major chronological periods of the Church Fathers?
3. List three characteristics of the writings of the Apostolic Fathers.
4. Who did Ignatius say was the best defense against heresy and the greatest promoter of unity? Why did he say that?

Chapter Three

DEFENDING THE FAITH: ENEMIES WITHIN AND WITHOUT

The blood of the martyrs is the seed of the church.
Tertullian

DEFENDING CHRISTIAN TRUTH has always been of foremost importance in church history. As the church moved into the late second century, this need was especially acute, for both inside and outside the church false teaching and error abounded. Thus God raised up a group of individuals—the Apologists—who defended the Christian faith and, in doing so, led the church toward deeper theological truth. Error forced the church to think more precisely about what it believed and to reach a consensus on what the Scriptures taught.

Most of the error was a crude mixture of Greek philosophy, Judaism, and other Eastern beliefs that assailed Christian teaching about Jesus Christ and His work. Nonbelievers often characterized Christians as atheists, cannibals, or immoral people. The first criticism arose because Christians refused to worship the emperor or the Greco-Roman gods. The second accusation resulted from a misconception about the Lord's Supper and the third from a misunderstanding of the love displayed within the early church.

HERESIES OUTSIDE THE CHURCH

Gnosticism

No other heresy threatened early Christianity more than Gnosticism. Reaching its height in the second century, Gnosticism had its origins at least a century earlier. At its center, this philosophy has a dualistic view of reality. The material world and the immaterial world were totally separate, the material being intrinsically evil and the immaterial being intrinsically good. For the Gnostics, it was inconceivable that a good God could have created such an evil, material world. Thus they argued that a divine spark, or emanation, from God created the physical universe. It was equally difficult for the Gnostics to believe that Jesus could have had a physical body. Many Gnostics argued Jesus only "appeared" to have a physical body.

These teachings were part of a special body of knowledge, or *gnosis*, that was necessary for salvation. This special knowledge God imparted only to an elite few. Because the soul alone was good, salvation was purely spiritual; there was no place for the resurrection of the body in Gnosticism. The very heart of Christianity was at stake!

Manichaeism

A bizarre cousin to Gnosticism, Manichaeism also was rooted in dualism. Following the teachings of Mani (216–276), this philosophy proclaimed that two opposing forces, light and darkness, were in eternal combat. Salvation was achieved by the children of light through a life of self-denial and celibacy.

Neoplatonism

Built on the teachings of Plato, this highly mystical challenge to Christianity taught that the goal of all humans was reabsorption into the divine essence. Reabsorption was accomplished through various processes including meditation, contemplation, and other mystical disciplines. Salvation was purely spiritual with no Jesus, no cross, and no atonement.

ERRORS WITHIN THE CHURCH

Marcionism

Marcion was a second-century heretic who established a vibrant rival church in Rome. He argued that there were two gods—a creator and a redeemer. The former was the god of the Old Testament, who was evil and capricious. The latter was the god of love and redemption, whom Jesus Christ revealed.

Because of his view of God, Marcion also developed his own canon of Scripture. He totally rejected the Old Testament for its portrayal of God. He likewise repudiated major segments of the New Testament, accepting only portions of Luke's Gospel and only ten Epistles of Paul.

Marcion thought that all the other books betrayed a Judaistic, Old Testament bias.

This man's ideas were poison to the early church. As a person of wealth and influence, he used both to establish a rival church in Rome that actually lasted for several centuries. In God's sovereignty, Marcion's influence was positive; he forced the church to think more carefully and systematically about the nature of the Godhead and about the canon of Scripture.

Ebionitism

This strange movement emerged late in the first century and continued into the fourth. In many ways, Ebionitism resembled the false teaching with which Paul did battle in the book of Galatians. Ebionites taught that Jesus was the prophetic successor to Moses—not the eternal second person of the Trinity. Furthermore, the Ebionites were legalists who viewed Jesus as an exalted man who perfectly kept the law. Coming from their dualism, they were ascetics, practicing a life of poverty, self-denial, and often elaborate rituals. Legalistic to the core, Ebionites challenged the free-grace Gospel of Christianity.

Montanism

Started by Montanus, this movement had its center in Phrygia (modern Turkey) in the second century. Central to Montanus was the revelation— the "New Prophecy"—that the coming of Christ was near. Obedience to the Paraclete (the Holy Spirit) through His messenger—Montanus— was the standard. Necessarily, the movement involved use of the sign gifts as evidence of anointing for the Second Coming. The movement also advocated a rigid asceticism that included celibacy and prolonged fasting. The Montanists challenged the authority of church officials and stood outside the developing New Testament canon. For these reasons, the church condemned the Montanists. The contribution of the movement was that it forced the church to think more precisely about the Holy Spirit's role in Christianity.

EMPIRE PERSECUTIONS

For the first few decades of the church, the Roman Empire regarded Christianity as a sect of Judaism and largely left it alone. However, with the growth of the church, this policy changed. Caesar Nero ruthlessly persecuted Christians in the late 60s. But the first empire-wide persecutions did not occur until the reign of Decius in 250, who attempted to enforce sacrifices to the Roman gods.

The most merciless persecutions occurred under Emperor Diocletian in the early 300s. He ordered the destruction of church buildings, the burning of the Scriptures, the closing of church meetings, and the imprisonment of Christians. Later he made the refusal to sacrifice to the gods a capital crime.

Increased persecution forced the church to determine what was really important. For what were church members willing to die? For what holy writings were members willing to die? The Apologists sought to determine the answers to these questions.

MAJOR APOLOGISTS AND THEIR WRITINGS

Justin Martyr

Justin was born about 100 in the biblical town of Shechem in Samaria. Extremely well educated for his day, Justin dabbled in all the popular philosophies—those of the Stoics, Plato, and Aristotle. He even committed himself for a while to the philosophy of the mathematician Pythagoras.

But, as he explained in his book *Dialogue with Trypho*, his search for truth ended when, while walking along the seashore near Ephesus, he met an elderly Christian who steered him toward the Scriptures. The correspondence between Old Testament prophecies and their fulfillment in Jesus Christ impressed him. At the age of thirty-three, he embraced the Christian faith.

He continued to pursue philosophical truth, but this time through the grid of the revealed truth of Scripture. Although he founded a Christian school in Rome, his ministry was largely an itinerant one of presenting the superior philosophical position of Christianity. It alone could bring the balanced and noble life that the ancients had sought in Greek philosophy.

Through this ministry, he gathered many disciples, among them Tatian, another famous Apologist. He also battled Marcion. Justin condemned Marcion's view of God as heretical and defended the Old Testament as God's Word. As he demonstrated the continuity of the two Testaments, Justin quoted or alluded to all four Gospels, Acts, eight of Paul's epistles, and 1 Peter. His defense of the integrity of God's Word was crucial to the developing conviction of the New Testament's authority.

However, Justin's greatest legacy was his writing. He wrote two *Apologies* and the penetrating *Dialogue with Trypho*. The two *Apologies* were directed to the Roman government and offered a brilliant defense of Christianity as far superior to any of the pagan religions or philosophies. He likewise targeted what he saw as the thoroughly unjust persecution of Christians.

His *Dialogue with Trypho* is essentially the narration of a conversation between Justin and Trypho, an educated Jew who was immersed in Greek philosophy. Quite central to the book is Justin's obvious passion to convince Jews that Jesus was the prophesied Old Testament Messiah. At the end of the book, Justin eloquently appealed to Trypho to accept the truth about Jesus and the Christian faith.

Like most of the early church leaders, Justin's theology was not well developed. He believed in the Trinity and the deity of Jesus, but he did not work out the complexities of the Godhead or the relationship between the deity and the humanity of Jesus. His background in Greek philosophy was often more of a hindrance than a help.

During a trip to Rome, about 165, Justin and six other Christians were arrested. After a mock trial in which they refused to recant their faith, they were all beheaded—hence the name, Justin Martyr.

Irenaeus

Irenaeus was one of the earliest and most distinguished opponents of Gnosticism. He was born in Asia Minor around 135. There he knew and was apparently influenced by Polycarp. Irenaeus may have been one of the early missionaries to Gaul (modern France), for by 177 he was the recognized bishop of Lyons. There he spent his life pastoring, teaching, commissioning missionaries to the rest of Europe, and writing. He was evidently martyred about 202.

Two major works of Irenaeus survive: *The Demonstration of the Apostolic Preaching* and *Against Heresies*. The first work detailed the Christian faith proved from Scripture and called for readers to defend proper doctrine against heresy. The second work clearly targeted the Gnostics. From his writing we can conclude much about the developing theology of the second-century church.

First, he was the earliest of the Apologists to have a fully developed view of scriptural authority. His arguments refer to both Testaments; in fact, he quoted or alluded to all but four of the New Testament books. He also saw great continuity between the two Testaments, presenting Jesus as the fulfiller of Old Testament prophecies.

Second, because the Gnostics had such a distorted view of Jesus, Irenaeus considered Jesus Christ the very core of theology. Christ was the basis for the continuity between creation and redemption. What human-ity lost in Adam is regained in Christ. In attacking Gnostic dualism, Irenaeus also argued for the literal nature of Jesus' physical body and the absolute centrality of the resurrection of the physical body.

Third, despite his orthodox positions on many central issues of the-ology, his beliefs held seeds of error that would later flower in medieval Catholicism. For example, in dealing with the Gnostics, he emphasized the physical presence of Christ in the bread and cup—an early form of transubstantiation. Also, his choice of words when it came to the ordi-nance of baptism seem to indicate that forgiveness accompanied the ordi-nance. Finally, as he contrasted Adam and Christ, he gave a special place to Mary, Jesus' mother, as the "new Eve." He taught that her obe-dience made possible the restoration of humanity. Such teaching was evi-dence of the developing veneration of Mary that would characterize mature Roman Catholicism.

Origen

Thoroughly committed to the inspiration and authority of Scripture, Origen wrote the first real systematic theology in church history as well as numerous commentaries on books of the Bible. He was born and lived part of his life in Alexandria, Egypt, one of the important intellec-tual and theological centers of the early church. After finishing his stud-ies, he became head of the Catechetical School at Alexandria, a position he held for twenty-eight years. Due to a struggle with the Alexandrian bishop, Origen ended up in Caesarea where he ministered for the remaining twenty years of his life. He suffered intense torture during the Roman persecutions and died around 254.

Because Origen wanted the church to combat the growing heresies, he committed himself to making the tools for Bible study available. Most significant was his extraordinary work called the *Hexapla*, an edi-tion of the Old Testament including the Hebrew text, the Greek translit-eration of the Hebrew text, and four available Greek translations in six parallel columns. A monumental work that took twenty-eight years to complete, it enabled Christians to study the Old Testament with all avail-able scholarship in one book. It also verified the accuracy of the Septuagint, the major Greek translation of the Old Testament.

Origen's interpretation of the sacred text got him in trouble. He taught that allegory was the key to unlock the mysteries of the text, and it was up to the interpreter to find the allegorical key. The centrality of Christ in Scripture gave his method its dynamic. For example, when it came to the Levitical laws and ceremonies, literalness did not help, he argued. Only allegory aided the interpreter in seeing Jesus in the Levitical system.

His championing of the allegorical method profoundly influenced scriptural interpretation for hundreds of years. Yet the influence of allegorical interpretation has been largely negative. Who is to decide if the proper hidden meaning has been found? What is the standard? As a tool for interpretation, allegory is simply too subjective.

Origen's zeal to serve the Lord also resulted in a deep devotion to asceticism—a life of self-denial—and greatly impacted the monastic communities of later centuries. In his commentary on the Song of Solomon, he stressed that material things and even other people can hinder a person from attaining the deeper spiritual life. Therefore, he denied himself adequate sleep, fasted, and walked barefoot.

The Apologists made their mark in church history as they contended for the faith and began to systematize theological truth. Through their work the church reached consensus on the twenty-seven books of the New Testament canon. The church also inaugurated its ecclesiastical structure, with the office of bishop becoming more significant. Most importantly, the Apologists laid the foundation for the mature theological reflection that characterized the Theologians, the topic of our next chapter.

FOR FURTHER DISCUSSION

1. Summarize Gnostic and Manichaean dualism. What does it mean? Why is it incorrect?
2. Explain why the Gnostic view of Jesus was wrong.
3. In what ways are Gnosticism, Manichaeism, and Neoplatonism similar?
4. What was the Ebionite view of Jesus?
5. Why was Marcion a threat to Christian beliefs about the Bible?
6. Where was the error of Montanism?
7. Summarize Justin's contribution as an Apologist.

The Apologists

Who?	Major Writings?	Main Focus?
Justin Martyr (circa A.D. 100–165)	*Two Apologies, Dialogue with Trypho*	Defense of authority of the Old and New Testaments
Irenaeus (circa A.D. 135–202)	*The Demonstration of Apostolic Preaching, Against Heresies*	Attacked the dualism of the Gnostics by defending the centrality of the physical resurrection of Jesus
Origen (circa A.D. 185–254)	*Hexapla*	Developed tools for Bible study

Chapter Four

THE ANCIENT CHURCH AND THEOLOGY

O God! Our souls find no rest until they rest in you.

<small>AUGUSTINE</small>

About the year 300, the winds of theological change were blowing through the church. Theological disputes over the nature of the Godhead, the nature of Jesus, and the doctrine of salvation caused the church to systematize its beliefs and reach consensus on what the Scriptures taught. Spiritual giants such as Athanasius and Augustine dominated this period and solidified the theology of Christianity. This period is profoundly important for our understanding of church history.

THE PREINCARNATE NATURE OF JESUS CHRIST

Controversy erupted in the early 300s over the teachings of a North African priest named Arius. Influenced by Greek rationalism, Arius argued for an absolute monotheism that denied the deity of Jesus and claimed that He was a created being. Similar to modern Jehovah's Witnesses, Arius contended that "there was a time when he was not" (Kelly, 228). Jesus was, therefore, of a different essence than the Father. Arius's commitment to Greek thought demanded that God, who is spirit and absolutely indivisible, could never truly identify with humanity, which is basically material. The two were forever irreconcilable. Thus only a creature, created within time, could possibly bridge that gap. That creature was Jesus Christ.

The Roman Emperor Constantine, himself a Christian who had ended the persecution of the church in A.D. 313, called the Council of

Nicea in 325 to deal with the uproar. Three positions were represented at Nicea: 1) Jesus was of a *different* essence from the Father (Arius); 2) Jesus was of the *same* essence as the Father (Athanasius); 3) Jesus was of a *like* essence to the Father (a compromise position).

The debate was heated and often bitter. But the creed that Nicea produced forthrightly condemned Arius as a heretic. Arguing that Jesus was of the *same* essence as the Father, the Nicene Creed declared Jesus to be "true God from true God" (Leith, 30). And denying one of the central tenets of Arianism, the council proclaimed Jesus as "begotten, not created" (Leith, 31).

Arius's arch opponent was Alexander, bishop of Alexandria, whose personal secretary was Athanasius. Athanasius played a small but important role at Nicea. But for the next forty-five years, he defended the Nicene formula. He taught that the members of the Trinity are coequal, coessential, and coeternal. He powerfully linked the doctrines of the Trinity and salvation. From Scripture he argued that God created humanity in His image, but through sin, humanity abandoned Him and His image. Thus a new creation was necessary, and only God could be the Savior of fallen humanity. No man could possibly provide this needed redemption. For Athanasius, then, the deity of Jesus Christ and the salvation of fallen humanity were inextricably linked. This Apologist was willing to suffer any punishment or persecution to defend that crucial bond, for to deny the deity of Jesus was to emasculate the Gospel.

THE THREE CAPPADOCIANS—DEFENDING THE TRINITY

One of the most profound truths of the Christian faith is the doctrine of the Trinity. It separates Christianity from all other world religions.

The Bible teaches in Deuteronomy 6:4 that God is one; yet from the New Testament it is clear that this one God consists of three persons—Father, Son, and Holy Spirit. The church has always affirmed this doctrine as orthodox, but wrestling with its theological and philosophical implications has been difficult. Especially in the early church, this struggle often produced heresy.

The ancient church of the third and fourth centuries was plagued with false teaching that challenged the deity of Jesus and the Holy Spirit. Whether it was the teachings of Arius or a group called the Pneumatomachians, the Son and the Spirit were regarded as subordinate to the Father. In order to preserve the oneness of God, others argued that Jesus was a man who was adopted as the Son of God; thus He was not eternally the Son.

Others contended that there was one God who revealed Himself in one of three modes—Father, Son, or Spirit. To decide the issue, the early church asked, "Is this what the Scriptures teach?" More specifically, what precise, descriptive words could guard against heresy when it comes to explaining the relationship between the Father, Son, and Spirit? Even into the fifth century, the church labored over these questions.

The orthodox doctrine of the Trinity was a product of a series of debates and councils, sparked in large part by heretical teaching from within the church. It was the collaboration of three friends, the Three Cappadocians—Basil of Caesarea (circa 330-379), Gregory of Nazianzus (circa 329-389), and Gregory of Nyssa (circa 330-394)—that produced the victory over many of these heresies. God clearly used them in a mighty way to formulate the truth about the relationship between the members of the Godhead. Until modern religious liberalism emerged in the nineteenth century, their work provided the definitive framework for thinking and speaking about the Trinitarian God we worship.

Brief biographical sketches place all three as key leaders in the Eastern church. Basil was born into a wealthy Christian family in what would be modern Turkey. Well educated in the schools of Greece, he was appointed bishop of Caesarea. His influence in the development of monasticism was enormous.

His brother, Gregory of Nyssa, became a teacher of rhetoric and was appointed bishop of Nyssa. While the Arians were in resurgence in the Eastern empire, he was deposed and sent into exile for five years. Their mutual friend, Gregory of Nazianzus, was also educated at the universities at Alexandria and Athens, where he met Basil. To one degree or another, each was philosophical, mystical, and monastic. But they shared a deep commitment to orthodox Nicene Christianity. Passionately, each defended the members of the Trinity as coequal, coessential, and coeternal.

Perhaps Basil made the most significant contribution in championing the orthodox view of the Trinity. The language used by theologians of the early church often depicted the Son as subordinate to the Father; He was thus in some way inferior. When it came to the Holy Spirit, there was very little discussion at all.

Basil showed that when we think of the Trinitarian God, we must always separate the terms "essence" and "person"; they are not synonyms. "Essence" is what makes God, God. Attributes such as omnipotence, omnipresence, and omniscience are involved here. "Person" is a term that defines the distinctions within that one essence. Thus we can correctly say "God the Father," "God the Son," and "God the Spirit," while maintaining that they are one and inseparable in being. Basil was also the first theologian to write a major treatise on the Holy Spirit in which he offered proofs for the deity of the Spirit.

Gregory of Nazianzus took the argument a step further. Agreeing with his friend Basil's contention of the difference between essence and person, Gregory showed that the difference between the three persons is relational. This relationship is delineated as eternally the Father, eternally the Son, and eternally the Spirit. Eternally there has been love and communion between the persons of one essence that constitute the Trinity.

Basil's brother, Gregory of Nyssa, also showed that the difference between the members of the Godhead is not one of essence or of substance. The difference can be grounded only on the inner relations and functions of each. Any language that results in the Son's being subordinate to the Father or of the Spirit's being subordinate to the Son is simply unacceptable.

Thus the Trinity is one God of three persons whose difference is relational and functional, not essential. We do not have three gods or three modes of God; we have one God. Ephesians 1:1-14 illustrates the point quite well—the Father chooses, the Son redeems, the Spirit seals (see also 2 Cor. 13:14; 1 Pet. 1:2). Each member of the Godhead is intimately involved in the drama of salvation. We thus can follow Paul and praise the Trinitarian God of grace!

It is difficult for us in the modern church to imagine how much the early church struggled with choosing the proper words when discussing the nature of the Godhead. But in each generation God raised up individuals to protect the church from error. The Three Cappadocians teach us the importance of precise thinking when it comes to the Trinity. Their precision won the day at the Council of Constantinople in 381 where the forces of heretical thinking were defeated.

DEFINING THE DOCTRINE OF THE GOD-MAN

The touchstone of theological orthodoxy is the person of Christ. Both His deity and His humanity must be affirmed, or the entire doctrine of salvation is affected. Only a Jesus who is truly God and truly man can provide a complete salvation for humanity.

A problem in the early church was explaining how Jesus' deity and

His humanity related. At any given point in His earthly life, how did His two natures blend? Was He more God or more man? How should we view the union of these two natures in the one person? The debate over Jesus' two natures troubled the church for more than 300 years, at least until 451 at the Council of Chalcedon, when the definitive statement about Jesus' two natures was written.

As one studies the early church, it becomes clear that the emergence of error usually prompted the church to seek a more satisfactory explanation of a theological question. This was true of the doctrine of Christ. Throughout the period from 325 to 451, major interpretations emerged, often heretical, that challenged the church to think more precisely about defining the relationship of Jesus' two natures.

The Alexandrian School

Two schools of theology, one in Antioch and the other in Alexandria, Egypt, framed the debate on the nature of Christ. The Alexandrian school claimed such luminaries as Athanasius and the great Origen. Influenced by Greek philosophy, especially Plato, the Alexandrians tended to elevate the spiritual—Christ's deity—at the expense of His humanity.

Following logically from the Alexandrian position came the heresy propagated by Apollinarius. He was a friend of Athanasius and Basil the Great as well as a teacher of the great Jerome. However, he taught that Jesus was fully God but that His "rational soul" was supplanted by the divine *Logos*. This meant that Jesus was not completely human.

The Council of Constantinople in 381 condemned Apollinarius as a heretic because his view affected the doctrine of salvation. How could Christ sufficiently die for humans if He was not totally a man Himself? The council thus concluded that Jesus had to be completely human and completely divine.

The Antiochene School

The second major school of theology, in Antioch, was influenced by Aristotle, who saw man as a unity of soul and body, not a dichotomy. This school gave far more importance to the unique distinction of Jesus' two natures than did the Alexandrians. The Antiochene emphasis logically produced the heresy Nestorianism, named after Nestorius, who further challenged the church's thinking about Jesus.

As Patriarch in Constantinople in 428, Nestorius held a powerful position in the early church. For several reasons he was uncomfortable with the way the Alexandrians were using certain phrases about Jesus, all of which he thought amounted to a dangerous mixing of the human and divine natures of Christ. His solution was to maintain an absolute distinction of the two natures to such an extent that the only connection between them was the will.

The best analogy of how Nestorius viewed Christ was as a Siamese twin. Because the patriarch could not imagine deity being involved in human suffering or change, he insisted that the two natures were artificially joined. Even though some modern scholarship doubts whether Nestorius actually taught this, this teaching was condemned as heresy at the Council of Ephesus in 431.

It was clear that neither the rigid two-nature model of Nestorius nor the careless one-nature theory of Apollinarius corresponded with the biblical data. In Jesus' confrontation with the Samaritan woman at the well in John 4, His two natures seemed to be in perfect communion. At any given moment in time, He was both God and man. Thus a position was needed that would combine the strength of both proposals.

A monk from Constantinople named Eutyches proposed a model for understanding Christ that attempted to reconcile Apollinarius and Nestorius. He refused to maintain a clear distinction between the two natures of Jesus; instead, he argued for a mixture of the natures such that a third confused mingling was the result. The analogy of dropping a few drops of oil into a pail of water illustrates the point—both the oil and the water are present, but the distinction between the two is not clear. The result of Eutyches' teaching was a confused mixture, not fully God or man.

The Council of Chalcedon

To settle this critical matter of how to view the two natures of Jesus, a major council of more than 400 church leaders was called at Chalcedon in 451. After much debate, these leaders affirmed a statement rooted in Scripture that has singularly remained the most important declaration about Jesus Christ in the history of the church.

The statement proclaimed Jesus to be both God and man in one person. It declared that both natures are joined in a miraculous way so neither nature is damaged, diminished, or impaired. His two natures are joined "unconfusedly, unchangeably, indivisibly, and inseparably" (Leith, 36). Salvation is thus secured for those who profess faith in Jesus because His sacrifice was as both saving God and identifying man.

From Chalcedon, then, the church taught that Jesus is undiminished deity plus perfect humanity united in one person, without any confusion of the two natures. In the absolute sense of the term, He is the God-man!

We live in a world where religious cults are threatening orthodox truth at every turn. If church history teaches us anything, it is this—precision of language in doctrinal matters is imperative. Any choice of words when describing Jesus that diminishes His deity or His humanity is incorrect and heretical.

The miracle of the Incarnation stretches our finite minds to the limit. The great legacy of the Council of Chalcedon reflects a consensus on the language that preserves both the complete deity and humanity of Jesus in His person. A complete salvation demands it; faith in the God-man, Jesus Christ, procures it.

AUGUSTINE—THEOLOGIAN OF GRACE

A quest for truth—no phrase better describes the work of the great theologian Augustine (354–430). After years of struggle with lust and doubt, he wrote of God: "You made us for Yourself, and our heart is restless until it finds rest in You" (*Confessions*, Book 1:1). His quest for truth found its satisfaction in the person of Christ, whose saving grace became the vital center of his theology. Augustine powerfully captured that personal search for truth in *The Confessions*, one of the truly profound spiritual autobiographies of history.

Born in northern Africa of a pagan father (Patricius) and a devout, godly mother (Monica), Augustine excelled as a student, especially in the ancient art of rhetoric. This introduced him to the genius of the Roman rhetorician, Cicero. Although Cicero was not a Christian, his writings started Augustine on his pursuit of truth and wisdom.

One of Augustine's greatest intellectual hurdles was the problem of evil—how could a good God permit a world filled with evil, pain, and suffering? He thought he had found the answer in Manichaeism. But when he examined Faustus, an important leader of the Manichees, his disillusionment with Faustus's arguments caused him to abandon the system. He tried other philosophies, but none satisfied his yearning for truth and wisdom.

Another intense battle of Augustine's early adulthood was with immorality and pride. For many years he kept a mistress, who bore him an illegitimate son. Because none of the philosophical systems he tried made demands on his personal morality, he believed his immoral lifestyle was justified. Too, his passion for personal fame in the academic world consumed him.

Seeking fame and fortune, Augustine traveled to Rome and Milan hoping to teach his beloved rhetoric. There he met Ambrose, the bishop of Milan. Ambrose's brilliance impressed Augustine, for Ambrose showed Augustine that his objections to Christianity were shallow and mistaken.

Augustine's conversion in 386 came, however, not through intellectual argumentation alone, but through an emotional encounter with the Almighty. In a garden outside Milan, he sat one day pondering the philosophical questions with which he had been toiling. As he tells it in his *Confessions*, he heard a child's voice say, "Take and read." He took up Paul's letter to the Romans (especially 13:13-14) and there found his questions answered. "All the shadows of doubt were swept away," he wrote (*Confessions*, Book 8:12). In God's Word, he found truth in the person of Jesus Christ. He also found the power to shatter his bondage to lust and self-seeking glory, and he found the peace and purpose for life that none of the intellectual fads of his day could provide. He experienced the power of God's grace that would define the rest of his life.

Augustine changed radically, breaking all ties with his immoral past. After Ambrose baptized him in 387, he returned to northern Africa where he embarked on a lifetime of study and devotion to Christ's church. He became a priest in 391 and in 395 the bishop of Hippo, a city west of Carthage. His enormous power and influence were felt for many years from that bishopric, especially through his voluminous writing.

Augustine's contributions to the church were extensive; in so many ways he was a transitional figure in church history. First, he defended the free-grace Gospel of Christ against many opponents, of which none was more threatening than Pelagius.

Pelagius, a British monk, taught a system that denied original sin and the need for God's grace in salvation, thereby championing a radical man-centered theology. Man, in effect, had the ability to save himself. Augustine leveled the definitive response at Pelagius. He affirmed the guilt and corruption of all humans because of Adam's sin and the absolute need for God's saving grace. Following Paul, Augustine formulated the doctrines of election and predestination that would powerfully influence Luther and Calvin centuries later. Augustine's theological system was God-centered, with salvation totally and causatively effected by God.

Second, Augustine's *Treatise on the Holy Trinity* is a magnificent theological masterpiece. In it he saw the God of the Bible as an eternal, transcendent, infinite, and perfect triune God. In defining God as a

Trinity in one essence, his work constituted the capstone of centuries of theological thought on the nature of God. There was little debate on the nature of the Trinity after Augustine.

In his work on the Trinity, Augustine also solved his personal struggle with the problem of evil. For him, the Bible taught that God created the universe out of nothing (*ex nihilo*) and created humans and angels with a free will. Free will explained how evil entered into a good universe—Satan, some angels, and humans chose to rebel against God. Grace was the only explanation of why God chose to redeem humanity through His Son.

Third, his *City of God*, rooted in a belief in God's sovereignty and providence, postulated the first genuine Christian philosophy of history. Written as a response to the destruction of Rome in 410 by the Visigoths, this work saw history as a story of two cities—the city of God and the city of man.

Each city is motivated by contrary loves—the city of God by love for God and the city of man by love of self. Both will continue until the end, when God will bring eternal condemnation on the rebellious city and eternal salvation to the obedient one. Therefore, Augustine argued, Rome fell, as will all cities of man, because it was sinful, idolatrous, and rebellious. Only God's city will triumph.

Other aspects of Augustine's theology deserve comment. Because of his ascetic lifestyle, he found repugnant any reference to a literal millennial kingdom on earth. He rebelled against the idea of God bringing in a kingdom of material goodness and physical abundance. So he allegorized passages like Revelation 20 and taught that these verses referred to the present age, not a literal thousand-year reign of Christ.

In an age when intellectual fads and promiscuous lifestyles continue to enslave, the life of Augustine remains a compelling one. He demonstrated that only God's grace can break the chains of sin, for Jesus alone provides the answers to life's vexing questions. Once Augustine found life's key, he stood as a model of erudition and brilliance explained only by the power of God's grace.

The Theologians achieved doctrinal consensus on what the Scriptures taught about the Trinity and Jesus Christ. The matter of the roles of God and man in the dynamic of salvation was not as easy. Increasingly, the official position of the Roman Catholic Church rendered man's role as equally important, so that salvation was taught to be a cooperative effort between man and God.

FOR FURTHER DISCUSSION

1. Summarize Arius's beliefs about Jesus.
2. What were the three theological positions represented at the Council of Nicea?
3. What three words best summarize Athanasius's position on the members of the Trinity?
4. Summarize the work of the Three Cappadocians on the nature of the Trinity.
5. Where was the error of each of the following—Apollinarius, Nestorius, Eutyches?
6. What was the importance of the Council of Chalcedon in 451?
7. Summarize the differences between Augustine and Pelagius.

Chapter Five

THE MEDIEVAL CHURCH

Jesus Christ . . . whose body and blood are truly contained in the sacrament of the altar under the figures of bread and wine, the bread having been transubstantiated into His body and the wine into His blood by divine power.

<small>FOURTH LATERAN COUNCIL, 1215</small>

IN CHURCH HISTORY THE medieval church comprised the period from about 600 to 1517. The collapse of the western Roman Empire in the fifth century left an enormous vacuum in Western Europe. The political, economic, social, moral, and intellectual structures of an immense civilization no longer existed. Undeniably, the institutionalized Roman Catholic Church filled this vacuum. The papacy gained legitimacy, monasticism became entrenched, Islam exploded across the Mediterranean, and the Crusades resulted. As the church grew in influence and power though, it became corrupt and ineffective. This is the story of the medieval church.

GREGORY I AND THE PAPACY

Protestant church historians generally maintain that institutionalized Roman Catholicism began with Gregory's appointment as bishop of Rome in 590. Though he refused the title of pope, administratively he organized the papal system of government that characterized the entire medieval period. Thus all the major bishoprics of the West looked to him for guidance and leadership. He likewise standardized the liturgy and theology of the burgeoning Roman church. Doctrines such as the veneration of Mary, purgatory, an early form of transubstantiation, and praying to departed saints found their infant pronouncements in his writings.

Gregory also promoted missionary activity among the Germanic tribes. The various Germanic groups that had destroyed the western empire needed to hear the Gospel. Gregory's zeal for missions led him to send dozens of monks to northern Europe, especially England. Many in England came to Christ, and Canterbury became the English center of Catholicism. Gregory laid the foundation for the great edifice known as Roman Catholicism.

Two other factors contributed to the growing power and prestige of the Roman bishop. First, an early king of the Franks, Pepin the Short (714–768), granted the pope extensive land in central Italy—the Donation of Pepin—making the Catholic Church a temporal and political power in Europe. Second, the Donation of Constantine allegedly gave power and authority to the Roman bishop when Constantine relocated his capital to the East. The document was later discovered to be a forgery. Both, however, solidified the position of the pope.

MISSIONARY ACTIVITY TO THE GERMANIC TRIBES

A number of independent Germanic kingdoms, each ruled by a pagan king, replaced the mighty Roman Empire. In an attempt to reach these kingdoms for Christ, missionary activity exploded across Europe. The English missionary named Boniface (circa 672–754) was the greatest of these missionaries.

Born in the Anglo-Saxon kingdom of Wessex in the early 670s, his original name was Winfrid. He was trained in a Saxon monastic school in Exeter and exhibited a mastery of the Scriptures and the ministry skills of teaching and administration. By the age of thirty, he was ordained. At this point he developed a fervor for missions. His ambition was to join another missionary, Willibrord, in Frisia (the Netherlands).

Winfrid sought the support of both the bishop of Rome (by now largely accepted as the pope of the church) and the ruler of the Franks. He received the endorsement of both, gaining the Roman name of Boniface in the process. From Frisia he launched his missionary thrust into Germany, which would consume his energy for the remainder of his life.

Boniface ministered in the areas of Hesse and Thuringia and led thousands of pagan Germans to the Lord. Furthermore, where there had been nothing but idolatrous heathenism, he planted scores of churches.

Symbolic of the triumph of Christianity over German paganism is the story of the felling of the Oak of Thor at Geismar in Hesse. Thor, the Nordic god of thunder, was revered by the Germans, and this oak tree was dedicated to his power and glory. With resolute zeal, Boniface chopped down the tree and used the wood for the foundation of a church dedicated to St. Peter.

He also brought remarkable organization to the burgeoning German church. In 732 the bishop of Rome appointed him archbishop over Germany. By pressing for an educated, disciplined, and pure clergy, Boniface systematically purged the German church of lazy, incompetent clerics and the lingering rites and rituals of German paganism. Using missionary volunteers from England, many of whom were women, he advanced organization and structure in the German church and filled it with zeal for obedience, service, and outreach.

Besides his administrative and missionary work, Boniface established monasteries throughout Germany, the most famous being at Fulda. Boniface was a Benedictine monk, who followed the Great Rule of Benedict of Nursia (the founder of monasticism in the West). The Benedictines emphasized poverty, chastity, and obedience to Christ. This rule became the norm for monastic communities throughout Europe. Monasteries became places of worship, devotion, prayer, and study— oases in the midst of pagan terror and decadence. Monks copied the Scriptures and early Christian classics. In fact, monasteries were the only educational centers during much of the medieval period. Over the hundreds of years of medieval civilization, however, these places of self-denial gradually became places of immorality, self-indulgence, and materialistic pursuit. The ones Boniface founded were largely places of education, hospitality, and missionary outreach. It is clear that God used them.

Boniface also nurtured the growing relationship between Franks and the church centered in Rome. The bishop of Rome needed protection, and the king of the Franks was willing to give it. Boniface secured special recognition from the pope for the Frankish king, Pepin, thereby nourishing what would flower into a powerful church-state alliance much later in the medieval period.

MISSIONARY ACTIVITY IN IRELAND

Similar pioneer work was done by Patrick (circa 389–461) among the Irish people. As Celts, the Irish people had never been a part of the Roman Empire. Although they had contacts with Britain, the Irish Celts were culturally, economically, and politically different. As Rome declined, it abandoned Britain as too difficult to defend; so the church filled the vacuum. The spiritual outreach to Ireland was primarily the work of Patrick.

He was born in Britain in 389, apparently to an affluent Christian family. Tragically, at the age of sixteen, he was kidnapped and sold into slavery in northern Ireland, where he worked as a shepherd and farmer. Yet in God's sovereignty, his conversion to Christ dates from this period. He wrote in *The Confession* that God opened his eyes and "showed him his sins."

After six years in slavery, he escaped, eventually ending up back in Britain. There, he apparently furthered his education and received a vision from the Lord calling him back to the Irish people who had enslaved him. As an itinerant minister, he understood the evangelistic dynamic of the Christian faith. He discerned that it alone offered what the Druid priests could not—peace to a land troubled by tribal warfare. He, therefore, developed a strategy for winning the tribal leaders of Ireland to Christ. All evidence indicates that many local lords and kings became Christians. As they converted, they guaranteed protection for the successful spread of the faith throughout Ireland. Some estimates suggest more than 100,000 converts as a result of Patrick's ministry.

Additionally, the Irish church became a missionary-sending church. From the strategic island of Iona, where a notable monastery existed, Columba (521–597) launched out to convert the Scots and Picts of Scotland and the Angles and Saxons of northern England. Columba became one of the greatest missionaries in church history. But without Patrick, there would have been no Columba, for Patrick led Columba's grandfather to Christ and baptized him.

God thus used Patrick to transform Ireland from a land saturated with the secretive magic and the occultist practices of the Druids to one devoted to Christ and His kingdom.

ISLAM

During the sixth and seventh centuries, the rise of a new monotheistic faith—Islam—drew great numbers of members away from the Roman Catholic Church. The religion centers on Mohammed (circa 570–632), the prophet of Allah, who claimed he had received a series of revelations from the angel Gabriel. Those revelations were later inscripturated in the Qur'an (Koran). The hub of the Qur'an, called the Witness, is that there is one God, Allah, and Mohammed is his prophet. To say this in faith is to become a Muslim, one who submits to God.

In addition to reciting the Witness, Muslims observe four other pillars of faith. Devout Muslims pray five times daily, pay alms to the poor, fast during the daylight hours of the month of Ramadan, and make a pilgrimage to Mecca. The theology of Islam thus concentrates on winning the favor of Allah through the practice of the faith.

Islam spread quickly. As Mohammed preached faith in Allah, he met tremendous resistance and in 622 fled from Mecca to Medina—the most important event in Islamic history. By 630 he had reconquered Mecca and established control over much of the Arabian peninsula. By 732 his successors had overcome Palestine, northern Africa, and Spain and were only stopped at the Battle of Tours in France. The military vacuum left by the collapse of western Rome and the jihad, or holy war, proclaimed by the Qur'an, help to explain the swift conquest of Islam. Huge territories once dominated by Christianity were lost, many of which have never been recovered.

"NE'ER THE TWAIN SHALL MEET"

After the fall of Rome, the Eastern and Western wings of the Roman Catholic Church faced differing circumstances. With no emperor to interfere, the Western popes gained power as they dealt with the chaos left by the barbarian invaders. By contrast, the Eastern Empire's ruler interfered in the affairs of the Eastern church, which also had to spend resources and energy fighting Islam.

The two branches of the church also took different positions on a number of issues. In the second century they had disagreed over when to celebrate Easter. They also differed on the issue of celibacy for clergy below the rank of bishop and on the use of statues and pictures of saints in churches. The most serious disagreement came in 867 when the Eastern patriarch accused the Western church of heresy for saying that the Holy Spirit proceeded from the Father and the Son rather than just from the Father.

Relations between the two churches became increasingly hostile until a minor issue brought the factions into a confrontation in 1054. All the bitter feelings and differences from the past erupted in the discussion. The meeting ended with the Roman delegates excommunicating the patriarch and his followers. Not to be outdone, the patriarch anathematized the pope and the Western church. From that time on the Roman

Catholic Church and the Greek Orthodox Church have gone in different directions.

THE CRUSADES

Muslims were predominantly Arabs until the eleventh century when the Seljuk Turks assumed control over much of Islamic territory. Much more fanatical and brutal, the Turks harassed Christian pilgrims and threatened the security of the Eastern church. Hence, in 1095 Pope Urban II issued a call to deliver the holy places of Palestine from Muslim hands. The response of Christian Europe was overwhelming. From 1095 to 1291, waves of Christian warriors set out to accomplish Urban's goal. Few of the Crusades were successful.

There were seven major crusades, with dozens of smaller ones. The first crusade (1095–1099) was the only successful one. The crusaders established the Latin Kingdom in Jerusalem, which lasted several decades. They built castles to defend their holdings and organized several orders of knights to protect the holy places. But their effort was in vain. Gradually, the Muslims regained control of Palestine and drove out the Christians.

The Crusades radically transformed Christian Europe. Culturally, as crusaders returned from the East, they brought new foods and clothing with them. Educationally, books from the ancient world that had been preserved by the Muslim Arabs became available to Europeans. Economically, trade revived, the church gained new wealth from the wills of soldiers lost in battle, and a new class—the middle class—began to take hold in the West. Politically, as kings taxed their subjects to gain revenue, their power increased. In many ways, the Crusades were a defining moment in the medieval church. People's loyalties were no longer directed solely toward the church. Over time the church was simply not as important in their lives as it once was.

ROMAN CATHOLIC SCHOLASTIC THEOLOGY

Key questions throughout church history have been these: Reason and faith—are they enemies or allies? Is the Christian faith reasonable, or is it simply a blind leap that is ultimately irrational? A major advance in answering these questions came with the emergence of a group of medieval theologians called the Scholastics. Prominent among them was Anselm of Canterbury (1033–1109) and Thomas Aquinas (circa 1225–1274).

Anselm devoted most of his adult life to suggesting reasonable arguments for theological propositions he had already embraced as truth by faith. His goal was not to attain faith through reason; rather, he wanted to use reason as a tool to better understand what he already believed. For Anselm, faith preceded and guided reason. He wrote in *Proslogion*, "I believe in order to understand." Through reason he sought to strengthen and give understanding to his faith. His was a "faith seeking understanding."

In his writings, Anselm gave reasonable proofs for God's existence and compelling reasons for God as the self-existent, incorporeal, almighty, compassionate, just, and merciful one. In his book *Why the Godman?* Anselm also demonstrated the crucial interrelationship between the incarnation of God's Son and His atonement for sin. His argument that Christ's atonement infinitely satisfied God powerfully influenced the thinking of Luther and Calvin centuries later.

The apex of Scholastic theology, however, was reached with Thomas Aquinas. His life of scholarship forever shaped the direction of institutionalized Catholicism. So profound was his influence that he earned the nickname "The Angelic Doctor." His magnum opus was *Summa Theologica*. In the *Summa* he maintained that philosophical reasoning and faith were perfect complements: Reason leads one to the "vestibule of faith."

Aquinas gave critical support to the distinctive doctrines of the Christian faith, including the attributes of God, the Resurrection, and *ex nihilo* creation. However, his defense of the veneration of Mary, purgatory, the role of human merit in salvation, and the seven holy sacraments through which God conveys grace are without biblical support. In addition, his idea that the Communion elements at the prayer of consecration become sacrificially the actual body and blood of Christ was rejected by Luther and the other sixteenth-century reformers as unbiblical.

THE CHURCH ON THE EVE OF THE REFORMATION

The Roman Catholic Church of the fourteenth and fifteenth centuries experienced a crisis of authority. Upheaval within and remarkable pressures from without undermined its credibility and legitimacy. The result was that the church was positioned for the Reformation of the sixteenth century.

Due to the politics of late medieval Europe, Clement V relocated the seat of the papacy to Avignon, France, in 1309. Under the dominance of France, the Avignon papacy was nicknamed the "Babylonian Captivity of the Church." Attempts to end this intolerable situation produced two duly-elected popes, one in Avignon and one in Rome, in what was called the Great Schism (1378–1417). Finally, the Council of Constance, with the insistence of the Holy Roman Emperor, ended the schism. The solution, however, raised serious questions about the authority of the papacy, further dividing the church leaders.

In addition to these political questions, the church was racked by corruption and fraud. Clergy bought and sold church offices (simony). Immorality among church leaders who professed celibacy further heightened the crisis of confidence. The church likewise spent a fortune acquiring thousands of relics for its cathedrals and paying for them with the selling of forgiveness (indulgences). The church thus became an object of ridicule and satire in pamphlets and books that were readily available with the invention of the printing press.

In the fourteenth and fifteenth centuries, mysticism also challenged the church from within. Most significant was the Brethren of Common Life and the Brethren's most famous spokesman, Thomas à Kempis. The Brethren stood in opposition to the Catholic monastic orders and breathed new spiritual life into the church. They stressed personal devotion to Jesus through study and meditation, confession of sin, and imitating Christ. They likewise emphasized obedience, holiness, and simplicity. In many ways, the Brethren prefigured the reformers of the sixteenth century.

Availability of the written Word of God also undermined the church. John Wycliffe (circa 1329–1384) believed that the Bible was the final authority for the believer and that each believer should have an opportunity to read it. But the only available version was the Latin Bible known as the Vulgate. So Wycliffe and his associates translated that Latin Bible into English. Wycliffe also wrote tracts arguing that Christ, not the pope, was the head of the church, that priests were unnecessary, and that the Catholic belief that the bread and wine became the literal body and blood of Christ was wrong.

The sixteenth-century world was one of astounding change. Medieval civilization dominated by institutionalized Catholicism was disappearing. Modern nation-states challenged the church for supremacy, and the voyages of discovery made the world appear smaller. In addition, the Renaissance of northern Italy had caused many to turn from Catholicism toward the glories of ancient Greece and Rome. Into this changing world stepped Desiderius Erasmus (1466–1536).

Erasmus found it quite easy to ridicule the Catholic church. In his most famous example, *Praise of Folly* (1509), he took jabs at the church's pervasive immorality, corruption, and decadence. He ridiculed its superstitions such as fanatical devotion to relics, stories of bleeding hosts, and the cult of saints. In another tract, he depicted Saint Peter castigating Pope Julius II for his life of luxury, military conquest, and opulence, and denying him entrance into heaven.

In 1516 Erasmus published his most influential work—his Greek edition of the New Testament. He examined and compared some of the available New Testament manuscripts and citations from the Church Fathers. The result was an accurate New Testament Greek text that became the New Testament of the Reformation. Although overstated, the old epigram, "Erasmus laid the egg that Luther hatched," captures the influence of Erasmus.

By the sixteenth century, reform of the church seemed imminent. All that was needed was the right individual. Martin Luther was that man. He provided the spark for the most significant reform in the history of the church.

FOR FURTHER DISCUSSION

1. Explain why Protestants consider Gregory I to be the first pope of the Roman Catholic Church.
2. What is monasticism, and what were some positive aspects of this movement?
3. How did God use Boniface and Patrick in the early medieval church?
4. Summarize the theology of Islam and explain why it spread so quickly.
5. Summarize the reasons why the church separated into East and West in 1054.
6. What were the Crusades and their results?
7. What were the contributions of Anselm and Aquinas?

Chapter Six

THE REFORMATION CHURCH

Unless I am convicted of error . . . by the Scriptures to which I have appealed, and my conscience is taken captive by God's Word, I cannot and will not recant of anything, for to act against our conscience is neither safe for us, nor open to us. Here I stand. I can do no other. May God help me! Amen.

MARTIN LUTHER, DIET OF WORMS, 1521

As the preceding chapter makes clear, by the sixteenth century, the spirit of reform permeated Europe. The only question was whether Christendom could survive intact. Events in sixteenth-century Germany answered the question.

MARTIN LUTHER

Luther was born November 10, 1483, in Eisleben, Germany, into an affluent copper miner's family. Steered firmly by his father, Luther decided to seek a degree in law. But one July day in 1505, a violent thunderstorm knocked him to the ground, and he screamed, "Help me, St. Anne! I will become a monk" (Bainton, 1950, 78). That vow changed his life.

To his father's consternation, Luther joined the Augustinian cloister in Erfurt. There he opened and studied the Bible for the first time. His fervent yearning to serve, please, and love God stemmed from a haunting fear of God's judgment. To win God's favor, he committed himself to a rigorous schedule of study, meditation, and fasting. But his

.1fe of rigid asceticism brought no peace. God was his judge, not his Savior.

In 1511 his Augustinian order sent him to the University of Wittenberg where he completed his Th.D. in October 1512. He then secured a permanent appointment there as a professor of Bible. But his struggle over God's holiness and justice deepened. Sometime between 1517 and 1519 Luther found the peace he sought. Through reading the New Testament, especially Romans, he came to understand that justification was not by works but through faith. Neither Luther nor the world would ever be the same.

Across the river from Wittenberg, a Dominican monk named Johann Tetzel was selling indulgences. These were small pieces of parchment that guaranteed forgiveness of sins for a price. Brazenly he trumpeted, "As soon as the coin in the coffer rings, the soul from purgatory springs." Such arrogance enraged Luther. He preached fervently against indulgences, and on October 31, 1517, he nailed Ninety-Five Theses for debate on the Castle Church door at Wittenberg. In them he argued that indulgences could not remove guilt, did not apply to purgatory, and provided a false sense of security. He later wrote, "The pope has no jurisdiction over purgatory, and if he does, he should empty the place free of charge" (Bainton, 1950, 81). The Reformation had begun.

From 1517 to 1521 Luther's stand against the church hardened. In 1520 when Pope Leo excommunicated him, Luther publicly burned the order. Furthermore, his writings from this period reflected a distinctly non-Catholic theology. He argued that Scripture allowed for only two ordinances—baptism and the Lord's Supper. He also rejected the Catholic dogma of transubstantiation. Justification came by faith alone; works played no role in salvation.

The most serious challenge to Luther came when the new Holy Roman emperor, Charles V, ordered him to answer charges at the imperial Diet of Worms. When asked to recant his writings, Luther responded, "Unless I am convicted of error . . . by the Scriptures to which I have appealed, and my conscience is taken captive by God's Word, I cannot and will not recant of anything, for to act against our conscience is neither safe for us, nor open to us. Here I stand. I can do no other. May God help me! Amen!"

With his life now in jeopardy, friends "kidnapped" him and took him secretly to Wartburg Castle. While there, he translated the New Testament from the Greek into German. Meanwhile, the revolt against the Roman Catholic Church spread. Towns all over Germany removed religious statues, abolished the mass, and forced priests from churches. As princes of the Holy Roman Empire chose to support the Lutheran cause, the Reformation became a political issue as well.

After a year at Wartburg, Luther went back to Wittenberg where he taught and preached for the rest of his life. In 1525 he married Catherine von Bora, a former nun, who bore him six children. He continued to write prolifically, including theology books, Bible commentaries, and music. As a pastor, he sought a method by which God's Word could endure in the hearts of his people. The singing of hymns met that need. He reshaped ancient tunes and melodies into dozens of hymns, such as "A Mighty Fortress Is Our God" and "Away in a Manger."

Luther's close friend and disciple, Philip Melanchthon (1497–1560), emerged as the theologian of Lutheranism. He authored the *Augsburg Confession* (1530) and its *Apology*, both forceful statements of early Protestant theology. But as a courteous and timid peacemaker, Melanchthon attempted to steer a middle course in early theological debates of the Reformation. Rarely did he satisfy anyone. In that sense, he personifies the tension caused by theological debate.

ZWINGLI

Ulrich Zwingli was born in Wildhaus, Switzerland, in 1484. Educated in the best universities and ordained a priest, Zwingli seemed destined to serve his life in the priesthood. But through theological inquiry and personal struggle, he came to saving faith in 1516. By 1523 he was leading the Reformation in Zurich. In 1526 his teaching and preaching convinced the city council to permit clergy to marry, abolish the mass, ban Catholic images and statues, dissolve the monasteries, and sever all ties with Rome. Additionally, the Zurich reformers published their vernacular New Testament in 1524 and the entire Bible in 1530, four years before Luther's translation became available.

Breaking his vow of celibacy, Zwingli secretly married Anna Reinhart in 1522. He made their wedding public in 1524. Like Luther, he demonstrated that spiritual leadership did not demand celibacy. His break with Rome was radical.

Zwingli was at the center of a major theological debate concerning the Lord's Table. Between 1525 and 1528 a bitter "pamphlet war" ensued between the Zwinglians and the Lutherans. Both sides rejected the Roman Catholic doctrine of transubstantiation—that the priest's prayer transformed the elements into the literal, sacrificial body and blood of Christ. Their disagreement centered on Jesus' words, "This is My body."

The Lutherans maintained that Jesus was present "in, with, and under" (from the *Augsburg Confession*) the elements and that participation in the sacrament strengthened the believer spiritually (consubstantiation). The Zwinglians regarded this as an unnecessary compromise with Catholicism. Instead, they concluded that because Christ's physical body was no longer present on earth, His words must be understood symbolically. The elements represented Jesus' body, and Communion was merely a memorial. The debate remains unsettled today.

Zwingli believed the state and church should reinforce one another in the work of God; there should be no separation. Therefore, the Reformation became increasingly political and split Switzerland into Catholic and Protestant cantons (or states). Warfare resulted. At the battle of Cappel (1531), a coalition of five Catholic cantons defeated Zurich. Zwingli, the chaplain for the Zurich forces, was killed during the battle. When his enemies discovered his body, they quartered and burned it. His ardor for reform had cost him his life.

CALVIN

With Zwingli dead, the Swiss reformers lacked a leader. John Calvin (1509–1564) filled that gap. As the reformer of Geneva, he inspired John Knox, the Dutch Reformation, the English Reformation, and the Puritans and Pilgrims of North America.

Calvin was born in France on July 10, 1509, and studied theology at the University of Paris and law at the University of Orleans. Sometime during the 1520s he trusted Christ and joined the young Protestant cause. An explosion of anti-Protestant fury forced Calvin to flee Paris. For three years he was on the run in France, Switzerland, and Italy.

During this time he also began writing. By March 1536 he had published *Institutes of the Christian Religion*. At first a slim volume, the *Institutes* went through five revisions. The 1559 edition is the definitive one containing four books of eighty chapters. With its theme of "God, the Creator and Sovereign Ruler of the World," it was the systematic theology of the Reformation.

Calvin eventually ended up in Geneva. The city council appointed him to lead the Reformation, but he never held political office and did not become a citizen until 1559. His goal was to make Geneva a "holy commonwealth" where the laws of God would be the laws of man. He preached every day and twice on Sunday. He established an academy for training the youth of the city and arranged for the care of the poor and the aged. Calvin's Geneva was a commonwealth of doctrine and practice and a model of Reformation living.

Because Geneva was so strategically located, Protestant refugees from all over Catholic Europe flooded into the city. They sat under Calvin's teaching, and when they returned home, they took his theology with them. This pattern explains the remarkable spread of Calvinism throughout the Western world.

In addition to his amazing preaching and teaching schedule, Calvin also wrote prolifically. He wrote lectures, theological treatises, and commentaries on thirty-three books of the Old Testament and the entire New Testament except Revelation. As Philip Schaff has written, "Calvin was the founder of the modern historical-grammatical exegesis" of God's Word (Schaff, 8:118-119). The reformer likewise carried on a massive correspondence with people all over Europe.

Calvin is often pictured as a disciplined, authoritarian fanatic. This idea is quite inaccurate. He loved life. He loved to play games and frequently visited the homes of his followers. He also spent many hours giving premarital counseling in his church. But it was his participation in the execution of Michael Servetus that contributed most to the image of Calvin as an extremist.

Servetus, a Spaniard, was already under the ban of the Catholic church for his heretical teaching—principally his denial of the Trinity. The Genevan city fathers imprisoned Servetus. In an attempt to convert him, Calvin made several unsuccessful visits to his cell. So with the full support of other Swiss Protestant cities, Geneva executed Servetus in 1553.

Because Calvin believed so strongly in the sovereignty of God, he held that God was directly involved in all aspects of the drama of salvation, including predestination and election. Calvinism, which was later systematized by his followers, is a God-centered system of theology. Today Calvinism is often summarized with the acrostic TULIP:

T	-	Total Depravity
U	-	Unconditional Election
L	-	Limited Atonement
I	-	Irresistible Grace
P	-	Perseverance of the Saints.

Calvinism today is found in historic Presbyterianism, Reformed faiths, and some Baptist groups.

THE ANABAPTISTS

As a term, *anabaptist* means "to again baptize." The Anabaptist movement stressed believer's baptism, as opposed to infant baptism. But the
term also refers to widely diverse groups of Reformers, many of which
embraced quite radical social, political, economic, and religious views.
The most respectable groups included the Swiss Brethren, the
Mennonites, the Hutterites, and the Amish.

When it comes to the tenets of Protestant theology, most
Anabaptist groups adhered to sound teaching on the Scriptures, the
Trinity, justification by faith, and the atonement of Jesus Christ. Many
Anabaptists, however, maintained several distinctives that made them
objects of persecution by both Catholics and some Protestants. First,
nearly all championed believer's baptism—a rejection of infant baptism, which Catholicism and most other Protestant groups affirmed.
Second, most argued for a gathered church concept as opposed to a
state church. Third, as a corollary, many defended the separation of
church and state. Fourth, some taught that Christians should live
communally and share all material possessions. Fifth, many supported
the position of nonresistance and sometimes pacifism. Finally, many
Anabaptists preached a strict form of church discipline. Each of these
marked Anabaptism as a movement quite distinct from all other
Reformation groups.

Zwingli's zeal produced intolerance, especially toward the
Anabaptists. Two of his disciples, Conrad Grebel and Felix Manz, were
impatient for radical reform. They became critical of Zwingli's relationship with the city council and broke with Zwingli over the nature of
baptism. Essentially, Grebel and Manz founded the Anabaptist movement. Because their beliefs were clearly antagonistic to Zwingli and the
city council, the Anabaptists were fined, imprisoned, and martyred by
the Swiss authorities.

THE ENGLISH REFORMATION

As a nation, England was ripe for reformation. The work of Wycliffe
and his followers, the Lollards, had prepared the way. The writings of
Luther circulated through the land. In addition, William Tyndale
(1494–1536) and Miles Coverdale (1488–1568) had each produced
highly accurate translations of the Bible that were widely available. But
the catalyst for the break with Rome came with the marital problems of
the English king, Henry VIII.

Henry's marriage to Catherine of Aragon had produced no sons; however, Henry's affair with Anne Boleyn resulted in her pregnancy. When Henry sought an annulment of his marriage, the pope refused. In 1534 Henry, therefore, removed England from the pope's jurisdiction and made himself head of the English church (now called the Anglican church). Henry also confiscated Catholic land.

As Protestant and Catholic forces in England struggled for control, confusion and crisis reigned for the next decade. But when Elizabeth I, Henry's daughter, came to the throne, she chose a middle road built upon national unity and not theological considerations. The core of her solution was that the Anglican church would be Protestant in its theology and Catholic in its ritual. She therefore neutralized Catholicism in England but did not satisfy her most vocal critics, the Puritans.

Puritanism was a complex movement that primarily yearned for the purification of the Anglican church. Puritans wanted to complete the Reformation in England. They claimed that Elizabeth had not gone far enough in her reforms. Congregational in church government and Calvinist in theology, the Puritans would later be expelled from the Anglican church. This, in turn, led to the emigration of many to North America.

JOHN KNOX AND SCOTLAND

Frequently shifting its allegiance between France and England, Scotland was caught in the vice of geopolitical conflict. The Reformation fed this instability. At the center of this conflict was John Knox (1514–1572).

Fearing the spreading Reformation, the Catholics in control of Scotland appealed to France for help. Therefore, on July 31, 1547, the French navy arrived at St. Andrews, seized the stronghold, and took all the occupants back to France. Among those seized was Knox. Efforts to propagandize him with Catholic doctrine failed. His enslavement became the watershed event of his life. He became a revolutionary for the cause of Christ.

Released from slavery after nineteen months, Knox fled to England where he joined the Reformation forces committed to Thomas Cranmer. For more than two years, he became an itinerant evangelist, proclaiming the Reformation gospel in Berwick and Newcastle. But the "Boy-King," Edward VI (a devout Protestant and enamored with Knox), died in 1553, making Mary Tudor (a steadfast Catholic) queen.

She became known as "Bloody Mary," and her reign centered on the systematic and ruthless persecution of Protestants. Hence, Knox fled to Germany.

During his exile in Europe (1554–1559), Knox pastored a church of exiles in Frankfurt, Germany, and developed a close relationship with John Calvin and other reformers. Knox's pastorate in Geneva was his most productive, for he helped translate the critical Geneva Bible, one of the first true study Bibles that included notes, maps, and prayers.

He also wrote his famous *The First Blast of the Trumpet Against the Monstrous Regiment of Women*, a biting polemic directed at Queen Mary and her Catholic following. In this pamphlet Knox developed his position on the rights of citizens in the face of an unjust ruler. Did they have the right to overthrow that ruler? Knox answered yes. He based his argument on Scripture, especially the case of Athaliah (2 Kings 11), who was overthrown and executed under orders from Jehoiada the priest. Knox also argued that when a ruler does not support the true church, referring to Queen Mary, that ruler's throne should be in jeopardy.

With the country on the verge of civil war, he returned to Scotland in May 1559 to lead the Protestant cause. As a result of complicated political moves on many fronts, the war did break out and soon drew in England and France. Knox was the heart and soul of the Protestant forces—as enlistment officer and even as a spy for the English behind French lines. The war ended in 1560, and the Treaty of Edinburgh recognized Presbyterianism. The new Parliament adopted the First Scottish Confession, written by Knox and others, as the theological confession of Scotland. It remained so until the famous Westminster Confession of 1647.

The spirit of reform impacted Catholicism as well. As the Catholic church responded to the advances of Protestantism, it built on reforms begun even before Luther appeared on the scene. That response is usually called the Catholic Counter-Reformation, the subject of the next chapter.

FOR FURTHER DISCUSSION

1. Why is October 31, 1517, so important to the Reformation?
2. Summarize Luther's disagreement with the Catholic church.
3. Zwingli's contribution to the Reformation centered on the Lord's Table. What was his view?

4. John Calvin's influence was immense. What was his role as leader in Geneva?

5. Summarize Calvin's teaching represented by the acrostic TULIP.

6. Who were the Anabaptists? What were some of the distinctive beliefs of this movement?

7. Detail the role that Henry VIII and his daughter Elizabeth played in the English Reformation.

8. Who was the undisputed leader of the Scottish Reformation?

Chapter Seven

THE CATHOLIC CHURCH RESPONDS

If anyone says that the sinner is justified by faith alone . . . let him be anathema.

Council of Trent, 1563

The Roman Catholic Church of the sixteenth century did not suddenly react to Protestantism. The spirit of reform was already present in Spain. However, the energy and zeal of Protestantism put Catholicism on the defensive and caused it to respond aggressively. That response was the Catholic Counter-Reformation.

SPAIN

In Spain the spirit of Catholic reform predated Martin Luther. The enthusiasm from evicting the Muslims and the persistence of medieval piety and mysticism fueled reform of the church there. When Queen Isabella began her rule of Castile in 1474, she brought a zeal to reform Spanish Catholicism and quickly gained papal approval for her fervor. Cardinal Francisco Jimenez (1436–1517), archbishop of Toledo, emerged as Isabella's key supporter in reorganizing Spanish Catholicism. In a campaign for holiness, Jimenez and Isabella set out to cleanse the monasteries and convents of Spain. They demanded renewal of monastic vows, enforced poverty among the clergy, emphasized the necessity of an educated clergy, and purged the monasteries of corruption and immorality.

Jimenez and Isabella also demanded high standards for scholarship, which both believed was the key to effective leadership. Therefore, they founded the University of Alcala, outside Madrid, which became an indispensable center of Spanish religious and literary life. The University of Alcala was likewise instrumental in publishing a new multilingual edition of the Bible, which included Scripture in Hebrew, Greek, and the Latin Vulgate—all in parallel columns. Jimenez said of the work that "this edition of the Bible . . . opens the sacred sources of our religion, from which flow a much purer theology than any derived from less direct sources" (Gonzalez, 2:112). Through this 1520 publication, Jimenez and Isabella affirmed the supremacy of Scripture over church tradition.

The Spanish Reformation was, however, hardly a model of tolerance. The pope gave Isabella and her husband, Ferdinand, authority to use the Inquisition, a church court, to enforce adherence to church doctrine and practices. The Jews were special victims of Spanish intolerance. In 1492 the Spanish crown decreed that all Jews must either accept Christian baptism or leave Spanish territories. Over 200,000 Jews fled Spain as a result, most losing their land, their possessions, and some even their lives. The Spanish crown passed similar laws aimed at Spanish Muslims, called Moors. Jimenez, now Grand Inquisitor, ruthlessly pursued the forced conversion of the Moors.

THE JESUITS

Several new monastic orders added to the energy emanating from Catholic Spain. None was more influential than the Society of Jesus (the Jesuits) founded by Spaniard Ignatius Loyola (1491–1556). Ignatius lived a life of luxury and pleasure until he was severely wounded in battle. That wound made him limp for the rest of his life. While recuperating from his wounds, he devoured religious literature, and in 1522 dedicated his life to God and the church. Such devotion led to the founding of the Jesuits in 1534. Patterned after the military, the Jesuit organization responded efficiently and rapidly to the challenges and opportunities of the Roman Catholic Church.

The mission of the Jesuits was threefold—education, fighting heresy, and missions. Through its teaching and preaching, the Jesuits regained control of parts of Germany and central Europe for the Catholic church. Francis Xavier (1506–1552) was the outstanding Jesuit missionary, ministering in Japan, the Far East, the East Indies, and parts of North America. Jesuit missionaries baptized thousands into the Roman Catholic faith.

Jesuit attacks against heresy meant attacks against Protestantism. Jesuits utilized two weapons—the Index of Prohibited Books and the Inquisition. By publishing a list of books Catholics were not permitted to read, the Index controlled the minds of the faithful. The Inquisition, a church court originally established in 1490, rarely followed due process and often utilized torture. Its major objective was to obtain a confession and the retraction of heretical beliefs from the accused heretic. If found guilty, the accused faced imprisonment or execution. The Inquisitor's court rarely showed mercy. In Italy, Spain, Portugal, and Belgium the Inquisition successfully eradicated any Protestant threat.

PAUL III

The most important pope of the Counter-Reformation was Paul III, who served from 1534 to 1549. An enigmatic man, Paul seemed to trust astrology more than Catholic theology. Like other popes of the Renaissance period, he was immoral and strove to make Rome a glorious city of wealth and prestige. But he was also a reformer. He recognized the Jesuits as a legal church order in 1540, appointed dedicated men as cardinals of the church, and organized a committee of nine to investigate abuses in the church and to recommend reforms. But most importantly, he called the Council of Trent in 1545.

THE COUNCIL OF TRENT

The Council of Trent was the definitive Catholic response to Protestantism. From 1545 to 1563, for a total of 25 sessions, the council of bishops deliberated. The council conceded that Protestantism resulted from the "ambition, avarice, and cupidity" of Catholic bishops. It also ordered the systematic education and training of the clergy in established Catholic seminaries. In the seminaries, the church promoted the study of Thomas Aquinas, making him the dominant Catholic theologian. In a direct response to the Lutherans, the council likewise abolished indulgence sellers, listed and defined clergy obligations, regulated the use of relics, and ordered the restructuring of bishops within the church.

The doctrinal work of Trent is summarized in the Tridentine Profession of Faith, which championed Roman Catholic dogma and provided the major theological response to the Protestants. Trent rejected justification by faith alone and promoted the necessity of meritorious works as necessary in the dynamic of salvation. It also reaffirmed the seven grace-conveying sacraments instituted by Christ—baptism, confirmation, communion, penance, extreme unction, ordination, and marriage—as needed for sanctification. Trent also reaffirmed transubstantiation and the sacrificial nature of the mass, clearly rejecting all Protestant positions on the Lord's Table. Finally, it declared the Vulgate Bible alone as acceptable for church use and maintained that church tradition was equal in authority with Scripture. Clearly, the Tridentine statement made reconciliation with Protestantism impossible.

CATHOLIC SPIRITUALITY

Medieval mysticism and spirituality also contributed a new energy to institutionalized Catholicism. Throughout Catholic Europe, an emphasis on prayer, meditation, examination of conscience, reading of Scripture, and fellowship with God surfaced. Much of this fresh vigor predated Martin Luther and was quite critical of the church hierarchy. Thomas à Kempis's *The Imitation of Christ* and Ignatius's *Spiritual Exercises* exemplify the literature of Catholic spirituality that burst across Catholic Europe.

THE THIRTY YEARS' WAR

The Reformation sparked a whole series of religious wars across the European continent. All were bloody and dreadful. The last of these was the Thirty Years' War (1618–1648). The Peace of Augsburg of 1555 had put Lutheranism on a legal basis with Roman Catholicism in Germany. The prince of a region was to determine the religion in his territory, but any dissenters could emigrate to another territory. To preserve Catholic domination of southern Germany, the agreement mandated that Catholic rulers who became Lutherans had to surrender rule. The agreement also left out Calvinists, Anabaptists, and other Protestants. In many respects, Augsburg solved nothing.

Beginning in Bohemia, the Thirty Years' War ravaged Central Europe and Germany and involved all the major European powers. The Peace of Westphalia, which ended the war in 1648, resulted from long and complicated negotiations. France and Sweden gained large amounts of territory, and German princes gained greater power and influence at the expense of the emperor. The treaty also recognized Calvinism, along with the Lutherans and Catholics, as a legal religion and permitted each ruler to determine the religion of his state. The Reformation was over.

But the effects of the War were devastating for Christianity. Religious issues were increasingly treated with indifference by political leaders. Secular, self-serving matters were now the chief concerns of the growing worldly nation-states. The barbarity and brutality of the war left many questioning the Christian Gospel. How could a faith that produced such atrocities be true? Doctrine took a backseat to doubt and skepticism.

In the Catholic Counter-Reformation institutionalized Catholicism honestly came to terms with its own shortcomings and responded to the threat of Protestantism. Most of the offensive tactics of the Counter-Reformation eventually ended—the Inquisition in 1854 and the Index in 1966. But the Tridentine Profession of Faith dogmatized Catholic theological distinctives and rendered reconciliation with the Protestants impossible. Now both Catholics and Protestants faced a new threat—the modern world. The intellectual framework for modernism is the subject of the next two chapters.

FOR FURTHER DISCUSSION

1. Why can we say that the Catholic Counter-Reformation began before Luther?
2. Why were the Jesuits so important to the Catholic response to Protestantism? What weapons did they use?
3. Which pope called the Council of Trent?
4. Why did the Tridentine Profession of Faith make reconciliation with the Protestants nearly impossible?
5. What religious war ended the Reformation? How did this last religious war affect Christianity?

The Seven Sacraments
of the Roman Catholic Church

Reaffirmed at the Council of Trent (A.D. 1545–1563)

 **BAPTISM**

 **CONFIRMATION**

 **COMMUNION**

 **PENANCE**

 **EXTREME UNCTION**

 **ORDINATION**

 **MARRIAGE**

Chapter Eight

THE CHURCH AND THE SCIENTIFIC REVOLUTION

Nature and Nature's Laws lay hid in Night;
God said, "Let Newton be," and All was Light.
ALEXANDER POPE

THE SCIENTIFIC REVOLUTION OF THE seventeenth century gave birth to modern culture. Modern science was both a product of the Reformation and the beginning of modern naturalism, which rejects the role of the supernatural in the physical world. How did this development occur?

THE REFORMATION AND MODERN SCIENCE

The Reformation challenged the authority of Roman Catholicism, which had dogmatized as theology a particular scientific view of the world. That view of the world is often called the Aristotelian-Ptolemaic model, built on the thinking of the Greek philosopher Aristotle (384–322 B.C.) and the second-century A.D. Greek scientist and philosopher Ptolemy. This view of the world became a part of Catholic theology through the work of Thomas Aquinas. According to this model, Earth was the center of the universe, the motion of heavenly bodies was perfect circular motion, and those heavenly bodies were immune to change, obeying different laws of motion than those of Earth. There were, then, two separate realms—the higher worlds of the heavens and the lower world of the Earth. The Scientific Revolution shattered this model.

Roman Catholicism argued that authority rested with Scripture, tradition, and the institutionalized church. The Reformation countered that authority resided only in Scripture. Luther's cry, "*Sola Scriptura,*" meant a clear rejection of the dogma of Catholicism as empty and erroneous, including the detailed arguments of the Scholastics. For many this rejection included speculations about science. The shift from the institutional church to the Bible as the source of religious authority played a crucial role in advancing the acceptance of new scientific ideas.

In addition, Protestants challenged the Western world to reject the philosophical speculations of Catholic theology that was developed apart from Scripture. Aristotle's philosophy, which had so strongly influenced Aquinas, led Catholicism down the road to vain and idle conjectures (e.g., the worship of Mary, purgatory, the mass). The natural operation of human reason, unchecked by the Bible, could only lead to error and vanity. That, Protestants claimed, was precisely what had happened to Catholic theology. Thinkers of the seventeenth century agreed and rejected along with theology the Catholic speculations about science.

Finally, Protestant affirmations about the sovereignty of God, especially in the dynamic of salvation, laid the groundwork for seventeenth-century thinking about science. Both Luther and Calvin maintained the absolute sovereignty and rule of God over His creation. The extent of human depravity was so immense that only God's active intervention by His grace could save a person. Hence, the doctrines of election and predestination.

God's sovereignty, with His active and dynamic involvement, meant no intermediaries, whether it was in salvation or in the natural world. Catholicism viewed the world as a hierarchy, with many intermediaries between God and the physical world. Not so with Protestantism. Luther and Calvin saw only Christ as an intermediary; the church as go-between had no biblical support. Similarly, God acted directly in nature. To study nature was to study God at work. Protestantism and the new science both held that truth came from studying God's Word and God's world.

A NEW MODEL FOR THE PHYSICAL WORLD

As the Reformation challenged Catholic assumptions, sixteenth-century scientists challenged natural assumptions. They all worked from a Christian worldview and did not see their work as threatening Christianity. Each believed that studying God's world proved that God was a God of order, purpose, and design. Through their study they likewise dismantled the old Aristotelian model and formulated a new model for the universe.

Modern science was born as philosophers asked new questions about how humans think and gain knowledge. An English philosopher, Francis Bacon (1561–1626), proposed a new method for arriving at knowledge and truth. That method involved the systematic recording of facts, which then led to tentative hypotheses that were tested by experiments. The end result of this inductive method was universal principles and scientific laws.

Even more significant was a French philosopher, Rene Descartes (1596–1650), who began his method with doubting everything, except that he was doubting. Since he doubted, he therefore existed: "I think, therefore, I am" (*Discourse on Method*, 120). Secondly, he believed that he could prove the existence of God. He found in his mind the idea of a "more perfect being." This idea, he concluded, could only have been placed there by God. Therefore, humans possess certain innate ideas that form the building blocks of understanding and knowledge. These innate ideas are sourced in God. Through the process of reason, Descartes further concluded, humans built upon these clear and distinct precepts and arrived at universal principles. This is the method of deduction.

In contrast to Descartes's concept of innate ideas was the empiricism of John Locke (1632–1704). He rejected Descartes's innate ideas and argued instead that knowledge is derived from experience. How does this view affect matters of faith? Locke argued that faith is an assent to knowledge derived from revelation rather than reason. Therefore, its knowledge is never certain, only probable. In 1695 Locke published *The Reasonableness of Christianity*, in which he claimed that Christianity is the most reasonable of faiths. The essence of the Christian faith is belief in God's existence and personal faith in Jesus as Messiah. But these truths are probable truths, not certain truths, he believed. Locke argued that one must separate probable judgments of faith from the certainty of empirical reason. Conduct and toleration of other beliefs are more important than the narrowness of Christian doctrine. The devastating implications of Locke's thinking for Christianity are obvious.

It was in the scientific discipline of astronomy that experimentation, observation, and mathematical reasoning found their union. Copernicus (1473–1543), in his *Concerning the Revolution of Heavenly Spheres*, argued that Earth revolved around the sun every twenty-four hours, thereby challenging the Earth-centered universe of Aristotle and Aquinas. Johannes Kepler (1571–1630) gave mathematical proof to Copernicus's theory and discovered that the planets move in an ellipse, not the perfect circle of Aristotle. Galileo Galilei (1564–1642), using the newly invented telescope, discovered mountains on the moon, observed sunspots, and discovered a moon of Jupiter. All of these discoveries demonstrated that not all heavenly bodies orbit Earth and that change is part of the heavens too.

The central figure of the Scientific Revolution, however, was Isaac Newton (1642–1727). Newton synthesized Kepler and Galileo by asserting that one all-embracing principle—the law of gravity— explained motion in the universe. This law applied to both Earth and the heavens. Newton thus proposed order, consistency, and uniformity throughout the universe. When it came to God's natural laws, there were no distinctions between heaven and Earth. So profound was Newton's work that Alexander Pope wrote in his *Epitaph. Intended for Sir Isaac Newton, In Westminster Abbey* (1730):

> *Nature and Nature's Laws lay hid in Night;*
> *God said,* "Let Newton be," *and All was* Light.[1]

THE REACTION OF QUAKERISM, GERMAN PIETISM, AND METHODISM

The Protestantism of the seventeenth century had become cold, impersonal, and, for some, stifling. Many reform movements developed in response. One was Quakerism. Founded in England by George Fox (1624–1691), Quakerism argued that it had discovered the true meaning of faith and Christianity. Hymns, orders of worship, sermons, sacraments, creeds, and ministers were all human hindrances to the true freedom of Christianity, which is found in the Spirit. Fox believed that a seed existed in all humans, called the "inner light," that each person must follow to find God. This inner light is the key to recognizing and accepting the presence of God and understanding His Word.

Fox's followers became known as "friends," and because of the trembling that often accompanied their worship, others referred to them as "Quakers." Because Quakers rejected worship structure of any kind, their worship took place in silence. When the Spirit moved them, men and women had the freedom to speak and pray aloud. In an age of conformity, structure, and orthodoxy, Quakerism developed as an expression of radical individualism. Persecuted intensely, many Quakers fled England for the freedom of the colonies, especially Pennsylvania.

Another important response to the formalism of mature Protestantism was German Pietism. *The Oxford Dictionary of the Christian Church* (p. 1089) defines Pietism as "a seventeenth-century movement in the German Church which had as its purpose the infusion of new life into the official Protestantism of its time." German Pietists such as John Arndt (1555–1621), Philipp Spener (1635–1705), August Francke (1663–1727), and Nicholas von Zinzendorf (1700–1760) revived German Lutheranism. They believed that Christians should meet in small house meetings to gain a better understanding of the Bible. The laity, not only professional ministers, should be allowed to exercise their spiritual priesthood. Although they believed in the importance of the mind, Pietists placed emphasis on the practical side of Christianity, highlighting personal holiness. Religious controversies needed to be handled with a spirit of love. Finally, Pietists believed that the pulpit should be for instructing, edifying, and inspiring believers, not for learned lectures on cryptic points of doctrine.

Pietism breathed new life into staid and stiff European Christianity and also influenced the development of American Christianity and modern missions (see chapters 10 and 11). But its influence on the experiential nature of Christianity often was at the expense of doctrine. Later developments in European Christianity would demonstrate the danger of this emphasis.

Another response to cold and detached seventeenth-century Christianity was Methodism. Founded by John Wesley (1703–1791), Methodism grew out of the Anglican church. A member of the Holy Club at Oxford University, Wesley struggled with personal holiness. He pastored and even served as a missionary in the new colony of Georgia. But it was not until he came into contact with the Pietistic Moravians that he met his Lord. On May 24, 1738, at a meeting of Moravians on Aldersgate Street in London, Wesley trusted Christ as his Savior.

Wesley devoted the rest of his life to preaching the Gospel. He traveled all over England, especially to the new industrial centers, where Methodism grew rapidly. He also utilized women and lay preachers to spread the message of salvation. Similar strategies brought Methodism to the American frontier, where it spread quickly. Methodism brought new life to English Christianity.

With the Scientific Revolution, the old model of the universe was dead. A new one had dawned. Earth was one of many planets that orbited the sun and not the center of the universe. Universal laws of physics applied to all planets and to all heavenly bodies. The seventeenth century increasingly viewed the universe as a machine operating according to physical laws that could be discovered and understood by reason and expressed mathematically. The question now was, what is the role of God? Did the Reformation view of Him as the Creator and Sovereign of the world still hold? If the physical laws of the universe were discoverable through reason, could reason yield a science of man as well as physics? Is truth something discovered or revealed? These were some of the questions the Scientific Revolution raised and with which Quakerism, Pietism, and Methodism struggled. But their answers were different from the Enlightenment's answers, the subject of the next chapter.

FOR FURTHER DISCUSSION

1. Briefly explain the model of the universe Aristotle defended. What Roman Catholic theologian made Aristotle's views part of Catholic theology?
2. Explain how the Reformation helped prepare the way for the Scientific Revolution.
3. Show the role each played in undermining the old model of the physical universe:
   a. Bacon—
   b. Descartes—
   c. Copernicus—
   d. Kepler—
   e. Galileo—
   f. Newton—
4. What were the key elements in the new worldview of the Scientific Revolution?

Chapter Nine

THE CHURCH, THE ENLIGHTENMENT, AND THEOLOGICAL LIBERALISM

The Enlightenment represents man's emergence from a self-inflicted state of minority. . . . Have the courage to make use of your own understanding is the watchword of the Enlightenment.

<small>IMMANUEL KANT, 1793</small>

THE EIGHTEENTH-CENTURY ENLIGHTENMENT was a movement of ideas that sought to release humanity from error and prejudice and to achieve truth, which in turn would produce freedom. Many Enlightenment thinkers targeted religion, for they saw it as embodying the error and prejudice they loathed. Specifically, they regarded Christianity and all other religions as irrational and inappropriate in a scientific age. The Enlightenment sought rational explanations for all of reality; religion was no exception.

THE ENLIGHTENMENT

Where the Scientific Revolution showed the order and rationality of the universe and discovered the laws governing the physical universe, the Enlightenment desired to examine human institutions to find the same kind of order and consistency and to posit laws that governed society. In short, they sought a science of man that would free him from all bondage. Some of the principal thinkers of the Enlightenment were

Voltaire (1694–1778), Jean Jacques Rousseau (1712–1778), Denis Diderot (1713–1784), and David Hume (1711–1776).

At bottom, Enlightenment thinkers were critical of everything. The method of the critic was the engine driving their analysis of society's institutions, including the church, the law, and even government. One French philosopher said, "all things must be examined, debated, investigated, without exception and without regard for anyone's feelings" (Gay, 1:128). With confidence in human reason and science, the Enlightenment championed the destruction of all barriers to human freedom and autonomy.

In addition, the eighteenth century was a period of skepticism, with many doubting the certainty of knowing absolute, universal truths. David Hume, the Scottish philosopher, epitomized this skeptical commitment. Central to Hume's position was the idea that no generalization about experience is ever rationally justified. As Norman Geisler has shown, Hume maintained that no proposition about experience is necessary, for one can easily imagine a world where the proposition would be false. As a generalization about reality, "the sun will rise tomorrow" is not necessary, for we can conceive of a world like ours where the sun will not rise tomorrow. For Hume, probability does not lead to certainty. Therefore, he denied the certainty of cause-effect relationships, attacked arguments for the existence of God, and authored a blistering attack on a belief in miracles.

John Locke (1632–1704) embodied the devotion to empiricism, a decisive characteristic of the Enlightenment. For Locke, humans were born with no sense of right or wrong or of any innate truths. Instead, the human mind is like a blank slate that throughout life is filled with data coming from the senses. Mysteries and doctrines of Christianity that could not be empirically proven were distrusted and often rejected. Following Locke, many Enlightenment thinkers repudiated all religion, including Christianity, as superstitious. They thought that religion needed to be replaced with a rational system of ethics.

Most of the Enlightenment thinkers, however, were not atheists; instead, many were deists. A philosophy difficult to summarize, deism proclaimed that one God created the world to operate on perfect natural law. But He no longer intervened in its present functioning, either by revelation or miracle. Thus deists rejected the Bible, gospel miracles, the Incarnation, and the Resurrection. Deism is a system in which God is an absentee landlord who has no involvement with His physical creation. He made the perfect clock and then left.

Voltaire's deism is perhaps most representative. He wrote: "I believe in God; not the God of the mystics but the God of nature, the great geometrician, the architect of the Universe, the prime mover, unalterable, transcendent, everlasting. . . . I shall always be convinced that a watch proves a watch-maker and that a universe proves a God" (Redman, 196). Voltaire rejected the special revelation of God in the Bible but embraced the God who created the physical universe. The deist's God was their Creator, but He was not their Savior!

The Enlightenment had a devastating effect on Christianity. First, because of Locke's empiricism, the Enlightenment affirmed the basic goodness of man. There was no doctrine of innate evil or original sin. Second, for the Enlightenment the human environment was determinative in shaping character and intelligence. Education was crucial in sharpening the senses, pursuing science, and changing human outlook and prejudice. It was the key to transforming people. Third, the Enlightenment was a thoroughly man-centered movement. Belief in the basic goodness of man held that under the proper circumstances, there was really nothing humans could not achieve.

Near the end of the eighteenth century, the doctrine of progress characterized the Enlightenment mind. Man was on an escalator, and nothing hindered him from going all the way to the top. Moral, spiritual, and technological progress seemed inevitable. Finally, the Enlightenment raised serious questions about the need for God. But with the emphasis on reason and science, God seemed irrelevant and unnecessary. With the rejection of objective revelation and skepticism about the supernatural, how can we know much about Him at all? This redefining of God laid the groundwork for the theological liberalism of the nineteenth century.

The Enlightenment also altered the connection between faith and reason for its followers. Near the end of the Enlightenment, Immanuel Kant (1724–1804) wrote several books attacking the traditional proofs for the existence of God. For Kant, the realm of knowledge was divided into two fundamentally separate domains, one that is knowable (the phenomena) and one that is not knowable (the *noumena*). Questions about God, immortality, and freedom of the human fell into the second category, and no empirical verification was thought possible. Kant therefore blocked the road to a knowledge of God through reason. One could not know God, he claimed, for there was no way to verify His existence rationally.

For Kant, then, what was religion? Religion was mostly human-centered in its orientation and grounded in a sense of duty and obligation. To Kant, religion was not an objective set of beliefs rooted in God's revelation to man. Instead, one lived *as if* God existed and was accountable to Him. Personal religion was a set of ethics, not propositional theology. As theologian Dr. Norman Geisler has remarked, "Kant kicked God out the front door and ran around and let Him in the back door" (from a lecture at Grace University). According to Kant, you do not know for certain that God exists, but you live as if He does!

THE ENLIGHTENMENT AND THEOLOGICAL LIBERALISM

As Kant blocked the road to God through reason for many, the only road left was the interior life, the realm of subjective experience. Friedrich Schleiermacher (1768–1834), the founder of modern theological liberalism, wrote in *The Christian Faith* (p. 125), "You reject the dogmas and propositions of religion. . . . Religion does not need them; it is only human reflection on the content of our religious feelings or affections. . . . Do you say that you cannot accept miracles, revelation, inspiration? You are right; we are children no longer; the time for fairytales is past." To Schleiermacher, religion was not knowledge as orthodox Christianity believed; nor was it a system of ethics as Kant implied. Rather, it was a "feeling" of dependence on God.

For Schleiermacher, "the feeling of absolute dependence" (*The Christian Faith*, 131) constituted the essence of religion. He believed Jesus was a man who exhibited such God-conscious dependence. Christ's work on the cross served as a model of self-denying love for us to emulate in all ways. Gone was any affirmation of Christ's deity, His substitutionary atonement, or propositional revelation from God.

If Christianity was reduced to feeling and Jesus was merely a suffering man, then the question for Enlightenment thinkers became, can we trust the New Testament accounts of Jesus? David Strauss's (1808–1874) book, *The Life of Jesus*, interjected the word *myth* into the discussion about the gospel accounts. He argued that the supernatural elements in the Gospels were not trustworthy. Miracles—for example, the Resurrection—were reflections by New Testament writers on Jesus' life. The Gospels were not history, said Strauss: "The life of Jesus was 'mythically' rewritten in order that writers might express their awareness of the significance of Jesus" (*The Life of Jesus*, 778).

If the New Testament then contains myth, what is the distinctive nature of Christianity? Theological liberalism reduced the Christian faith to righteous behavior grounded in the ethic of love. Albrecht Ritschl (1822–1889) maintained that the man Jesus Christ embodied this ethic. For Ritschl, the center of Jesus' teaching was the kingdom of God and its ethics, "the organization of humanity through action based on love" (Ritschl, 1:13). Furthermore, Adolf von Harnack (1851–1930), in his groundbreaking book *What is Christianity?*, asserted that the essence of the Christian faith was "the fatherhood of God and the brotherhood of man." To Harnack, Christianity was the commandment of love. To make the theology of Jesus more important than the work of Jesus was a "great departure from what Jesus thought and enjoined" (Fletcher, 62-63). To Harnack, the history of doctrine was the movement from the teachings of Jesus to the teachings about Jesus.

Was Christianity unique? Not to liberal theology. Between 1880 and 1920, in what was called the History of Religions School in Germany, Christianity was regarded as a human religion like all others that needed to be studied historically. Jesus was a historical figure but not the one pictured in the New Testament. In addition, the liberals said that Paul, influenced by Greek Gnosticism, probably distorted what Jesus taught. There was, then, no continuity between the Old Testament and the New Testament. For most of the leaders of this school, the Old Testament had little influence in shaping Christianity.

Liberal theology next began a quest for the historical Jesus. Its theologians asked, since we cannot trust the New Testament, what is the ground on which we can build our understanding of Jesus? Rudolf Bultmann (1884–1976) called for the "demythologizing" of the Gospels, the peeling off of the husks, to find the kernel of truth. That Jesus existed, Bultmann argued, is about all that can be claimed as certain. The anti-supernaturalism of the Enlightenment reached its peak with Bultmann.

One major German theologian, Karl Barth (1886–1968), turned away from theological liberalism. Trained in this school of theology, Barth struggled in the pastorate. He concluded that he had nothing to offer his people. He abandoned much of liberal theology and espoused a more orthodox, reformed interpretation of Christianity. He affirmed the utter transcendence of God and the chasm that existed between God and man. Only Jesus, the revelation of God, bridged that chasm, he argued. The Bible, then, is the revelation of God because it gives a witness to Jesus. Man meets God in a "crisis" when the Word of God "becomes" real to man. It is this crisis experience that formed one of the distinctives of Barth's neo-orthodoxy. In the end his interpretation satisfied very few people.

The antisupernaturalism of the Enlightenment produced the theological liberalism of the nineteenth and twentieth centuries. Kant separated faith and reason, declared man self-reliant, and claimed that absolute truths about God were unknowable. Faith for many now had no foundation. In attempting to find a new underpinning, theological liberalism cut all ties to the Bible as historical and trustworthy. Christianity became an ethical system, not all that different from other religions. But that is not the only story. Despite liberalism's major inroads into Christianity, God's program of redemption continued with the eruption of the modern missions movement throughout the world—the subject of the next chapter.

FOR FURTHER DISCUSSION

1. Why can we say that the Enlightenment was an attack on organized religion, especially on Christianity?
2. What was deism?
3. How did the Enlightenment challenge some of Christianity's teachings?
4. Explain Immanual Kant's view on the relationship between faith and reason. Why was this so harmful to Christianity?
5. Theological liberalism was a child of the Enlightenment. Show how each of the following built on the foundation of the Enlightenment:
   Friedrich Schleiermacher—
   Albrecht Ritschl—
   Adolf von Harnack—
   Rudolf Bultmann—
6. In what ways did Karl Barth disagree with liberalism?

Chapter Ten

THE CHURCH AND MODERN MISSIONS

Expect great things from God; attempt great things for God.

WILLIAM CAREY

The Great Commission of Jesus Christ defines the church's mission. But church history demonstrates that the church has not always taken that mission seriously. Although the ancient and early medieval church took the Gospel to the Germanic tribes, the medieval church neglected missions for centuries. Fighting for survival, the Reformation church also lacked missionary zeal. During the last two hundred years, a passion for reaching the world for Christ has enriched the modern church. This is especially true of the nineteenth century, which has been called the "Great Century of Missions." That missionary passion produced the first truly universal church, in which all races and nations had a part. This is the story of that passion.

ROOTS OF THE MODERN MISSIONS MOVEMENT

The roots of the modern missions movement reach back to the revivals of the eighteenth century (see next chapter). These movements of God's Spirit gave the fervor and energy so necessary for cross-cultural ministry. But other factors provided a fuller context. The voyages of discovery that opened the western hemisphere raised theological questions about where the people of this hemisphere came from and whether they were redeemable. The trading companies that settled North America demanded a spiritual emphasis in their charters. Also the Catholic church, especially the Jesuits, had modeled missionary activity for several centuries.

These developments coincided with the rise of industrial capitalism in Europe and the United States. As capitalism spread, the need for raw materials and markets for the finished products spawned a need for conquest of the remaining continents—Africa and Asia. The major European powers—France, England, and the Netherlands—competed to plant colonies on those continents. The nineteenth century was thus a century of imperialism. Most Europeans, including Protestant Christians, looked at imperialist activity as taking the benefits of capitalism, democracy, and Christianity to the needy world. Author Rudyard Kipling called this the "White Man's Burden." Trade, hospitals, roads, and industrial development did come to these continents, but so did racism and exploitation.

WILLIAM CAREY—"THE FATHER OF MODERN MISSIONS"

As colonists expanded into Africa and Asia, they took the Gospel with them. Early missionary societies were the sending agencies—the Danish-Halle Mission (1704), the Scottish Society for Propagating Christian Knowledge (1707), and Moravian Missions (1732). All of these societies owed their existence to the Pietistic revivals of the eighteenth century. But it was William Carey (1761–1834), founder of the Particular Baptist Society for Propagating the Gospel Among the Heathen, who became "the father of modern missions."

As a teacher, Carey was captivated by the stories of Captain Cook's discoveries in the Pacific. The intersection of these stories and his Baptist faith produced a deep conviction that the church had an obligation to proclaim the news of Jesus Christ to the unreached peoples of the world. He joined with others of a like mind and formed the Particular Baptist Society. In 1793 he and his family went to Calcutta, India. The work was difficult but fruitful, and his enthusiasm and intensity did much to cause others to venture out to other lands. His famous dictum, "Expect great things from God; attempt great things for God," still inspires people today.

Carey's ministry in India provided the model for modern missions. First, it depended on donations from private individuals and churches. Second, Carey regularly communicated with home churches and individuals, which generated increased interest in missions. Third, he made the Bible available to the Indian population. With an innate gift for learning languages, Carey translated the Bible, or parts of it, into thirty-five different languages. Fourth, in addition to planting churches, Carey's work and that of his followers promoted medical help and education as a part of the ministry. Finally, the gospel message had social and cultural implications. Carey personally toiled to end the burning of widows on their husbands' funeral pyres. Others insisted that India's caste system was wrong. Members of India's lowest caste, the Untouchables, and Indian women found Christianity personally liberating.

Others followed in Carey's path. Adoniram Judson (1788–1850), a Baptist missionary from America, did pioneer work in Burma very similar to Carey's. A group of English Congregationalists, among them David Livingstone and Robert Moffat, founded the London Missionary Society (1795), which did pioneer work in southern Africa.

MISSIONS IN EARLY AMERICA

The Haystack Prayer Meeting launched the missionary movement in America. In 1806 students at Williams College in Massachusetts took refuge from a thunderstorm under a haystack for their prayer meeting. Their motto was, "We can do it if we will." The resulting society eventually became known as the American Board of Commissioners for Foreign Missions (1810). By the end of the Civil War, fifteen mission boards serviced the major denominations of America.

THE EXAMPLE OF J. HUDSON TAYLOR

The modern missions movement, however, found its greatest power and influence in the faith missions movement, founded by J. Hudson Taylor (1832–1905). Born in England, Taylor underwent a deep spiritual conversion at the age of seventeen. He felt a distinct call to the nearly closed empire of China, where he began his ministry in 1854. Forced to return to England due to ill health, he devoted himself to founding and then leading the China Inland Mission (CIM). Strongly interdenominational and dependent on God for support, CIM became the vanguard for spiritual awakening in China. Taylor went back to China where he meticulously led the opening of each province to the Gospel. By 1895 there were 641 CIM missionaries in China. Through his writings and world speaking tours, Taylor's influence extended far beyond China. Today the faith missions movement he founded includes at least fifteen thousand missionaries representing more than seventy-five different faith missions.

Other faith missions that followed Taylor's model included the Christian and Missionary Alliance founded by A. B. Simpson in 1887, the Evangelical Alliance Mission founded by Fredrik Franson in 1890, and the African Inland Mission founded by Peter Cameron Scott in 1895. Through the first several decades of the twentieth century, dozens more would be founded.

THE CONTRIBUTIONS OF MODERN MISSIONS

The achievements of the modern missionary enterprise have been staggering. First, literally millions of people have found eternal life. Every ethnic, racial, and language group is now represented in the universal church of Jesus Christ. Second, national churches, with scores of local churches, now exist in virtually every nation of the world. Third, mission agencies planted thousands of educational institutions throughout the world. Fourth, Christianity became a liberating force for women and other underprivileged groups in the native cultures. The social and ethical implications of the Christian faith have often had profound, transforming effects on the native culture. Fifth, Christian mission agencies usually built medical facilities, including large hospitals, to care for the medical needs of the native population. Finally, the modern missionary movement has made the Bible available in hundreds of languages throughout the world. The Wycliffe Bible Translators, founded in 1934, is the best example of this extraordinary effort.

The modern missionary endeavor has literally changed the world.[1] North America has provided the majority of missionaries for this movement, and the revivals that have dotted American history provided the catalyst for this army of change-agents.

FOR FURTHER DISCUSSION

1. What were some of the factors that explain why modern missions exploded in the nineteenth century?
2. Summarize the importance of William Carey.
3. Summarize the importance of Hudson Taylor to faith missions.
4. List the positive effects that modern missions has had on the church and the world.

The Growth of the Gospel

GOD IS BUILDING HIS CHURCH—RAPIDLY

Across the centuries, Bible-believing Christians have become an ever-larger proportion of the world population. In A.D. 1430, only one person in one hundred was a Bible-believing Christian. Today, one in nine is. This means 600 million out of 5.7 billion people in the world are Bible-believing Christians. This huge body of believers is growing at a rate of *more than three times* that of the world population!

MILESTONE DATES IN THE GROWTH OF TRUE CHRISTIANITY

—At the dates indicated, a comparison of
1) the number of Bible-believing Christians and
2) the total number of people in the world:

One per hundred (**1%**) by	**A.D. 1430**	(One to **99** after **1430** years)
Two per hundred (**2%**) by	**A.D. 1790**	(One to **49** after **360** years)
Three per hundred (**3%**) by	**A.D. 1940**	(One to **32** after **150** years)
Four per hundred (**4%**) by	**A.D. 1960**	(One to **24** after **20** years)
Five per hundred (**5%**) by	**A.D. 1970**	(One to **19** after **10** years)
Six per hundred (**6%**) by	**A.D. 1980**	(One to **16** after **10** years)
Seven per hundred (**7%**) by	**A.D. 1983**	(One to **13** after **3** years)
Eight per hundred (**8%**) by	**A.D. 1986**	(One to **11** after **3** years)
Nine per hundred (**9%**) by	**A.D. 1989**	(One to **10** after **3** years)
Ten per hundred (**10%**) by	**A.D. 1993**	(One to **9** after **4** years)
Eleven per hundred (**11%**) by	**A.D. 1995**	(One to **8** after **2** years)

"Bible-believing Christian" refers to those people who read, believe, and obey the Bible whether or not they are yet as active as they ought to be in helping out with world evangelization.

WHERE DO THESE AMAZING NUMBERS COME FROM?

Major milestone dates down through history were supplied by the Lausanne Statistics Task Force, headed by David Barrett, Ph.D., author of the *World Christian Encyclopedia*. The intermediate values here were then calculated (exponentially) for these specific milestone dates. From the January-February, 1996 edition of *Mission Frontiers*, The Bulletin of the U.S. Center for World Mission, Pasadena, California. Used by permission.

Chapter Eleven

THE CHURCH AND REVIVALS IN AMERICA

The whole theory of revivals is involved in these two facts; viz., that the influence of the Holy Spirit is concerned in every instance of sound conversion, and that this influence is granted in more copious measure and in greater power at some times than at others. When these facts concur, there is revival of religion.

JOEL HAWES, 1871

BECAUSE REVIVALS HAVE BEEN SO frequent in America, one could easily study American history solely from their perspective. Each century has seen at least one period of renewal that molded the nation's development. The purpose of this chapter is to reconstruct the decisive impact revivals have had on the development of American society.

Undeniably, American civilization of the seventeenth century was tied almost exclusively to the Protestant Reformation. The Pilgrims and Puritans who settled New England were devout Calvinists. Baptistic groups came to Rhode Island and the middle colonies. Presbyterians established churches in both the middle and southern colonies. The Anglican church was central to the planting of Virginia, the Carolinas, Georgia, and New York. Lutherans also settled in the middle colonies. The only exception to Protestant dominance was Maryland, a quasi-Catholic colony, and Pennsylvania, a Quaker colony that practiced remarkable religious tolerance.

THE FIRST GREAT AWAKENING

By the eighteenth century, it was clear that the church needed renewal. There was an acute shortage of spiritual leadership in the churches, and few opportunities for adequate ministerial training existed in America. In addition, the reordering of the political relationships with the British Empire caused an unsettledness among many colonials. Finally, the second and third generations that now inhabited the American colonies had lost the original vision that had sent their forefathers to the New World. God in His grace, therefore, sent a revival to His church. That revival is usually called the First Great Awakening.

The move of God apparently began in the 1720s among the Dutch Reformed churches in the colony of New Jersey. A Dutchman named Theodore Frelinghuysen (1691–1748) came to minister there and preached moral purity and the need for a profound, not perfunctory, commitment to Christ. The churches began to grow in numbers, and members deepened in piety. Frelinghuysen found friends of like mind in the Tennent family, committed Presbyterians who believed that proper theological training was the key to bringing life to dead churches. William Tennent, Sr., (1673–1746) began to train young men for pastoral ministry in a school that became known as the Log College in the 1730s. The "graduates" of that college fanned out across the middle and southern colonies with the Gospel. They laid the groundwork for spiritual renewal in America.

Jonathan Edwards (1703–1758) gave pivotal leadership to the revival in New England. At seventeen Edwards graduated from Yale and took a pastorate in Northampton in 1727, where he served until 1750. His famous 1741 sermon, "Sinners in the Hands of an Angry God," epitomized the power of words in an age when sermons were usually read in a monotone voice. Edwards's preaching power contributed to the revival that swept through the entire Connecticut River valley. He also made a powerful defense of the emotionalism that often accompanied revivals, seeing this as evidence of the sovereign God at work. His involvement with George Whitefield (1714–1770) deepened the New England awakening.

As the best-known Protestant of the eighteenth century, George Whitefield gave an exceptional degree of unity to the colonial revival. A friend of John and Charles Wesley, Whitefield was a member of the Holy Club at Oxford University in the 1720s and 1730s. He made seven tours of the colonies, preaching up and down the coast of America. His impact on the New England revival was especially marked. It was his preaching style that appealed to the common American colonial. He used plain language that was easy to understand, and he contributed immensely to the more democratic and popular style of Christianity that was developing in late colonial America.

Largely through the leadership of Isaac Backus (1724–1806), New England Baptists grew and became institutionalized in the culture. In addition to championing adult baptism, Baptists stood for the separation of church and state; they resisted the traditional New England support of the churches by the government. The need for trained leaders led to the founding of a Baptist College in Rhode Island in 1764, later known as Brown University.

The Baptist work in the southern colonies was led by Shubal Stearns (1706–1771) and Daniel Marshall (1706–1784), who together founded a Baptist Association of churches at Sandy Creek, North Carolina, in 1755. Through this Association, Baptist churches burst across the South. The typical Baptist preacher was not well-educated; instead, he was often a farmer who preached on Sunday to his small country church. Such a Baptist model was appealing to the rural South and largely explains Baptist growth.

Lastly, the Methodist church, under the leadership of Devereaux Jarrett (1743–1801), gained strength in Virginia and North Carolina and laid the groundwork for the eruption of growth that would follow under Francis Asbury. Like the Baptists, Methodists appealed to the poor and uneducated of the South. Methodist ministers, with their simple gospel message, were often willing to go where the educated clergy would not.

The impact of the First Great Awakening on American civilization was staggering. Because of theological controversy generated by the revivals, Presbyterians and Congregationalists split. Two new denominations gained a strong foothold in America—the Baptists and the Methodists. Further, a new zeal and energy characterized American churches. New converts and new churches dotted the evangelical landscape of America. Missionary work among the slaves and the Indians resulted. David Brainerd (1718–1747) endured great hardships to take the Gospel to the Seneca and Delaware Indians. Evangelists Samuel Davies (1723–1761) and George Whitefield both ministered to slaves during this period. The Awakening built important bridges to Native Americans and African-Americans.

The Awakening, as the first truly national event, likewise had powerful cultural implications for the new nation. Either through his preaching or his writing, George Whitefield touched virtually every American.

His preaching tours throughout the colonies gave a measure of cultural unity unlike anything else at that time. This linkage often transcended ethnic barriers and provided a growing distrust of England and the Anglican church. Finally, the revivals resulted in a new form of spiritual leadership in the colonies. Gone were the days when only a highly educated clergy had legitimacy. Now the itinerant minister, often without formal education, preached that a person's relationship with God was more important than status or social standing. In many ways, the Awakening helped foster a growing commitment to democratic-republican ideals. That is why religious words such as *liberty* and *virtue* had strong social/political connotations as well.

THE SECOND GREAT AWAKENING

The American Revolution (1776–1783) profoundly changed American society. Not only did the colonies become an independent country—the United States of America—but the churches of America played a vital role in supporting the independence cause and giving leadership to it. The political ideology of the Revolution, called Republicanism, shared common tenets with Protestant Christianity. Both viewed history as a struggle between good and evil, with America clearly on the side of the good. Both viewed power and tyranny as the enemy of liberty. America, each argued, symbolized liberty and Britain, tyranny. Therefore, preachers of Congregational, Baptist, and Presbyterian congregations openly supported the independence cause as the cause of Christ and His kingdom.

However, with the nation established and the new Constitution written, a growing secularism took hold in America. In fact, through pamphlets and books, the deism that had fueled Enlightenment thinking filtered down to the masses. In addition, the new territories west of the Appalachian Mountains were generally devoid of any gospel witness. Economically, the nation faced hard times, even coming close to defaulting on its debts. Prices for staples soared, a plague of worms destroyed the corn and fruit crops, and diseases, including smallpox, ravaged the population. In many ways a crisis mentality characterized the nation. But from about 1790 to 1810, a broad-based revival swept across the new nation. It was the most significant revival in American history.

The southwestern phase of the revival began from the desire of one man to reach the frontier for Christ. James McGready (1758–1817) pastored three small churches in rural Logan County, Kentucky. Impressed by the writings of Jonathan Edwards, he led his people in a monthly fast and weekly prayer meetings for revival. Once a year he brought all the churches together on a mountainside to observe the Lord's Table. An outpouring of the Spirit at one of these gatherings drew many people from other churches. That Communion service birthed the first camp meeting, the form revival mainly took on the frontier. Camp meetings offered days and often weeks of gatherings where Presbyterian, Baptist, and Methodist preachers proclaimed the Gospel to eager listeners. In addition, Methodist circuit riders and Baptist lay preachers spread the Gospel throughout the South and the West, transforming the denominational landscape and spiritual climate of these regions.

The eastern phase of the Awakening centered on the college campuses. Timothy Dwight (1752–1817), newly appointed president of Yale, led a revival on that campus that brought hundreds to Christ. These students in turn carried revival throughout New England, New York, and the West. Similar developments occurred at the southern Presbyterian college of Hampden-Sydney.

Although the First Great Awakening dramatically affected the colonies, the Second Awakening had a more lasting effect on American life. First, Methodists, Baptists, and the newly formed Disciples of Christ spearheaded the revival, leaving the Congregationalists, Presbyterians, and Anglicans far behind. Methodists, Baptists, and the Disciples went on to dominate American Protestantism for decades.

Second, the Awakening produced durable institutions that impacted American culture well into the twentieth century. Institutions such as the American Bible Society (1816), the American Sunday School Union (1824), the American Tract Society (1825), the American Society for the Promotion of Temperance (1826), and numerous others owed their reform vision to the transforming zeal of the Second Awakening.

Finally, the Awakening represented a fundamental shift in American theology. Where the Puritans of the seventeenth century focused on a God-centered theology that stressed man's inability to save himself, the early nineteenth century embraced a man-centered theology that emphasized the free will and responsibility of man in salvation. In many ways, the Second Awakening marked the death knell of Calvinism as a major force in American religious life.

CHARLES GRANDISON FINNEY

This shift away from a God-centered theology accelerated with the revivalistic and evangelistic preaching of Charles Finney (1792–1875). Finney trusted Christ in 1821 and changed his vocation from lawyer to minister.

Throughout the remainder of the 1820s and into the 1830s, Finney conducted revival meetings in key Northern cities. These ventures gained him national prominence. In addition, some of his converts founded key reform movements, especially those dedicated to the abolition of slavery.

Charles Finney radically altered the direction of American Christianity. First, he introduced many "new measures"[1] into American evangelism. Because he believed so strongly in human free will, he thought that the evangelist, if he followed the proper methods, could reap a harvest of converts. Therefore, he utilized the protracted meeting; the anxious bench for repentant sinners; long, emotional prayers; and organized choirs—all designed to break the stubborn will of the prospective convert.

Second, Finney advocated a strong postmillennialism in his theology. He believed that the church, through its efforts at reforming society, could usher in the kingdom of God now! The kingdom could come in three years, he often said.

Finally, Finney's man-centered theology led him to advocate a perfectionism when it came to sanctification. Finney taught that some Christians could reach a permanent sanctified state in which they do not knowingly sin. He truly believed that Christians who were entirely sanctified could bring about a thorough reform of society so that the kingdom of God would come to America. Such optimism dovetailed perfectly with the individualism and self-sufficiency of the new nation.

THE LAYMAN'S PRAYER REVIVAL OF 1858

One of the most remarkable American revivals took place in 1858. Lacking any one leader, this renewal was thoroughly lay-oriented and took place largely in the cities. Praying, not preaching, sparked the movement that started in a noonday prayer meeting in New York. Soon interdenominational prayer meetings started up in most of the major cities of the North, with more than two thousand people jamming Chicago's daily prayer meeting at the Metropolitan Theater. The revival then spread to rural areas, including the South, to Europe, especially England, and even to Australia. The awakening helped establish the historical context for Moody, the Salvation Army, and the rise of the faith missions movement, all after the Civil War.

D. L. MOODY

D. L. Moody (1837–1899) and Billy Sunday both built their ministries on the "new measures" foundation of Charles Finney. Each represented the triumph of mass evangelism in Protestant America. Increasingly, as mass production triumphed in business, the same techniques crossed over into evangelism.

Born in Northfield, Massachusetts, Dwight Lyman Moody was a successful shoe salesman in both Boston and Chicago. Converted in his late teens, Moody started a Sunday school in the Chicago slums in 1858 and by 1866 was president of the Chicago YMCA. For Moody there was no dichotomy between social work and the Gospel. He rented four pews in Chicago's Plymouth Congregational Church and filled them with men from Chicago's streets. During his work with the burgeoning Sunday school movement, he met Ira Sankey (1840–1908), whom he enlisted as a song leader in his evangelistic meetings.

In 1873 Moody and Sankey embarked on a two-year preaching tour of Great Britain. Returning to the states as an established evangelist, Moody conducted evangelistic tours of Brooklyn, Philadelphia, New York, Chicago, and Boston from 1875 to 1879. Throughout the eighties and into the nineties, Moody transformed evangelism as he preached throughout the United States and Europe.

D. L. Moody was the focal point for urban revival in America and Europe. His preaching style and organizational skills brought a new level of refinement to revivalism. As a businessman, his managerial techniques appealed to the growing middle class of industrial America. The business community avidly supported his campaigns and gave his meetings a middle class flavor. His preaching was simple, pleasant, and straightforward—setting forth ruin by sin, redemption by Christ, and regeneration by the Holy Spirit. He laced his sermons with stories that cut to the heart of America's struggles with the loss of agricultural simplicity and the pressures of industrial, urban civilization. He traveled over a million miles and preached to more than 100 million people.

Moody not only transformed evangelism, but he also left an important institutional legacy. Believing that education was foundational for Christianity, he established two schools—Northfield Seminary for girls and Mount Hermon School for boys. In addition, in 1886 he established the Chicago Evangelization Society, later known as Moody Bible Institute. Finally, he started the Northfield summer Bible Conference in 1880, a forerunner of the Bible conference movement that swept across late-nineteenth-century America.

BILLY SUNDAY

Moody's successor in the development of mass evangelism was William (Billy) Ashley Sunday (1862–1935). Born near Ames, Iowa, Sunday at first pursued a baseball career; but in 1886 he was converted to Christ at Chicago's Pacific Garden Mission. In 1891 he walked away from baseball to become a full-time minister, first with the YMCA and then with J. Wilbur Chapman (1859–1918), another pioneer in mass evangelism. But after 1896, Sunday was on his own.

At first his emphasis was on small Midwestern towns, but gradually by 1915 larger cities all over America held Billy Sunday crusades. The hallmark of his urban crusades was the huge wooden tabernacle. Sunday's preaching style, which included colorful, bombastic antics and well-planned theatrics, gained him fame and attention. In addition, the Sunday crusades were a genius of organization. Before each crusade, an advance team of at least twenty specialists descended on the town arranging publicity, music, and business support. The team recruited thousands of church volunteers. At the center of such strategic planning was Sunday's wife, Helen Amelia Thompson.

Sunday's simple message reached over 100 million people, with about one million converts. But his influence extended far beyond conversions. He stood undaunted against alcohol use. In fact, he bears significant responsibility for the passage of the Prohibition Amendment to the U. S. Constitution. He likewise championed patriotism during World War I, arguing that "Christianity and patriotism are synonyms" and that "hell and traitors are synonyms" (Noll, 115-119). He helped raise millions of dollars for the military effort. Few Christian leaders have ever had a more significant impact on shaping American culture.

BILLY GRAHAM

Present-day evangelism and revivalism centers on Billy Graham (b. 1918). Born in North Carolina, Graham evidenced preaching skills even at an early age. After ordination as a Southern Baptist preacher and a brief pastorate, Graham became the first full-time employee of Youth for Christ in 1944. Graham's 1949 twelve-week Los Angeles crusade was a watershed in modern evangelism. Athletes, mobsters, and Hollywood stars professed faith in Christ. National attention resulted. Therefore, in 1950, Graham organized the Billy Graham Evangelistic Association and the *Hour of Decision* radio program. His 1954 crusade in England gained him international acclaim.

Billy Graham's message was the same as that of other evangelists, but his style differed. At first his hatred of communism mixed a forceful patriotism with the gospel message. He even befriended presidents such as Truman and Nixon. But Nixon's resignation caused Graham to back away from the perception of partisan politics. Graham's 1959 New York crusade marked the other determinative characteristics of his style. He included representatives of mainline Protestant churches in planning the crusade, causing many of the more conservative Protestants to label him a liberal. Graham also integrated African-Americans into his ministry and crusades and achieved the support of Roman Catholics as well. Finally, he penetrated Communist countries with the Gospel several years before the collapse of communism in Europe. He has also visited Communist China and North Korea, preaching and meeting with prominent Communist leaders.

In an age of few heroes, Graham has been a sterling example of integrity. Rarely responding to criticism, he has remained focused on proclaiming the Gospel. His use of technology has allowed him to preach to more people than any other individual in history. Arguably, he stands out as the evangelical statesman of the twentieth century.

Revivalism and evangelism in this century are a far cry from similar movements of colonial America. Theology seems less important to the twenty-first-century evangelist than it did to Jonathan Edwards in the eighteenth century. Perhaps the emphasis on method and technology has cost the church much when it comes to theological maturity and discipleship. Is the modern church stressing "just believe" and ignoring the importance of doctrine? This question is difficult to answer. But it reflects one of the central issues of today—the struggle of the church with modernity.

FOR FURTHER DISCUSSION

1. Summarize the three phases of the First Great Awakening.
2. Show why Jonathan Edwards and George Whitefield were so important to the Awakening.
3. Discuss several effects of the First Awakening.
4. How were the First and Second Awakenings different?
5. What was the Layman's Prayer Revival of 1858?
6. What is mass evangelism? How did D. L. Moody and Billy Sunday influence its development?
7. How did Billy Graham influence the development of evangelism in the modern age?

What If Edward Kimball Had Not Told a Shoe Clerk in Boston About Christ?

If Sunday school teacher Edward Kimball had not been faithful to share his faith with a Boston shoe clerk, the world might not have heard about Dwight L. Moody, Billy Sunday, or Billy Graham. But Kimball was faithful, and in 1856 Dwight L. Moody came to faith in Christ, and the world has never been the same. God called Moody into evangelism, and in 1879 while he was preaching in England, an evangelistic fervor was awakened in the heart of Frederick B. Meyer, the pastor of a small church.

Years later while Meyer was preaching on an American college campus, a student named J. Wilbur Chapman professed faith in Christ. Chapman went on to hold evangelistic meetings across America. He later hired a new convert (and former major league baseball player), Billy Sunday, to work as an advance man in his ministry. In a few years Chapman went into the pastorate, and Sunday began to lead his own evangelistic crusades.

In 1924 Billy Sunday held a crusade in Charlotte, North Carolina. After the meetings about thirty men formed the Charlotte Men's Club, which met on a regular basis for prayer. Ten years later the club met for a day of prayer and fasting in a grove of trees at Frank Graham's dairy farm. The main focus of the day was to prepare for an upcoming crusade to be held in Charlotte. One of the men, Vernon Patterson, prayed that "out of Charlotte the Lord would raise up someone to preach the Gospel to the ends of the earth." Patterson had no idea that the answer to his prayer was a few hundred yards away, pitching hay into feeding troughs. During the crusade led by Mordecai Ham, Frank Graham's son Billy committed his life to Christ.

Because Edward Kimball was faithful, the world has been blessed by the ministries of Dwight L. Moody, J. Wilbur Chapman, Billy Sunday, Mordecai Ham, Billy Graham, and thousands of other men and women the world has never heard of, like Vernon Patterson. Church history is in large part a record of the faithfulness of people like Edward Kimball and Vernon Patterson.

Based on information from the *Encyclopedia of 7,700 Illustrations: Signs of the Times,* Paul Lee Tan, ed. (Rockville, Md.: Assurance Publishers, 1979) and *A Prophet with Honor: The Billy Graham Story* by William Martin (New York: William Morrow, 1991).

Chapter Twelve

THE CHURCH AND MODERNITY

What is the relation between Christianity and modern culture; may Christianity be maintained in a scientific age?
J. GRESHAM MACHEN,
CHRISTIANITY AND LIBERALISM, 1923

THE MODERN WORLD HAS NOT been kind to the church. As earlier chapters have shown, the antisupernaturalism of the Enlightenment had devastating results for theology and by the twentieth century had filtered down to the ordinary church member, especially in the mainline denominations. The term "modernity" involves accommodating Christian theology to antisupernaturalism. So modernity asks: Is the Bible really the Word of God? Can the church really trust the first three chapters of Genesis? Are science and the Bible friends or enemies? What exactly is salvation, and how is it defined?

THE SOURCES OF MODERNITY

Before Charles Darwin (1809-1882), most people in Western civilization believed that the design they observed in the physical world proved the existence of God and that everything had a fixed order or place. Each species was separately created by God, and each had a specific purpose in the mind of God. Darwin's 1859 publication of *Origin of Species* shattered these assumptions for many. Those who accepted Darwin's theory thought that he had undermined the authority of Scripture, especially in terms of Creation. Darwin argued that a struggle for existence characterized the natural world, resulting in all organic beings adapting to the changing dynamics of their environment. Thus, by natural selection unfavorable variations and those possessing them are eliminated. He thought that this process of natural selection over vast periods of time explains how different species evolve.

Darwin's theory of evolution had catastrophic effects for Christianity. First, it questioned the literal interpretation of the Bible, especially of Genesis 1. Does "day" mean a twenty-four-hour day? Natural selection also argued against a special Creation of God as recorded in Genesis. Doubt about the Bible's authority resulted. Second, natural selection removed the idea of purpose and design from nature. Chance was now seen as the powerful force controlling natural selection. People now thought that the intricacy and interconnectedness of nature did not necessarily demonstrate the handiwork of God. Third, the idea of order and fixity in nature was questioned. For Darwin, nature was in a state of flux and change via natural selection; the word was change, not permanence. Fourth, Darwin's hypothesis was destructive to the idea of the uniqueness of man, so central to Christian theology. For Darwin, man was a product of time and chance. Key doctrines, such as the image of God in humankind, the entrance of sin into the race by the Fall, and the need for a Savior, were all brought into question. Darwin shook Christianity at its very foundation.

A second source of modernity was the social gospel. With the rise of industrial capitalism came massive social problems—vast urban industrial centers teeming with workers who lived in slums. These urban centers festered with dirt, exploitation, crime, and poverty. In addition, immigrants of different ethnic, racial, and religious backgrounds flowed into the cities where child labor predominated. Christian leaders, therefore, asked what the role of the Gospel was in those conditions. Could Christianity and socialism be reconciled? What was the social dimension of Christianity? As Christians struggled with these questions, a response known as the social gospel emerged.

The social gospel was liberal Christianity's response to the crisis of modern industrialism. Men like Walter Rauschenbush (1861–1918) and Washington Gladden (1836–1918) theologically revised the Gospel. Sin was defined as corporate and environmental, not individual and inborn. The problems of humanity were caused by the conditions of society, they said, not by the sin nature of each individual. Therefore, salvation was redefined to involve changing a person's surroundings, helping to organize labor unions, and working for legislation to improve human conditions. The social gospel defined sin and salvation as external, with no real emphasis given to the internal corruption of humanity.

The third source of modernity centered on further undermining of the Bible's authority. Coming from Germany, a movement called higher criticism questioned the authorship of biblical books, as well as the traditionally accepted dates and purposes for the biblical texts. German scholars doubted Mosaic authorship of the Pentateuch, for example. Julius Wellhausen (1844–1918) argued that these books were really written by four unknown authors (he identified them by the letters J, D, E, P), not Moses. In New Testament criticism, F. C. Baur (1792–1860) asserted that Paul wrote only Romans, Galatians, and the Corinthian letters. In addition, Baur placed all four Gospels in the second half of the second century. These critics questioned the authority of God's Word, saying it could not be trusted.

Because many of the Protestant scholars in America studied in Europe or used European scholarly texts, Darwinism, the social gospel, and higher critical thinking became a part of seminary education in America. By the opening of the twentieth century, most of these ideas were common in mainline Protestantism. Pastors taking the pulpits in America reflected these ideas, and their preaching and counseling likewise exhibited a commitment to what was then called "modernism."

FIGHT FOR CONTROL OF THE DENOMINATIONS

Between 1910 and 1930, among the largest of the Protestant denominations—Northern Baptists, Northern Presbyterians, and Northern Methodists—a struggle for control ensued between the fundamentalists and the modernists. On the surface, issues such as administration of foreign missions and control of denominational magazines defined the conflict. However, the real concern centered on theology. The modernist wing of Protestantism had abandoned the inerrancy of Scripture, the Virgin Birth, the deity of Christ, His Second Coming, and His substitutionary atonement. The fundamentalists, through writing, preaching, and teaching, defended adherence to these fundamental doctrines as central to Christianity. In every major case, the fundamentalists lost control of the denominations.

The successes of nineteenth-century revivalism had lulled fundamentalism into complacency. The Bible conference movement, begun in the 1870s and 1880s, often separated those committed to historic Christian orthodoxy from the mainline churches. In addition, the Bible institute movement, begun in the same time period, provided practical, abbreviated, and efficient biblical education to laypeople. These schools trained missionaries and gave extraordinary opportunities to women, but they also reinforced the separatism taking place. The preaching ministries of Moody and Sunday widened the chasm between fundamentalists and modernists. Publications such as *The Scofield Reference Bible* (1907) and *The Fundamentals* (1910) defined the theological issues of the struggle.

With control lost, what did the fundamentalists do? First, many formed new denominational groups. The Presbyterians formed the Orthodox Presbyterian Church, the Bible Presbyterian Church, and the Reformed Presbyterian Church. Some Baptists formed the General Association of Regular Baptist Churches, the Conservative Baptist Association, and the Baptist Bible Fellowship. In addition, the numbers of independent churches exploded across America. Second, conservative fundamentalists formed interdenominational groups such as the Independent Fundamental Churches of America (1930) and the National Association of Evangelicals (1942) that worked together to promote conservative theological causes.

The formation of parachurch ministries was a third response of the conservatives. Ministries founded for youth work, such as Word of Life (1941), Young Life (1941), and Youth for Christ (1944), were designed to reach a whole generation of young people. College ministries—Inter-Varsity Christian Fellowship of America (1941) and Campus Crusade for Christ (1951)—represented concerted efforts to reach the universities. Evangelical Teacher Training Association (1930) was started to help standardize and develop a curriculum to train Bible teachers in colleges, Bible institutes, and local churches. The radio became a powerful teaching tool through the ministries of *The Old Fashioned Revival Hour* of Charles Fuller, *Back to the Bible* of Theodore Epp, and *Radio Bible Class* of M. R. DeHaan.

THE FRAGMENTATION OF CONSERVATIVE PROTESTANTISM

By the 1950s, fundamentalist Protestantism was rife with tension. In the judgment of many conservative Christians, the fundamentalist-modernist controversy of the twenties and thirties had left the fundamentalists bruised, defensive, suspicious, and increasingly separatistic. Therefore, a group of conservative Christians, later known as neo-evangelicals and led by Harold John Ockenga (1905–1985), broke with fundamentalism. Together with Billy Graham and Carl Henry (b. 1913), Ockenga sought to reform fundamentalism to be more scholarly and to put more emphasis on apologetics and the social dimension of

Christianity. They founded Fuller Theological Seminary in California to champion this reform. *Christianity Today*, a magazine founded by Billy Graham and his father-in-law, L. Nelson Bell, in 1955, was considered the unofficial voice of the movement.

Over issues such as the inerrancy of Scripture, questions about eschatology, and the role of the social sciences in meeting people's needs, a further fragmentation of conservative Christianity occurred in the 1970s and 1980s. A younger generation of evangelicals, represented in publications such as *The Wittenberg Door* and *Sojourners* magazine, argued that neo-evangelicalism did not go far enough. As political and social activists, these evangelicals, led by individuals such as Ron Sider and Tony Campolo, pressed the church to consider its social responsibility and to give less emphasis to theological questions. The result is that today conservative, evangelical, fundamentalist Christianity is increasingly divided.

Further fragmentation of Protestantism is evident in the explosion of "renewal" movements in the twentieth century. Originating in the early years of the century, Pentecostalism challenged Protestants to think about the issues of sanctification and the Holy Spirit in a new way. Proclaiming the connection between baptism of the Holy Spirit and speaking in tongues, the Azusa Street Revival in Los Angeles (1906) spread throughout the world and eventually led to the formation of several new denominational groups such as the Assemblies of God, the Church of God (Cleveland, Tenn.), the Church of God of Prophecy, and the Church of God in Christ. Over time the Pentecostal movement gained respectability and legitimacy as these denominations experienced rapid growth in the United States and overseas. But the mainline denominations were largely left untouched by Pentecostalism.

In the late 1950s and into the 1960s, groups such as those led by businessman Demos Shakarian (1913–1993) and Pentecostal preacher Oral Roberts (b. 1918) committed themselves to penetrating the mainline churches with what came to be known as the charismatic renewal. To model that goal, Roberts joined the United Methodist Church in 1968. Throughout the 1960s and 1970s, charismatic renewal groups formed in every major denomination—Methodist, Presbyterian, Lutheran, Episcopalian, and the Roman Catholic Church. The charismatic movement emphasized not only the gift of tongues, but also words of knowledge and prophecy as well as faith healings. Nationwide conferences throughout this period demonstrated that what united the various renewal movements was more a shared experience of the Spirit than theology.

In the 1980s, a "third wave" of renewal spread across the church, heralded by individuals like John Wimber (1931–1997) and Fuller Seminary professor C. Peter Wagner (b. 1930). The third wave movement identified "the signs and wonders" of the New Testament book of Acts as legitimate demonstrations of God's power today. These signs were seen as authenticating Christ's ambassadors. Hence, proponents speak of "power evangelism" and "power encounters" that prove God's existence and validate the gospel message. The "Signs and Wonders" movement expressly appeals to evangelicals who have traditionally rejected such demonstrations of power as appropriate only for the first century. The most significant example of this was the embrace of the third wave by former Dallas Theological Seminary professor Jack Deere.

THE GROWTH OF THE BLACK CHURCH

The Black church in America had its origins in the slave religion of the American South. Deprived of their identity, oppressed by their masters, and unable to establish their own institutions, many slaves turned to Christianity. Faith in Jesus Christ gave them hope for the future when His justice would right the wrongs done to them. Negro spirituals embodied the vibrant faith of a subjugated people who looked to God for justice and mercy.

The Black church began to organize into denominations quite early in the national period. The African Methodist Episcopal Zion Church was formed in 1816 with Richard Allen (a former slave) as its first bishop. The National Baptist Convention of the USA, formed in 1915, was an amalgamation of three Baptist groups that today, after additional mergers, has a membership in excess of 6.5 million members. Many Pentecostal groups also formed during the twentieth century. One of the fastest growing churches in America and the fifth largest denomination is the Church of God in Christ (COGIC). Founded by Charles Harrison Mason in 1897, the church adopted its Pentecostal distinctives and its current name in 1907. Currently with membership of over 6.75 million, COGIC churches grew more than 48 percent between 1982 and 1991.

The modern civil rights movement largely grew out of the Black church. Leaders such as Dr. Martin Luther King, Jr., were themselves Baptist preachers who believed that the Bible condemned discrimination and racism. King, the undisputed leader of the nonviolent civil rights movement, organized African-Americans and whites to pursue justice for all Americans regardless of race. Using the Bible and nonviolence, the movement impacted all aspects of American society.

ROMAN CATHOLICISM AND MODERNITY

The modern world has not been kind to Roman Catholicism either. In fact, the twentieth century witnessed a crisis of authority in Catholicism. During the nineteenth century, the Roman Catholic Church (RCC) attempted to consolidate its authority through a series of decisive declarations aimed at defining doctrine and papal power. In 1854 the RCC declared the immaculate conception of Mary. Through the merits of Jesus, the RCC pronounced that Mary was preserved from the effects of original sin and therefore sinless. In 1869 it issued the Syllabus of Errors, which announced that when the Pope spoke *ex cathedra* (from his chair), he was speaking infallibly. Finally, Vatican Council I (1869–1870) affirmed papal infallibility. The papacy utilized this power only once, in 1950, when Pope Pius XII proclaimed the dogma of Mary's bodily assumption into heaven.

During the twentieth century, Roman Catholicism experienced its greatest struggles since the Reformation. Largely through Vatican Council II (1963–1965), the RCC answered the challenges of modernism. In the documents that resulted from the council, the RCC embraced the ecumenical movement. The RCC has thus been in dialogue with various Protestant denominations and the Eastern Orthodox Church. Vatican II likewise avowed papal infallibility and the equality of Scripture and church tradition as sources of authority for Catholics. However, it was in the practical areas that Vatican II had its most revolutionary impact. The council made optional some traditional expressions of Catholicism—Latin in the liturgy, meatless Fridays, Lenten fasts and abstinence, the cult of the saints, and the regular practice of confession to the priests. Vatican II thus removed many of the cultural distinctives of Catholicism.

Today the Roman Catholic Church under Pope John Paul II is struggling with how to respond to liberation theology in Latin America, the charismatic movement in western Europe and America, pressures to allow the ordination of women into the priesthood, and ethical questions such as abortion, contraception, euthanasia, and divorce. The RCC has officially taken strong stands on each of these questions, but many Catholics reject the official position, thereby heightening the crisis of authority.

The modern world has brought profound challenges to the church of Jesus Christ. This chapter has highlighted some of those challenges and reviewed how the church responded. The twenty-first-century world is one of continuous and permeating change. One thing that can be learned from history is that the church needs to remember its mission and its Head. With that focus, the church will not lose its way and will remain the instrument God uses to bring people to Himself in salvation.

FOR FURTHER DISCUSSION

1. Summarize how each of the following contributed to modernity and challenged the church:
   Darwinism—
   Social gospel—
   German higher criticism—
2. What was the fundamentalist-modernist controversy in the American denominations? Who won the struggle?
3. List some of the responses of fundamentalists to the loss of control of the major denominations.
4. Summarize the differences between Pentecostalism, the charismatic movement, and the "Signs and Wonders" movement.
5. What is the difference between a fundamentalist and an evangelical?
6. Summarize the developments in Roman Catholicism in the last century.

NOTES

CHAPTER 8: THE CHURCH AND THE SCIENTIFIC REVOLUTION

1. Butt, John, ed. *The Poems of Alexander Pope* (New Haven, Conn.: Yale University Press, 1963), p. 808.

CHAPTER 10: THE CHURCH AND MODERN MISSIONS

1. For more information on the history of missions, see Hulbert, Terry C., and Mulholland, Kenneth E., *World Missions Today* (Wheaton, Ill.: Evangelical Training Association, 1990).

CHAPTER 11: THE CHURCH AND REVIVALS IN AMERICA

1. "New measures" was a phrase used by critics of Finney in the 1820s. See Mark Noll, *History of Christianity in the United States and Canada* (Grand Rapids: Wm. B. Eerdmans Publishing Co., 1992), p. 175.

GLOSSARY

Apology—When used as a theological term, it refers to making a defense of what is held to be true. Apologetics has to do with the study of evidences from Scripture and nature used to present a logical defense of the truth of Christianity.

Bishop—From the Greek word *episkopos* (ep-is'-kop-os), it means "overseer." In early church history, a bishop was a minister who was responsible for the oversight of several churches.

Catechetical School—Catechetical comes from the Greek word *katecheo* (kat-ay-kheh'-o), which means to "teach" or to "instruct." The Catechetical Schools in the early church followed the Socratic approach of teaching, which utilized a question-and-answer methodology.

Church—From the Greek word *ekklesia* (ek-klay-see'-ah), it means "called out ones" or simply "assembly." In reference to the Christian church, *church* has two meanings. The first is the universal or invisible church, which is made up of all born-again believers in Jesus Christ. The second usage (most prevalent in this book) is used to refer to the visible, organized church, which is made up of both believers and unbelievers.

Circa—When used with a date, it means "approximately," indicating uncertainty about the ability of historians to pinpoint it with absolute precision.

Diet of Worms—The formal assembly of German princes that had legislative authority. Martin Luther was tried before this body in 1521 in the German city of Worms.

Emasculate the Gospel—To remove the very heart from the gospel message of salvation and thus make it ineffective.

Erudition—Refers to extensive knowledge, usually gained from the study of books.

Free-grace Gospel—The good news of salvation based fully on the unmerited favor of God being bestowed upon believers through no self-generated activity.

Monasticism—An approach to life that calls for physical isolation from the world and usually is accompanied by the taking of vows such as chastity and poverty. Monasticism is characterized by an emphasis on obedience and authority as well as a desire for seclusion, order, and routine.

Veneration—Means to "worship." Often used by the Roman Catholic Church as in the "veneration of Mary" or the "veneration of the saints."

BIBLIOGRAPHY

CHAPTER 1

Bruce, F. F. *New Testament History*. New York: Anchor, 1972.

Cairns, Earle E. *Christianity Through the Centuries*. Grand Rapids: Zondervan, 1981.

Foh, Susan. *Women and the Word of God*. Philadelphia: Presbyterian and Reformed, 1979.

Hoehner, Harold. *Chronological Aspects of the Life of Christ*. Grand Rapids: Zondervan, 1977.

CHAPTER 2

Lightfoot, J. B. *The Apostolic Fathers*. Grand Rapids: Baker, 1978.

CHAPTER 3

Frend, W. H. C. *The Early Church*. Philadelphia: Lippincott, 1966.

Gonzalez, Justo L. *A History of Christian Thought*, Vol. 1. Nashville: Abingdon, 1970.

CHAPTER 4

Brown, Peter. *Augustine of Hippo*. Berkeley: University of California Press, 1967.

Kelly, J. N. D. *Early Christian Doctrines*. New York: Harper and Row, 1978.

Leith, John H., ed. *Creeds of the Churches*. Atlanta: John Knox Press, 1982.

CHAPTER 5

Gonzalez, Justo L. *A History of Christian Thought*, Vol. 2. Nashville: Abingdon, 1971.

Southern, R. W. *Western Society and the Church in the Middle Ages*. New York: Penguin, 1970.

CHAPTER 6

Bainton, Roland H. *Here I Stand: A Life of Martin Luther*. New York: Abingdon, 1950.

_____. *The Reformation of the Sixteenth Century*. Boston: Beacon, 1952.

Schaff, Phillip. *History of the Christian Church*. New York: Charles Scribner and Co., 1871.

Spitz, Lewis W. *The Protestant Reformation, 1517-1559*. New York: Harper, 1985.

CHAPTER 7

Gonzalez, Justo L. *A History of Christian Thought*, Vol. 2. Nashville: Abingdon, 1971.

Olin, John C. *The Catholic Reformation*. New York: Harper, 1969.

CHAPTER 8

Deason, G. B. "The Protestant Reformation and the Rise of Modern Science." *Scottish Journal of Theology* 38:221-40.

Gonzalez, Justo L. *The Story of Christianity: The Reformation to the Present Day*. New York: Harper, 1984.

Hall, A. R. *The Scientific Revolution, 1500-1800*. Boston: Beacon, 1962.

CHAPTER 9

Fletcher, William C. *The Moderns: Molders of Contemporary Theology*. Grand Rapids: Zondervan, 1962.

Gay, Peter. *The Enlightenment: An Interpretation*. New York: Knopf, 1966-69.

Geisler, Norman. *Christian Apologetics*. Grand Rapids: Baker, 1976.

Gonzalez, Justo L. *A History of Christian Thought*, Vol. 3. Nashville: Abingdon, 1975.

McGrath, Alister E. *The Making of Modern German Christology: 1750-1990*. Grand Rapids: Zondervan, 1994.

Redman, Ben Ray, ed. *The Portable Voltaire*. New York: Viking, 1949, 1963.

Ritschl, Albrecht. *The Christian Doctrine of Justification and Reconciliation*. Clifton, N.J.: Reference Book Publishers, 1996.

CHAPTER 10

Latourette, Kenneth Scott. *A History of the Expansion of Christianity*. New York: Harper, 1941-1944.

CHAPTER 11

Murray, Iain. *Revival and Revivalism: The Making and Marring of American Evangelicalism, 1750-1858*. Carlisle, Pa.: Banner of Truth, 1994.

Noll, Mark A. *A History of Christianity in the United States and Canada*. Grand Rapids: Eerdmans, 1992.

Smith, Timothy L. *Revivalism and Social Reform: American Protestantism on the Eve of the Civil War*. Gloucester: Peter Smith, 1976.

Weisberger, Bernard A. *They Gathered at the River: The Story of the Great Revivalists and Their Impact Upon Religion in America*. Chicago: Quadrangle, 1966.

CHAPTER 12

Noll, Mark. *A History of Christianity in the United States and Canada*. Grand Rapids: Eerdmans, 1992.

THE TRUTH
ABOUT
WORLDVIEWS

CONTENTS

Chapter One

POSTMODERNISM
AND THE NEED FOR
WORLDVIEW ANALYSIS

THE NATION THAT IS often hailed as the wealthiest, most powerful, and best-educated nation on earth is still one of the most religious—but in intriguing new ways. Nearly two-thirds of Americans say religion is very important in their lives, and close to half say they attend worship services at least once a week—the highest percentages since at least the 1960s. Other surveys indicate that belief in God and devotion to prayer are at historic highs. Further, voluntary giving to religious institutions—estimated to exceed $55 billion annually—surpasses the gross national product of many countries. From Los Angeles to New York City, there are more churches, synagogues, temples, and mosques per capita than in any other nation on earth (one for every 865 people).[1]

Additionally, more than four of every five Americans say they have "experienced God's presence or a spiritual force" close to them, and 46 percent say it has happened many times.[2] There appears to be a deep spiritual hunger in America. The modern world has failed many Americans who are reaching beyond themselves to find meaning and purpose in life.

But being religious today in America looks entirely different than it did only one hundred years ago when Protestantism, Catholicism, and Judaism dominated the religious landscape. America is now becoming the most religiously diverse nation on earth. Since the Immigration Act of 1965 eliminated quotas linked to national origin, Muslims, Buddhists, Hindus, Sikhs, Jains, Zoroastrians, and others have arrived in increasing numbers. Added to this reality is the fact that three in four Americans believe all religions have at least some elements of truth, even though few say they know much about any religions other than their own. Further, nearly 70 percent think spiritual experiences are the most important aspect of religion, not a written text or set of dogmas.[3]

With increased religious diversity has come increased emphasis on toleration. In a 2002 *US News & World Report*/PBS poll, 71 percent, including 70 percent of Christians, said Christians should be tolerant of people of other faiths and leave them alone. Only 22 percent (24 percent of them Christians) thought it was a Christian's duty to convert members of other faiths.[4] The point is that American culture, with its pluralistic nature and its diverse faiths, is changing—radically so.

A recent issue of *Time* magazine (October 13, 1997) focused on the growing appeal of Buddhism in America. In the words of one of its adherents, Buddhism is "a path of enlightenment into a lay culture without priests and temples and structures. . . . [It is a] daily practice of everyday life. . . . It's beneficial to all of us. It will go down in history as one of the best things that happened to civilization."[5] How can this be? Buddhism advocates the abandonment of logic and reason, glorifies emptiness and the illusion of selfhood, and looks toward the end of desire and liberation from rebirth. How could multitudes of Americans, including media gods like Steven Segal, Richard Gere, Tina Turner, and Phil Jackson, now embrace a system considered irrational not all that long ago? The answer is that America is now a postmodern, post-Christian civilization.

THE POSTMODERN WORLDVIEW

The whole Western world is in the midst of a paradigm shift from modernism to postmodernism. It is imperative that the church and its leaders understand this shift, for it impacts how we both relate to the culture in which we live and how we represent the Lord Jesus Christ in that culture. Postmodernism is not a generation of people; it is a way people view reality, a worldview. As a worldview it seeks to redefine truth and the place of the individual in the scheme of things.

Postmodernism is a reaction against modernism (or modernity). The modern period in Western history began with the Renaissance in northern Italy and northern Europe but exploded with the eighteenth-century Enlightenment. According to Millard Erickson[6] modernity abandoned the transcendent concept of reality, replaced supernaturalism with naturalism, championed humanism and individualism, and saw human knowledge as certain, objective, good, and attainable through the scientific method.

Theologian Stanley Grenz[7] poignantly sees modernism's human archetype in Mr. Spock, key hero in early versions of the popular TV series, *Star Trek*. The assumptions of the modern mind were that knowledge is certain and reasonable, objective and dispassionate, good and, therefore, optimistic. "Spock was the ideal Enlightenment man, completely rational and without emotions (or his emotions were in check). . . . According to the creators of *Star Trek,* in the end our problems are rational, and therefore, they require rational expertise." As with Spock, the Enlightenment saw human reason as the path to universal truth and universal morality. By contrast, postmodernism rejects the cold rationality of Mr. Spock and embraces a fuzzy tolerance of all truths.

Postmodernism as a worldview is complex and not easy to define; however, its ideas are pervasive and all-encompassing. What follows is an attempt to define the five specific characteristics of this emerging worldview now dominating Western civilization.

1. *A radical hermeneutic.* Rooted in the deconstructionist movement of post-World-War-II Europe, the postmodern hermeneutic (the science of interpretation; how humans interpret and understand the written word) sees words as power; words manipulate and control. This new hermeneutic argues that in communication, there is no final or true meaning to words. Therefore, the reader is sovereign. The reader determines the meaning of the text while the author's intent is nearly irrelevant. According to Alister McGrath,[8] "All interpretations are thus equally valid, or equally meaningless (depending on your point of view)."

For biblical Christianity, such a position is troublesome. Because authorial intent (i.e., God's verbal revelation in the Bible) is unknowable and irrelevant for the postmodernist, it is senseless to discuss the Bible as the Word of God. The postmodernist considers such a statement offensive and an attempt to control and manipulate. It is insensitive to those who see other sources of "truth," since in postmodernism, all claims to truth are equally valid; there is no universal vantage point for viewing truth. With this mind-set, a postmodernist will argue that it is arrogant and unacceptable for a Christian to claim the Bible as God's Word, as truth or as a source for truth. To accept the postmodern view of the written word is to destroy the foundation of genuine, biblical Christianity.

2. *A radical relativism.* Here is the focal point of postmodernism: the doctrine of the autonomous self living in community. In postmodernism, the self defines reality. There are virtually no boundaries for behavior, and there are few authority figures that matter anymore. For example, the entire May 7, 2000, issue of *The New York Times Magazine* was devoted to this concept of autonomy. Autonomy impacts all aspects of culture—entertainment, business, law, leisure, and religion. I, the self, define all

aspects of reality. There really is nothing transcendent that defines it for me; I am autonomous. This claim has a haunting ring of familiarity to it; in the book of Judges is the refrain, "Every man did what was right in his own eyes"(17:6; 21:25).

When individual autonomy is mixed with America's deep-seated commitment to rights and liberties, one sees how lethal this thinking becomes in the areas of sexuality, ethics, and morality. There are no boundaries or absolutes. Instead, the right of the individual is absolute. This belief frames discussion on the key cultural issues of our day—abortion, homosexuality, cohabitation before marriage, the use of genetic and reproductive technologies, and the right to "die with dignity." When "every man does what is right in his own eyes," the limits to freedom and rights are boundless.

A 2002 Zogby International poll of college seniors demonstrates the impact of this radical relativism. Nearly 73 percent of students surveyed said that when their professors taught ethics, the consistent message was that uniform standards of right and wrong do not exist.[9] Instead, what is right or wrong depends on differences in each individual and in the individual's culture. So, if all beliefs are equally valid, there is nothing to debate. Nothing separates personal "truth" from self-delusion. If students currently enrolled in college are convinced that ethical standards are simply a matter of individual choice, what hopes can we have that they will be reliably ethical in their future careers? This is the end result of a radical relativism.

3. *A radical pluralism.* The first two characteristics naturally lead to the third: a culture with a smorgasbord of religious choice where no worldview has a corner on truth. There are many "truths" and, since there is no certainty anyway, it does not matter which worldview you choose. Postmodernism stands for radical pluralism and universalism. In the postmodernist's mind, all religions are social constructs, and none is inherently superior to another. All religions are equally valid, and all paths lead to God. Religion, says the postmodernist, is not based on something external but stems from internal needs and subjective personal experience. Religious people are therefore not discerning truth but rather are the source of their own truths, says the postmodernist. Something is true if it is true for me!

Such a tenet explains why postmodern jargon is so pervasive in our culture. People often use terms with positive connotations—"diversity," "inclusion," and "multiculturalism"—to reinforce the claim that there is no truth and that no one can claim truth. Everyone's opinion is equally valid and worthy. Hence, increasingly Christians are bombarded with charges of being bigots and hatemongers because of the claim that Jesus is the way, the truth, and the life (John 14:6) and that Jesus is the only name under heaven by which men are saved (Acts 4:12). This is exclusive truth penetrating an inclusive world. It is exclusive truth, embodied in Jesus and proclaimed as such by His followers.

4. *A radical morality.* Postmodernism argues that moral and ethical behavior is not the result of any final reality such as God. Rather, morality comes from the needs of society. Every culture develops its own morals, and no other culture has the right to judge another's value system. True ethics are based on the needs of the moment, not final truth.

Let me illustrate: Two recent articles in the *Chronicle of Higher Education* reveal that college students are often unwilling to oppose large moral horrors, including human sacrifice, ethnic cleansing, and slavery, because they believe no one has the right to criticize the moral views of another group or culture. Professor Robert Simon, who has taught philosophy for twenty years at Hamilton College in Clinton, New York, indicates that his students acknowledge that the Holocaust occurred but cannot bring themselves to say that killing millions of people is wrong. Between 10 and 20 percent deplore what the Nazis did, but their disapproval is expressed as a matter of taste or personal preference. One student responded, "Of course I dislike the Nazis, but who is to say they are morally wrong?" Another professor, Kay Haugaard of Pasadena College in California, wrote of a student in a recent literature class who said of human sacrifice, "I really don't know. If it was a religion of long standing. . . ." Haugaard was stunned that her student could not make a moral judgment: "This was a woman who wrote passionately of saving the whales, of concern for the rain forests, of her rescue and care for a stray dog."[10]

The result of postmodern pluralism and relativism is tolerance. You must respect the beliefs and distinctives of others. The only wrong belief is saying that someone else's beliefs are wrong. Postmodernism has replaced the ethic of truth with the ethic of tolerance. Toleration extends to lifestyle questions and practices. No wonder criticizing the homosexual lifestyle is labeled as bigoted and hate-filled. No wonder condemning abortion is labeled as threatening a woman's rights. No wonder challenging doctor-assisted suicide as dangerous is labeled naive.

But the Bible repudiates this type of thinking. It contains transcultural principles that form the ethical foundation for all civilizations. It is always wrong to murder, to lie, to commit adultery—no matter what culture one belongs to.

5. *A radical pragmatism.* Since there are no absolutes and every decision is based upon the needs of the moment, whatever works becomes "the new truth." The triumph of pragmatism therefore marks postmodernism. It does not matter if the United States president is immoral as long as he keeps the economy growing. If state-sponsored gambling causes destructive and addictive behavior, so be it; the profits are going to education and care for the elderly. Same-sex marriages are between consenting adults; if it works for them, fine. No one is being harmed by such practices.

Pragmatism is not a valid test for truth, for it can produce an end-justifies-the-means ethic. Following the tenets of postmodern pragmatism, the culture can justify the destruction of human embryos as a source for stem cells or gender selection of children in order to prevent hemophilia. Such practices will eventually empower parents to select their children as they select a car or a house. Give the specifications, and it is yours. God's revelation to the human race, recorded in the Bible, is the beginning point for truth's pursuit, not a pragmatic, end-justifies-the-means ethic.

THE NEED FOR WORLDVIEW ANALYSIS

The apostle Paul, in Colossians 2:8, issued a penetrating exhortation: "See to it that no one takes you captive through philosophy and empty deception, according to the tradition of men, according to the elementary principles of the world, rather than according to Christ." The relevance of this admonition is clear. We live in a world where "the tradition of men" and "empty deception" are pervasive. Wading through the current sea of worldly philosophies and traditions can be both perplexing and overwhelming—not to mention dangerous! How can a Christian keep from being deceived by worldviews that are opposed to the knowledge of Christ and His Word? How does one discern the differences between the competing worldviews of our postmodern age?

First, it is important to understand what a worldview actually is. A worldview is the core of what we believe. It answers the basic questions of life: How did we get here (creation and the universe)? Where are we going (the meaning of history)? What is the nature of reality (physical or spiritual or both)? What is the nature of God, or transcendent reality? What is the nature of truth (objective or subjective)? What is the nature of human beings? What happens to human beings when they die? What guidelines determine human behavior (ethics)? This book analyzes each of the major world religions, cults, and philosophical systems as a worldview. The history, major teachings, and ethical implications of each worldview will be considered. The ultimate thesis of this book is that only genuine biblical Christianity provides consistent answers to worldview questions. Only Christianity presents the truth.

Additionally, this book will suggest connection points, or bridges, for sharing the gospel within each worldview. The overall goal is to inform and equip Christians to live and witness the truth of the gospel in this postmodern world where all worldviews are tolerated.

BUILDING BRIDGES

Because Christianity proclaims exclusive truth, Christians must know how to build bridges to the postmodern world. Christians must understand this world and know how to make connections to it, while at the same time maintaining their distinctiveness as Christians. As Jesus counseled, we must "be in the world but not of the world" (see John 17:13-18).

The task of "building bridges" to the larger culture with its postmodern pluralism is very much a New Testament idea. Alister McGrath writes that the New Testament church is really a "colony of heaven. . . an outpost of heaven in a foreign land."[11] It speaks the language of that homeland and is governed by its laws. Yet, as Paul demonstrated in Acts 17:22-31, we are to seek common ground with citizens of earth, to be all things to all people that we might win some. For example, though the dangers of postmodernism are clear, this worldview is not all negative. Postmodernism allows an openness to supernatural realities and spiritual experiences that modernism would have scoffed at. The value postmodernists usually place on authentic relationships and community, an acceptance of diversity, personal experience, and practical living are not necessarily contrary to Christian values. The Christian must seize the opportunity and find this common ground with postmodernists.

Ultimately, we must speak and live the truth of the gospel in the world and into the worldviews of others. Using 1 Peter 3:15, Ken Boa[12] suggests a pattern for building bridges that will be helpful as you form relationships with those from different worldviews:

• "Sanctify Christ as Lord in your hearts." In other words, be certain Jesus is Lord of your life and affirm your utter dependence upon Him. Remember that when you are talking with someone embracing another worldview, this is a spiritual battle. Your task is to be faithful in proclaiming the truth. It is God's business to change the person.

• "Always be ready." Know God's Word and know how and when to use it. In doing so, you will be prepared to correct misconceptions about biblical Christianity.

• "To make a defense." Always keep the discussion focused on Jesus and His finished work on the cross. Stay away from minor issues and do your best to prevent the other person from focusing on his or her misconceptions. Stay focused in a friendly, God-honoring manner, and do not be sidetracked by the other person's unique claims or errors.

• "To every one who asks you." Pray that God will give you opportunities to share your faith in this pluralistic culture. Above all, be a good listener and ask for permission to express your view in the discussion. Do not be pushy or arrogant.

• "To give an account for the hope that is in you." It is your personal relationship with the living God that is the source of your power and strength. Do not be afraid to recount your personal experiences of all that God has done for you. He is your hope and strength.

• "Yet with gentleness and reverence." Show patience, respect, and love as you talk. Always look for common ground and seek to develop a relationship of trust and confidence that God can use to bring that person to Himself.

Never forget that Christians have the truth! Only genuine biblical Christianity provides consistent answers to worldview questions. This should give us confidence as we seek to gain understanding about different worldviews, build relationships, and make a stand for the truth in an age of many truths.

FOR FURTHER DISCUSSION

1. Summarize the cultural and ethnic changes that have occurred in America since the 1960s. What do you see as positives and negatives about these changes?
2. Cite real-life examples of each of the following five aspects of postmodernism from current news headlines, your own community, or past experiences.
   • Its radical hermeneutic
   • Its radical relativism
   • Its radical pluralism
   • Its radical morality
   • Its radical pragmatism

3. What is a worldview? Name some reasons why you think it is impor-
    tant to have a Christian worldview.
4. What are some "empty deceptions" the world gives as answers to
    the basic worldview questions?
5. In examining Ken Boa's pattern for building bridges, which points
    do you think would be the most challenging for you to practice?
    Why?

Chapter Two

NATURALISM
(OR SECULAR HUMANISM)

IN HIS BOOK *Culture Wars,*[1] sociologist James Davison Hunter argues that American culture is experiencing a crisis of moral authority. One side of the cultural cleavage, "the progressive," claims that the individual self is the source of moral authority, while the other side, "the orthodox," claims that something transcendent is the source of moral authority. This struggle to define America's cultural center informs the debate over abortion, euthanasia, sexuality issues, education, law, and the role of government in our lives. It is a battle for the future.

The progressive side of this cleavage argues from a naturalistic perspective. There is an inherent antisupernaturalism in this position. For most people committed to modern thinking, physical matter is all there is. God does not exist, and religion is irrelevant. As religion fades, the progressive hopes, peace and harmony will reign. This sentiment is perhaps best captured in John Lennon's song "Imagine." In the lyrics, Lennon calls upon us to envision a time when there is "no heaven," "no hell," "no religion," and "nothing to kill or die for." What he calls the "brotherhood of man" will bring in an age of "no possessions," wealth, or greed; a time when the world "will be as one."

When did this worldview originate? What is its origin? One must go back to the Enlightenment of the eighteenth century for the answers.

THE EIGHTEENTH-CENTURY ENLIGHTENMENT: MODERN HUMANISM'S ORIGIN

The Enlightenment was a movement of ideas that saw its task as the release of humanity from error and prejudice, toward the achievement of truth, which in turn would produce freedom. Many Enlightenment thinkers targeted religion, for they believed it embodied the error and prejudice they loathed. They regarded Christianity and all other religions as irrational and inappropriate in a scientific age. The Enlightenment sought rational explanations for all of reality. They especially desired to examine human institutions to discover rational laws that governed society. Some of the principal thinkers of this age were Voltaire (1694-1778), Jean Jacques Rousseau (1712-1778), Denis Diderot (1713-1784), and David Hume (1711-1776).

Enlightenment thinkers were critical and skeptical of everything. Nothing in society escaped their analysis, including the church, the law, and the government. One French philosopher said, "all things must be examined, debated, investigated, without exception and without regard for anyone's feelings."[2]

Many of them also doubted the certainty of knowing absolute, universal truths that stemmed from religion. David Hume, the Scottish philosopher, epitomized this skeptical commitment by denying the rational certainty of experience, attacking arguments for God's existence, and authoring a blistering attack on a belief in miracles. Near the end of the Enlightenment, Immanuel Kant (1724-1804) also disputed traditional proofs for God's existence, claiming that one could not know God through reason, for there was no way to empirically verify His existence.

Finally, John Locke (1632-1704) embodied the devotion to empiricism, a decisive characteristic of the Enlightenment. For Locke, humans were born with no sense of right or wrong or any innate truths. Instead, the mind is like a blank slate that, through life, is filled with data coming from the senses. Following Locke, many Enlightenment thinkers repudiated all religion, including Christianity, as superstitious. It needed to be replaced with a rational system of ethics.[3]

THE INTELLECTUAL GODFATHERS OF HUMANISM

Three key historical figures have provided the underpinnings of this modern humanism that focuses strongly on the human mind to reason and solve problems. Each has solidified the modern conviction that religion, especially Christianity, has no place in a scientific age. Each has regarded religion as the enemy to progress and the higher achievements of the human race. Each has detested genuine biblical Christianity.

1. *The scientific attack.* Charles Darwin (1809-1882) undermined the authority of Scripture in the minds of many people, especially in terms of its account of Creation. Before Darwin, most people in the Western world believed the design they observed in the physical world

proved the existence of God and that everything had a fixed order or place. Each species was separately created by God, and each had a specific purpose in God's mind. Darwin's 1859 publication of *Origin of Species* shattered these assumptions. He argued that a struggle for existence characterized the natural world, resulting in organic beings adapting to the changing dynamics of their environment. Thus, by natural selection, unfavorable variations and those possessing them are eliminated. This process of natural selection over vast periods of time explains how different species evolve, he thought.

Darwin's theory of evolution had catastrophic effects for Christianity. First, it questioned the literal interpretations of the Bible, especially Genesis 1. Does "day" mean a twenty-four-hour day? Natural selection also argued against a special Creation of God as recorded in Genesis. As a result many doubted the Bible's authority. Second, natural selection sought to replace the idea of divine purpose and design in nature. Chance was offered as the powerful force controlling natural selection. Third, Darwin questioned the idea of order and fixity. For him nature was in a state of flux and change via natural selection; the word was *change*, not *permanence*. Fourth, Darwin's hypothesis was destructive to the idea of the uniqueness of man, so central to Christian theology. For Darwin, man was a product of time and chance. Key doctrines such as the image of God, the entrance of sin into the race through the Fall, and the need for a Savior were all questioned. Darwin shook Christianity at its foundation and made atheism respectable. Without Darwin, it is doubtful humanism would have been a viable option.[4]

2. *The political and economic attack.* Karl Marx (1818-1883), the founder of ideological communism, detested religion of all forms. He led one of the fiercest political and economic attacks on religion, specifically Christianity, in the modern world. He regarded religion as similar to opium; it drugged people. Because religion focused so much on heaven, it kept the working class down and, in Marx's view, was the excuse for their exploitation by the rich. For Marx, only the revolution energized by the working classes (the proletariat) would produce the perfect, communal society that he expected to emerge at the end of history. He believed the revolution would purge society of the evils of capitalism and produce the classless society that would bring history to its end.

3. *The psychological attack.* Sigmund Freud (1856-1939) led an unrelenting psychological attack on religion. An avowed atheist, Freud argued that religion was merely a psychological projection. Like a child

runs to its father for protection in times of trouble, so humans project their earthly father into the heavens and run to him when things get tough. Freud believed that religious teaching had no basis in truth and that religion was really a sign of neurosis. Only his method of psycho-analysis, which probed beneath the subconscious, could help the person enslaved to religious dogma achieve the freedom Freud believed possible. His books, *The Future of an Illusion* and *Moses and Monotheism* provide his scathing attack on religious teachings.[5]

The scientific, political, economic, and psychological attack leveled by Darwin, Marx, and Freud have provided the intellectual basis for the ongoing revulsion most humanists have for religion, and especially for biblical Christianity. In some ways, the Christian church of North America is still reeling from these blistering attacks.

MODERN HUMANISM AS A WORLDVIEW: ITS THEOLOGY

What exactly does modern humanism or naturalism mean? At least historically, "a humanist" can be an "academic humanist" who studies the humanities—history, art, philosophy, or the classical languages. Such a scholar can be a Christian. Modern humanists should not be confused with "humanitarians," people who do good things for others. The humanists (naturalists) that this chapter addresses are those represented in the American Humanist Association, an organization created during the Enlightenment.

In 1933 a group of thirty-four liberal U.S. humanists drafted *The Humanist Manifesto I,* a document considered radical for its time. Committed to reason, science, and democracy, the document rejected orthodox religious dogma and argued for a "new statement of the means and purposes of religion."[6] This document was followed in 1973 by *The Humanist Manifesto II,* which not only reaffirmed the tenets of the 1933 document, but also raised the issues of civil liberties, equality, human survival, world economic growth, population and the environment, war and peace, and the building of a world community.

These two documents encapsulate the worldview of modernism. In short, modern humanism despises conventional religion and traditional morality. It rejects any belief in God and, instead, affirms a dogmatic and optimistic belief in humankind. Modern humanists see the problems of the world—racism, oppression, militarism, war, and poverty—as resolvable by humans working together for the maximum fulfillment of all. Traditional religion, whatever its form, they argue, has not made progress in solving these human problems. The modern humanist claims that we must put faith in ourselves and aggressively attack the problems of the human race. Such a spirit is evident in organizations such as the Americans for Democratic Action, the American Civil Liberties Union, and the National Organization for Women.

Despite the antisupernaturalism of modern humanism, this worldview still has a "theology." Here are its salient themes:

1. *Creation and the universe.* Humanists contend that the physical world was formed from chaos and that only man's reason has brought some order to this chaos. There is no divine plan or purpose. For the humanist, the only thing eternal is matter. Carl Sagan, who popularized the humanist approach to science and cosmic evolution, argued, "The Cosmos is all that is or ever will be."[7] Humanists say that all the matter of the universe has always existed in some form. In addition, this matter has no relationship to any transcendent creator.

The universe as we know it is a closed system, maintains Sagan.[8] It cannot be reordered from anything or anyone from outside itself. Of course, there is no transcendent God; humans are unable to reorder matter either. Sagan argues that because humans are matter and because there is no such thing as a soul (or anything supernatural), the laws of the universe apply to humans as well. Humans do not transcend the universe in any manner whatsoever. The universe is a closed system based on a uniform set of cause-effect relationships; humans are a part of that system.

2. *God.* Humanists insist that there is no personal God who created the universe or who gives any kind of meaning to it. They also reject the idea of God as sovereign, as one who organizes and oversees the course of history. As *The Humanist Manifesto II* asserts, "We find insufficient evidence for belief in the existence of the supernatural; it is either meaningless or irrelevant to the question of the survival and fulfillment of the human race. As nontheists, we begin with humans and not God, nature and not deity."[9] Thus, humans make their own history without any master plan. There is no accountability to God and no fear of judgment from Him.

3. *Humanity.* The human race is a cosmic accident, say the humanists. Humans come from nothing and, when they die, go to nothing. But that does not mean man is insignificant; indeed, humans are the key to a better world. Born with basic goodness, their intellects and attitudes only need to be positively shaped through their environment and education. *The Humanist Manifesto II* contends that "reason and intelli-

gence are the most effective instruments that mankind possesses."[10] That
is why modern humanism believes that compassion, cooperation, and
community will bring about a better world. For that reason, economic
well-being is possible in a world of "shared human values." There is no
such thing as eternity; so modern humanism affirms that happiness is the
only core value for the human race.

Humanism as a philosophy contends that "man is the measure of all
things." In themselves, humans are the ultimate norm by which values
are determined. They are the ultimate beings and the ultimate authority; all reality and all of life centers on human beings.

Curiously, although humans emerge from nothing and move toward
nothing at death, somehow humans acquire supreme dignity. Yet,
despite the humanist's belief in human progress, what is the real reason for hope? Why should we affirm human dignity? Why should I fight
to solve the problems of racism, war, or poverty? If nothingness is my
ultimate destiny, then human dignity is an illusion. Although emotionally satisfactory, humanism is intellectually dishonest and unten-
able.

4. *Ethics.* Modern humanism maintains that there are no absolutes
to guide humans ethically. *The Humanist Manifesto II* demands that ". . .
moral values derive their source from human experience. Ethics is
autonomous and *situational,* needing no theological or ideological sanction. Ethics stem from human need and intent. To deny this distorts the
whole basis of life. Human life has meaning because we create and
develop our futures. . . . We strive for the good life, here and now."[11] For
that reason, all human acts are ethically neutral, except for their influence on others for good or ill. But human standards are constantly
changing, fluid, and vary from culture to culture. Hence, humans
must create their own standards and then live consistently with them.
Humanism rejects any dependence on absolute ethics; instead, sexual
freedom, personal autonomy, and the unbridled pursuit of personal
peace and happiness are the vital center of the humanist's ethical standard.

For decades humanism was the dominant worldview in most colleges
and universities. It pervaded the discipline of science and underscored
the humanities throughout Western civilization. It gives the impression
of being objective, unbiased, and modern. Because modern scholarship
has been so closely associated with humanism's tenets, to disagree with
it is to appear backward and naive.

Today, however, in the typical college or university, postmodernism is competing with humanism. Where humanism has generally argued that truth is knowable, certain, and obtainable through the scientific method, postmodernism steps away from humanism's claim and argues that truth in any absolute or certain sense is not attainable. For that reason tolerance of all beliefs, worldviews, and systems is the reigning tenet of postmodernism. Both postmodernism and humanism seek human autonomy with no accountability. The relativism and pluralism of postmodernism mesh perfectly with the antisupernaturalism of humanism. The difference between the two is how each views the possibility of attaining absolute truth.

UNITARIANISM: HUMANISM AS AN ETHICAL SYSTEM

In many ways, the religious institutionalization of humanism (or naturalism) is the Unitarian worldview. The Unitarian worldview has its origins deep in early church history when many denied the triune nature of God. However, its modern form has its origin in late eighteenth- and early nineteenth-century New England. The theological descendants of the Puritans (the Congregationalists) denied the doctrine of the Trinity. The official movement was founded in 1825 as the American Unitarian Association, which merged with the Universalists in 1961. The movement acknowledges that it is no longer a part of the Christian worldview.

The Unitarian worldview has beliefs that make it the religious embodiment of naturalism (or humanism):

1. Unitarians deny that the Bible is God's Word. At best, it is a great piece of literature.

2. God is not triune. In fact, He is not a person. At best, Unitarians regard Him as a Force, or some Prime Mover. Unitarians often embrace atheism comfortably.

3. For the Unitarian, Jesus is a mere man. He is often thought of as a great teacher or ethicist but never as deity.

4. Unitarians argue that humans must look to themselves for their "salvation," which means nothing more than the development of good character and living a good life. They reject the doctrine of hell and of God as a judge.

5. In short, Unitarians regard human reason as the sole authority for guidance and purpose in life. This worldview is naturalistic humanism dressed up as a religion with buildings, pastors, and teaching centered on the power of human reason.[12]

BUILDING BRIDGES TO HUMANISM

Bridge #1

Humanism affirms the value of human life and sees human happiness as its core value. This meshes with biblical Christianity, which also affirms the value of human life. However, humanism has no basis for its claim for the value of human life, for helping people, or for showing compassion. Why engage in such things if humans are simply the product of chance? Christianity affirms the value of life because humans bear God's image (Gen. 1:26ff). It provides the reason for compassion, care, and concern that is missing in humanism. Humanism is most vulnerable on this point and we must lovingly press it.

Bridge #2

Humanism claims that in terms of religious beliefs and ethical standards, it is impossible to have absolutes. In other words, there are absolutely no absolutes. In making such a claim, humanism affirms something absolute. That is a glaring inconsistency, and Christians can point this out. Christians can press humanists to seriously reflect on the inadequacy of a lack of standards for truth and ethics. Are humanists willing to bank everything on the belief that there is no God? What if there is? What if there is accountability? The Holy Spirit can use this inconsistency within humanism to bring conviction.

Bridge #3

Humanism teaches that at death there is extinction. The only "immortality" for the human, says *The Humanist Manifesto II,* is to "continue to exist in our progeny and in the way our lives have influenced others in our culture."[13] There is no hope of seeing loved ones, of life after death, or of an eternal destiny. Humanism provides no real incentives for living or for dying. This physical world is all there is, they argue, and we must live for the moment. If there is no God, then there is no accountability and no motivation for virtue or goodness. Most people cannot live with this kind of teaching.

Here Christianity's message is compelling. It offers hope because there is life after death; there is hope of seeing loved ones and friends. Christianity also offers the certainty of salvation, which guarantees heaven, eternal life with God. Humanism offers no counsel to a family who has lost an infant in death, to someone with a terminal illness, or to a wife who has lost her husband in an automobile accident. The humanist can offer nothing; Christianity offers everything. It is in the real world that humanism's bankruptcy becomes evident.

Naturalism (or humanism) pervades Western civilization and is still currently institutionalized in many of the academic centers. It remains powerful, influential, and informs much of contemporary education. It will retain its position of importance only as long as Westerners seek their purpose and meaning from technology, science, and reason. Its anti-supernaturalism is difficult for most people, however, because the average person cannot live without some sense of a transcendent realm, belief that there is something beyond death, that the physical is not all there is. Only genuine biblical Christianity answers that quest for meaning and purpose.

FOR FURTHER DISCUSSION

1. What were some of the goals and characteristics of the eighteenth-century Enlightenment?
2. Why was it difficult for the Enlightenment person to embrace religion, especially biblical Christianity? What evidence do you see of this same tendency in people you know today?
3. Crystallize the essence of *The Humanist Manifesto I* and *The Humanist Manifesto II* into one or two sentences. What would you say as a possible rebuttal to these documents?
4. How is the humanist's view of humanity similar to and different from the Christian view? Use Scripture to support your observations.
5. Which humanist views or humanist figures (Freud, Marx, Darwin, etc.) do you see as most influential today?
6. What bridge (from the book or your own ideas) might you use to build a connection with a Unitarian friend?

Chapter Three

HINDUISM

HINDUISM IS PERHAPS the most complex and difficult worldview to understand, especially to the Western, rational mind. It seems to hold frequently contradictory tenets and is the most difficult to summarize in a short book. Hinduism gradually grew over a period of five thousand years, absorbing and assimilating the religious and cultural movements of India. It has been likened to "a vast sponge, which absorbs all that enters it without ceasing to be itself. . . . Like a sponge it has no very clear outline on its borders and no apparent core at its center."[1]

In order to understand the basic tenets of Hinduism, we need an outline of the main Hindu scriptures and its history. After this brief review of Hinduism's history, we will review its theology and its ethical implications.

HINDUISM: ITS SCRIPTURES AND ITS HISTORY

Scriptures

The Hindu scriptures, mainly written in Sanskrit, were composed over a period of more than 2,000 years. The name for the most sacred scriptures of Hinduism is the "Vedas," meaning "book of knowledge." There are four Vedas: the Rig-Veda, the Sama-Veda, the Yajur-Veda, and the Atharva-Veda. These sacred texts written before 1000 B.C. contain the life, customs, and beliefs of early polytheists who inhabited ancient India. They also contain the liturgies, chants, prayers, and litanies associated with the worship of their many gods. Hindus usually regard the Veda texts as verbally and unerringly authoritative.

From 1000 to 800 B.C. another group of holy texts emerged called the Brahmanas. The focus of these texts is the sacrifices that Hindus must perform. The Brahman priests were given the authority and responsibility to perform animal sacrifices to the gods to appease them and ensure salvation.

Mature philosophical Hinduism emerged with the writing of the best-known Hindu texts—the Upanishads—written between 800 and 600 B.C. These texts have little regard for the ritual, formal religion of the earlier holy books; instead, they are philosophical writings that emphasize an understanding of the world and the realm of the transcendent. With the Upanishads, the important Hindu term "Brahman" came to designate the one Reality or World-Soul. Brahman (sometimes identified as "Atman") is the absolute, infinite, eternal, omnipresent, impersonal, indescribable, neuter Being of the universe. Individual human souls, the Upanishads teach, are to merge with Atman to achieve salvation (more about this later).

About 250 B.C., the Code of Manu emerged as a sacred text. The Code gives the commandments and prohibitions that regulate the daily living of the Hindu through all of life's stages. Social regulations, dietary rules, and interpersonal rules of behavior reinforced the emerging caste system within ancient India. Indeed, the four-fold caste system is presented in the Code with great elaboration and approval.

Among the many sacred Hindu texts, the Bhagavad-Gita is perhaps the most revered. It is part of the epic devotional literature that emerged around the time of Christianity's origin. The Gita records the ongoing discussion between the Hindu hero-warrior-god Krishna and Arjuna, his kinsman, friend, and disciple. The dialogue reinforces a commitment to India's historic caste system and reincarnation, and can be summarized as "Do your caste duty, and trust your God for the rest of your salvation." With the Gita, Hinduism had become devotional and duty-oriented.[2]

History

Ancient Hinduism (2000-500 B.C.). In this period we see the worship of half-personified forces of nature such as fire, wind, and rain, and a primitive conception of the Absolute, the One. All things were a part of this impersonal One. Another important development of this period is the conception of a cosmic order of which the Hindu gods were the guardians. A professional class of priests became necessary to propitiate these gods with sacrifices.

During this time the Upanishads were written, which turned the Hindu searchlight inward. Hindus discovered that at the center of their being, beyond the senses, beyond the mind, and beyond understanding is a divine spirit. The goal of Hinduism is to liberate the human divine spirit—the true end of man. At the end of this period in history, the gods and sacrifices faded into the background. What emerged was the focus on self, the law of karma, and the commitment to reincarnation.

The Sutra and Epic Period (500 B.C. to A.D. 300). During this period the epics of Hinduism, especially the Bhagavad-Gita, promoted a great religious revival throughout India as the stories, legends, and teachings of the Upanishads became popular and understandable among the people. Also during this period, the multiple gods and goddesses from the various parts of India became incorporated into the Hindu pantheon of gods. The use of images, temples, pilgrimages to sacred places associated with deities, and festivals took hold in Hindu India. Thus the main tangible features of Hinduism found in modern India came into being.

Medieval Hinduism (A.D. 300 to 1400). During this long period, Hinduism faced three enemies—Buddhism, Jainism, and Islam. Although still found in India today, Buddhism and Jainism, both of which emerged from within Hinduism, were defeated as challenges to Hindu supremacy. But that was not the case with Islam.

Islam raced throughout India from A.D. 1000 through 1400, causing a period of turmoil in the course of Hindu history. Hindus suffered terribly from Islamic fanaticism. There were forced conversions, destruction of temples, and the desecration of holy places. Major parts of Hindu India were lost to Islam.

Modern Hinduism (A.D. 1400 to the present). The British takeover of India, which lasted about a century and a half, was quite unlike the Muslim conquest. The British broke the isolation of India and brought Hinduism into contact with European history, science, and literature, and exposed it to European political and social institutions, customs, and manners. The British rule profoundly changed India and Hinduism.

During this period, the caste system was severely criticized, as were practices such as the burning of widows on the funeral pyres of their husbands. Also, during the modern period, Hindu ideas and thoughts began to influence Western thinking as well. We see that influence in Ralph Waldo Emerson and the Transcendental movement of nineteenth-century New England.

Finally, Mahatma Gandhi changed India and Hinduism. Gandhi, in leading the fight for independence from Britain, extended the virtue of nonviolence to communities and nations and developed a suitable technique of action for it. According to Gandhi, truth is God, and nonviolence is the means of reaching it. Perfect nonviolence is perfect self-realization. His nonviolent methods produced the democratic India that still exists today.[3]

HINDUISM AS A WORLDVIEW: ITS THEOLOGY AND ETHICS

Hindu theology is complex and difficult for the Western mind. Foundational to Hinduism is the concept of Brahman. Brahman is the unchanging reality of the universe. It is the unity that is in the universe and yet beyond it. All objects, animate and inanimate, are included in it. Gods, humans, demons, animals, etc. are all part of Brahman. (The term "Brahman" derives from a language root that means "to expand," denoting an entity that cannot be limited in magnitude or expansion.)

In the Upanishads, Brahman is represented in two aspects—in an unqualified state named *Nirguna* Brahman, and in a qualified sense named *Saguna* Brahman. Nirguna Brahman is indescribable in human terms. Nirguna is attributeless. It is described by negation (i.e., by that which it is not—no body, no form, no attributes). It is beyond space, time, and causation; it is infinite and unknowable. The Upanishads describe Nirguna as:

> Where one sees nothing else, hears nothing else, understands nothing else—that is the Infinite.
>   Where one sees something else, hears something else, that is the finite.[4]

Central to Hinduism's understanding of Brahman is that Nirguna Brahman is veiled; that is, its "maya" (veil) hides the true nature of Brahman and causes the perception in humanity that the physical world is true reality, when in fact Nirguna Brahman, the realm of the true Infinite, is reality. Thus, Saguna Brahman is the veiled Brahman.

Because of Saguna Brahman, Hindus can speak of creation and its various deities. Saguna Brahman is the personal "god" who watches over the physical universe and acts as its ruler. When one speaks of attributes of deity, one is speaking of Saguna Brahman. For that reason, as well, Saguna Brahman is familiarly known as Brahma the Creator, Vishnu the Preserver, and Shiva the Destroyer. All three of these "gods" are simply different ways of looking at Saguna, the veiled Brahman.

The "Avataras" are the incarnations of the gods. The Avataras are crucial especially to understanding Vishnu. One of his most popular

Avataras is Krishna, the hero of the epic Bhagavad-Gita. The following chart attempts to visualize the difficult theology of Hinduism.[5]

NIRGUNA BRAHMAN
(Impersonal Brahman)

THE VEIL OR "MAYA"

SAGUNA BRAHMAN
(Personal Brahman with attributes)

BRAHMA   VISHNU   SHIVA

For the Western, rational mind, one major question looms in Hinduism: How can there be beliefs in different gods (Hindu polytheism) along with the belief in oneness so central to the Hindu idea of Nirguna Brahman? Malcolm Pitt argues that

> Because of the relative unreality of God himself in the theistic sense, the realization that all concepts of God are human and all creatures are Brahman, it seems to be only natural that the Hindu can tolerate the worship of any form of any kind as a manifestation of Reality. This is the framework that allows the most advanced Indian philosopher to feel that the most primitive animist, in living up to his best light, is *on the path* to the realization of Reality.[6]

Although Hinduism seems polytheistic, in reality its theology contends that there is one monistic Nirguna Brahman. Ultimately all religions and all beliefs reflect some kind of "path" to that Reality. Hence the "sponge" we know as Hinduism.

What follows are some cardinal definitions essential to understanding Hinduism:

• "God"—In Hinduism the Supreme Being is the Impersonal Nirguna Brahman, a philosophical Absolute beyond all impediments, either ethical or metaphysical.

• "Humanity"—The human is an emanation or temporary manifestation of the Impersonal Brahman. Humans are not inherently or permanently valuable; nor is the human accountable to "god."

• "The World"—The physical world is a temporary, worthless illusion due to the veil (or "maya") that hides the Impersonal Brahman.

• "Reincarnation" or "samsara" is the belief in the transmigration of the soul. There is a cycle of rebirth after rebirth after rebirth of the soul. One could be reborn as a wealthy aristocrat or as an animal, a beetle, worm, vegetable, etc.

• "Karma" is the cause of what is happening in one's life now. The Law of Karma (*karma* means "works, deeds") is the law that one's thoughts, words, and deeds have an ethical consequence fixing one's lot in future existences. Karma is what determines the nature of the next birth in the cycle. The Law of Karma is at the heart of the Hindu ethical system.

• "Moksha" is the release from the cycle of reincarnation, the cycle of life. It is salvation from illusion and release into the true reality of Nirguna Brahman.

• "Nirvana" is not a place but a state in which self-awareness is lost and oneness with Brahman attained.

• The "caste system" originated around 500 B.C. and constituted the fundamental social system of Hindu India. There were four main castes and a group called the "outcastes," or the "untouchables," obviously outside the four main castes. As Hinduism developed, the Law of Karma was tied to the caste system. Today the caste system is technically illegal in India, but its manifestations linger in the Indian social order.[7]

INROADS FROM THE EAST

Many Hindu concepts and practices have penetrated the Western world. In some ways, Hinduism has mainstreamed into Western thinking. Here are several examples:

Yoga. Yoga is not unique to Hinduism but is a fundamental technique for achieving Hindu spirituality. Norman Anderson describes yoga as "the physiological and psychological technique by which all bodily and psychic energy is controlled in order to achieve spiritual perfection."[8] Ultimately spiritual perfection is reunion with Brahman. Through the control of body and mind, the human can achieve a state of being that transcends space and time. The soul is thereby freed from attachment to the physical world of illusion. In the purest form of yoga, all mental activity stops, and the mind is completely still.

As a means of relaxation, to relieve stress, or even prescribed medically for muscle relaxation, yoga is popular in the West today. Christians must be careful and discerning about practicing yoga.

Reincarnation. Reincarnation tied with the Law of Karma has also been popularized in the West. It is manifested in three ways: (1) For some, karmic reincarnation provides an explanation for birth defects, physical handicaps, poverty, social injustice, and suffering. (2) Many today argue that humans "remember" their past lives in previous reincarnations. Feelings of *deja vu,* or a strong sense that one has been somewhere before, are additional proofs for reincarnation, some argue. (3) Some even argue that the Bible teaches reincarnation. John the Baptist and Melchizedek are viewed as reincarnations of Elijah and Jesus. The doctrine of being "born again" in John 3 is pointed out as evidence of Christianity accommodating Hindu reincarnation. The late Edward Cayce popularized such teachings in his books and lectures.[9]

Transcendental Meditation (TM). TM is the brainchild of Maharishi Mahesh Yogi, who was born in North Central India in 1917 and forty years later traveled to Europe and America preaching his gospel of TM. Different from yoga, TM practitioners use a "mantra," a secret Sanskrit word that is repeated over and over silently in the mind to achieve expanded consciousness. TM is often portrayed as a nonreligious exercise to relieve stress and to relax. TM promises greater clarity of perception, expanded awareness, and full development of the individual. The goal is natural bliss and happiness.

TM is presented as being nonreligious, but that is far from the truth. To Maharishi, humans are innately good, and TM enables one to reach that state of goodness through meditation using the mantra. Such teaching clearly contradicts the biblical teachings on sin, salvation, and the nature of humanity.

BUILDING BRIDGES TO HINDUS

The Christian gospel is clear and straightforward, but it is the convincing and convicting work of the Holy Spirit that brings a person to Christ. As we share Christ in both word and deed, it is imperative to remember that our prayers and our dependence on the Spirit bear the fruit of the gospel. Nonetheless, there are critical bridges or contact points of similarity between Christianity and Hinduism that the Spirit can use:

Bridge #1

As with Christians, Hindus believe that ultimate reality is spirit. John 4:24 teaches that "God is spirit and those who worship Him must worship in spirit and truth." That there is a spiritual world and that that world is ultimate reality is a powerful commonality between the two faiths.

Bridge #2

Central to Hinduism is the idea of a unity to all things, a unity centered in the belief in Nirguna Brahman. Given this conviction, the Christian can build the bridge that natural revelation reveals this unity, focused on God Himself (see Psalm 19 and Romans 1:18ff.). The next critical step is, of course, to get the Hindu to focus on the special revelation in Jesus Christ.

Bridge #3

Rooted in the Law of Karma, Hinduism also teaches that there is a sense of justice that permeates the universe. If the Hindu falls short of karma's requirements, he or she is condemned to the endless cycle of reincarnation. For the Christian, that sense of justice has been met in the finished work of Jesus Christ on Calvary's cross.

Bridge #4

Seeking to break the cycle of the soul's transmigration, Hinduism has a passion for freedom. For Christianity, Jesus provides that longing for freedom. Faith in Jesus Christ provides the freedom from sin and its bondage (see John 8:32).

Bridge #5

Hinduism teaches and respects the significant cost there is to the religious life. The typical Hindu honors and defers to the devout, the holy, and the ascetic leaders of the Hindu faith, for they are close to breaking the Law of Karma and achieving the freedom from reincarnation. Although Christianity rejects the extreme asceticism of Hinduism, it does teach "death to self," other-centeredness, and self-sacrificial love as paramount virtues. Hindus can identify with these teachings and witness the liberation from legalism that biblical Christianity brings.

These five bridges are most helpful in sharing Christianity with Hindus, but there are three significant barriers to which Christians must be sensitive. Only God's Spirit can break down these barriers, but Christians must be conscious of them and their power.

1. Most Hindus believe that ultimate truth is a synthesis of many truths. They separate the Jesus revealed in history from the Christ of the Christian faith. To them, Jesus is not the only path to truth or to salvation. Christians reject this syncretism, believing God's revelation is the only source for truth.

2. Many Hindus believe that all religions lead to the same goals and

that none possess full truth. Often Hindus contend that Jesus is *a* way to salvation but will not tolerate the claim that He is *the* way of salvation. This is perhaps the most formidable barrier between Christianity and Hinduism. For Christians Jesus is exclusive, and His path of salvation is exclusive (John 14:6).

3. Hindus believe that there is divine revelation in all religions and that none can claim exclusivity. Therefore, Christianity is not unique. But, because it is rooted in revelation, Christianity is unique and exclusive. With love and compassion, this truth must be shared. Only God's Spirit can break down this barrier.[10]

As stated at the beginning of this chapter, Hinduism resembles a sponge, soaking up teachings, absorbing them, and then redefining them according to its syncretistic teachings. If Christians are to reach Hindus, we must understand their thinking, build the bridges, and then allow the Holy Spirit to do His supernatural work. There is no other way to reach the Hindu for Jesus Christ.

FOR FURTHER DISCUSSION

1. What does the author mean when he compares Hinduism to a sponge?
2. Compare and contrast the sacred texts of Hinduism with the Christian Scriptures.
3. Which period of Hinduism's history was most interesting to you? Why?
4. Describe three of the following terms according to Hindu theology. Compare and contrast these terms with Christian theology.
   - God
   - humans
   - the world
   - reincarnation
   - Moksha
   - The Law of Karma
5. Which of the three "inroads from the East" do you think has had the most influence on Western culture? Give an example of this influence.
6. Keeping in mind some of the bridges and barriers to Hinduism cited in this chapter, write a paragraph on how you would share your faith with a Hindu. Spend time in prayer for opportunities to witness to Hindus.

Chapter Four

BUDDHISM

FOR THE TYPICAL WESTERNER, Buddhism is the faint memory of people prostrated before a large statue of a smiling man sitting cross-legged or of men in yellow robes with their hands together, meditating. Yet 300 million people call themselves Buddhists in Asia, and the numbers are increasing in the Western world. It is a religion that predates Christianity by almost six centuries. What is this curious faith called Buddhism? Why do so many Westerners find it appealing? How should we as Christians seek to reach the Buddhist with the gospel of Christ?

Richard Gard defines Buddhism as follows:

> Conceived in Asia, Buddhism is an historic expression of a universal human ideal. It offers any individual or society a voluntary way of thought and conduct, based upon an analysis of conditioned existence, dependent upon supreme human effort, and directed toward the realization of freedom in perfect existence.[1]

From its beginnings, Buddhism differed from most other religions. Rather than focusing on moral evil, it concentrated on pain and suffering; unlike other religions, Buddhism did not ask for devotion to or ritual toward a supreme god or gods. Buddhism is essentially a philosophy rather than a religion, an Eastern form of spirituality. David Bentley Taylor characterizes Buddhism as "a non-theistic ethical discipline, a system of self-training . . . stressing ethics and mind-culture to the exclusion of theology."[2]

BUDDHISM: ITS HISTORY

Buddhism was born in the sixth century B.C., one of the most significant centuries in human history. Babylon had collapsed as a world power in 538 B.C. only to be replaced by two Eastern powers—India and China. In this century, India moved from tribal oligarchies to a monarchy and an empire. Within India at this time a monetary system, trade and commerce, and a class of merchants and royal advisors emerged. Hinduism was being challenged, and a new, reflective, and meditative form of Hinduism was emerging, illustrated especially by the Upanishads (see chapter 3).

In addition, within Hinduism a movement of celibate asceticism developed. These new ascetics lived by begging and did not worship any deities. They maintained that the ascetic lifestyle of self-denial brought about liberation from reincarnation. According to Richard Robinson and Willard Johnson, these ascetic Hindus "believed in transmigration [i.e., reincarnation] and maintained that life is misery and liberation from the cycle of birth and death is supreme good."[3]

Into this historical context Siddhartha Gautama, the founder of Buddhism, was born in northern India. Although disputed, his probable dates are 566 to 486 B.C. Early Buddhist thought and history were transmitted through oral tradition and not written down until later. So the life of Siddhartha contains extensive legends mixed with historical fact. Apparently born into a wealthy family, Siddhartha lived in comfort through his youth, until he was confronted with a crisis. When challenged with "the four most impressive sights"—a man advanced in age, a sick man, a dead body, and an ascetic hermit—he abandoned his comfort, his wife, and child to seek life's meaning, specifically to answer the questions of suffering and death.[4]

Siddhartha sought answers in Hinduism. He shaved his head, put on a yellow robe, and tried asceticism for five years. John Noss describes some of his devotional acts during this period:

> He lived for periods on all sorts of nauseous foods, dressed in chafing and irritating garments, stood for days in one posture . . . sat on a couch of thorns, lay in the cemetery on charred bones among rotting bodies, let dirt and filth accumulate on his body till it dropped off of itself, and even ate his own excrement in the extremity of self-discipline.[5]

However, after five years, he realized the futility of asceticism and abandoned the effort. According to legend, Siddhartha's awakening came while he was sitting under a Nigrodha tree (or Bo tree). There he won his battle with desire and attained the knowledge of perfect contentment, becoming a *Buddha*, which means "enlightened one." He had discovered a "middle path" between those who taught sensuality (indulging oneself) and those who taught asceticism (denying oneself). His

Buddhist monastic order (i.e., the order of the enlightened ones) had begun. It spread quickly throughout India, and Buddha spent the rest of his life preaching the "middle path." He died at the age of eighty.

Siddhartha Buddha was profoundly concerned with explaining suffering—its cause and how to escape it.[6] His answer was the Four Noble Truths:

1. Suffering is universal. The act of living is suffering, and each person's incarnation is suffering. Therefore, "salvation" (Nirvana) is release from this cycle of suffering.

2. The cause of suffering is craving (selfish desire). The endless cycle of reincarnation is tied to this desire, this craving, because humans are attached to this world.

3. The cure for suffering is to eliminate craving. Buddha's great discovery was that to live is to suffer, and craving causes suffering; therefore, remove craving, and suffering will cease.

4. Eliminate craving by following the Middle Path—the Noble Eightfold Path. This Eightfold Path consists of three categories: understanding, morals, and concentration:

- *Understanding:* right viewpoint, right aspiration
- *Morals:* right speech, right behavior, right occupation, right effort
- *Concentration:* right-mindedness, right meditation.

Buddha taught that those who followed this Eightfold Path would eventually attain Nirvana, the release from the endless cycle of birth and death.[7]

Buddha's teaching about the Four Noble Truths and the Eightfold Path was extremely general, readymade to fit with other moral codes of behavior. Buddha spent his life trying to explain them. According to John Noss, Buddha's rules were simple. All followers were to wear a yellow robe, shave their heads, carry a begging bowl, take part in daily meditation, and subscribe to the Buddhist confession: "I take refuge in the Buddha; I take refuge in the Dharma (the Law); I take refuge in the Order." Buddhists were also to obey the Ten Precepts: Refrain from destroying life, don't take what is not given, be chaste, be honest, do not drink intoxicants, do not eat after noon, do not watch dancing or singing or drama, do not wear ornaments or scents or garlands, do not have a high or broad bed, and do not possess any silver or gold.[8]

Buddhism spread rapidly throughout Asia. Siddhartha strongly opposed India's caste system, so closely tied to Hinduism. He taught that Nirvana was for everyone, regardless of caste. Hence Buddhism appealed to the lower castes of society. In addition, unlike the vague, often contradictory ideas of Hinduism, Buddhism offered a precise definition of the human condition with an exact plan of "salvation." Finally, Buddhist monks took their new religion along the trade routes of China, Japan, and Tibet. Today more than 300 million Buddhists live in the areas from Sri Lanka to Japan because of these traveling monks.[9]

Buddhism is divided into two major sects, with many other variations. Those two sects are Hinayana Buddhism and Mahayana Buddhism:

• Hinayana (Theravada) Buddhism means "the doctrine of the lesser way," suggesting that only a fortunate few will find Nirvana—those who commit wholeheartedly to Buddha's teachings. This sect (sometimes called Theravada Buddhism) stresses the monastic life and has become wealthy through gifts of land and money for the monasteries. It is dominant today in Sri Lanka, Myanmar, Thailand, Cambodia, and Laos.

• Mahayana Buddhism means the teaching of the "greater way." Its followers know that Buddha taught that salvation is for all people, but they believe that Buddha himself was special. In fact, in this branch of Buddhism, Buddha is deified. They argue that Buddha remained on earth for forty-five years after his enlightenment despite the fact that he could have gone on to Nirvana. He chose to save humans. Therefore, Buddha is not only a teacher (as he is in Hinayana), but he is a savior-god for all people. He is still accessible through prayer and worship and continues to impart insight and revelation to his followers. This sect of Buddhism is far more popular and influential. Today it is dominant in China, Tibet, Japan, Vietnam, and Korea.[10]

BUDDHISM AS A WORLDVIEW: ITS THEOLOGY

God: Despite the manifold divisions within Buddhism, there is a basic metaphysical worldview underlying the entire Buddhist framework. Although in many ways Buddhism is nontheistic (as evidenced by no definable belief in a supreme being or god), it promotes pantheism. Pantheism is the belief that God (ultimate reality) is the world, and the world is ultimate reality (i.e., God); God is all and all is God. However, within Buddhism any religious devotion or piety is not directed to this pantheistic "god." There are no prayers or sacrifices to deities in Buddha's teachings. For Buddha, the universe abounded in gods, goddesses, demons, and other nonhuman powers and agencies, but all were without exception finite and subject to death and rebirth.[11] So Buddhism is foundationally pantheistic but practically nontheistic.

Salvation: For the Buddhist, salvation centers on the individual, on his or her own powers, on redemption through spiritual self-discipline. Buddha was not interested in philosophical speculations regarding salvation. He was immensely interested in the practical and the psychological dimensions of life, namely suffering and how to escape it. Although he rejected Hinduism and all it represented, Buddha did adopt (with alterations) two prominent religious thoughts from Hinduism— the Law of Karma and rebirth.

Concerning the Law of Karma (the law of cause and effect), Buddha viewed it as operating remorselessly and without recompense in the life of unchecked desire. The desires and lusts that caused so much suffering would act in determining the next cycle's destiny for the human. But if the person got control of his desires through the Middle Path that Buddha taught, the cycle of rebirth could be broken.

It is clear that Buddha believed in the doctrine of reincarnation. However, in his teachings, he refused to discuss exactly what happened to the self—the true essence of the person—at death and at the next cycle of reincarnation. For the Western rational mind, there is simply no analogy or satisfactory explanation for Buddha's reincarnation teaching. John Noss offers a helpful perspective:

> Wherever we observe it, the living world, whether about us or within ourselves, is constantly in flux, in a state of endless becoming. There is no central planning world-self, no sovereign Person in the heavens holding all together in unity. There is only the ultimate impersonal unity of Being itself, whose peace enfolds the individual self when it ceases to call itself "I" and enters the featureless purity of Nirvana, as a drop of spray is merged in its mother sea.[12]

For Buddhists, "salvation" is this "drop of spray merging in its mother sea." "Salvation" is the breaking of the reincarnation cycle, the liberation from pain and suffering, the merging with "the ultimate impersonal unity of Being," and the attainment of Nirvana. Nirvana to the Buddhist is a state of perfect, painless peace and joy, a self-achieved freedom from misery of any kind. Nirvana is an eternal state of neither being nor nonbeing; it is the end of all finite states. As Noss argues, "Human knowledge and human speech could not compass it."[13] Nirvana divests self of self in any sense of the word.

Scripture: The Buddhist idea of scripture and revelation do not correspond to most other faiths, including Christianity. Buddhist teacher, Subhadra Bhikshu, writes:

No; there are no divine revelations. It is a groundless assumption, utterly rejected by Buddhism, that the truth should be revealed by God or an angel, to a few inspired favorites. The only revelation we have ever received is from the mouth of those sublime teachers of mankind, who themselves have worked out their own perfection and deliverance, having shown others the way to do it. . . .[14]

Subhadra Bhikshu summarizes Buddhism's theology:

Buddhism teaches the reign of perfect goodness and wisdom without a personal God, continuance of individuality without an immortal soul, eternal happiness without a local heaven, the way of salvation without a vicarious Savior, redemption worked out by each one himself without any prayers, sacrifices, and penances, without the ministry of ordained priests, without the intercession of saints, without Divine mercy. Finally, it teaches that supreme perfection is attainable even in this life and on this earth.[15]

BUDDHISM: ITS ETHICS

Fundamentally, Buddhism is about ethics. It is a religion founded on human ethical behavior as the sole basis for attaining Nirvana. If one were to put it in Christian terms, Buddhism is a works-righteousness system of salvation. Nirvana (salvation) is totally dependent on what the Buddhist achieves while pursuing the Middle Path of Buddha's teaching. A person who follows the Four Noble Truths and the Eightfold Path will attain Nirvana. If a person remains captive to human desires, the Law of Karma will remain active, resulting in ongoing reincarnation.

By maintaining a commitment to the Four Noble Truths and observing the Eightfold Path, Buddhists naturally follow Buddha's Ten Precepts (discussed previously). Buddhists live between self-indulgence on the one hand (which is condemned) and extreme practices of ascetic self-denial (which are equally condemned). Buddha claims that this balance produces the psychological freedom within this life and the hope of release from reincarnation that awaits the faithful. More than any other religion, except perhaps Confucianism, Buddhism is a religion of ethics, a religion of what the faithful *ought* to do.

BUILDING BRIDGES TO BUDDHISTS

The ultimate reason for seeking an intelligent understanding of Buddhism, or any worldview, is to find bridges we can build to reach people with the gospel. Jesus did this constantly as He regularly adapted His message to His hearers.

Bridge #1

First and foremost, Christians must set consistent examples. What we believe—our convictions—must be demonstrated in a Christlike life. Because Buddhism is fundamentally an ethical faith with no real emphasis on the supernatural, the authentic life of Christ speaks volumes to followers of Buddha. Authenticity will get the Buddhist's attention.

Bridge #2

Both Buddhism and Christianity address the issue of suffering. For the Buddhist, suffering encompasses all of life from birth to death. Clinging to the pleasures of life is considered foolishness and vain. The Christian worldview shows some harmony with Buddhism on this point. Christianity recognizes the reality of suffering and ties it to the consequences of human sin (Gen. 3). For that reason the book of Ecclesiastes may be the best starting point, for it declares the futility of life "under the sun" (1:1-11). The author of Ecclesiastes points out that life is unfair, futile, confusing, and transitory. It is only belief in a sovereign, personal God that brings sense to all of this. For that reason, life is seen, for the Christian, as a good gift from a good God who ultimately makes sense even out of suffering. Perhaps books like Philip Yancey's *Where Is God When It Hurts?* or C. S. Lewis's *The Problem of Pain*, both of which deal with suffering, can be of help to the Buddhist.

Bridge #3

When the Buddhist asks the question, "What is life all about?" he looks inside himself for the answers. When the Christian asks the same question, he turns to God for the answer. Buddhists focus on dwelling on and mastering self in an effort to eradicate self. The haunting question for the Buddhist is: How does one achieve selflessness through occupation with self? It is a paradox.

Jesus solves the paradox: "He who has found his life shall lose it and he who has lost his life for my sake shall find it" (Matt. 10:39; Mark 8:35; Luke 9:24). We find our true identity by losing ourselves in the One who created us, namely Jesus Christ.

Bridge #4

Buddhism claims that all humans should be treated well. But why? There is no absolute standard in Buddhism. By paying respect to everything in life, a Buddhist gains personal peace and lives in harmony with the world. Buddhists must realize that there are people in the world who get ahead through evil means. We must press the Buddhist: "What is goodness? How do we know what is good?" Moral law points to a moral Lawgiver, namely the true God.

Bridge #5

For the Buddhist, ultimate reality is within the human self. But for the Christian, ultimate reality is in the absolute truth of a God who is outside of human beings. For the Buddhist, reality is thoroughly subjective and inner; for the Christian, it is objective and God-centered. Ultimate reality is revealed only through Jesus Christ, who said, "I am the way, the truth, and the life; no one comes to the Father but through Me" (John 14:6). This is ultimately the choice the Buddhist must make—is it self, or is it Christ?

Reaching the Buddhist with the gospel of Jesus Christ can be difficult. These suggested bridges can be used by the Holy Spirit to pierce the heart of the Buddhist. Both Buddhists and Christians use the metaphor of light to describe the path to truth. A Buddhist journeys into himself for the purpose of negating himself to achieve enlightenment. The Christian journeys into Jesus Christ, the light of the world, to find true enlightenment. That is the message we must take to the Buddhist.

FOR FURTHER DISCUSSION

1. Why is Buddhism considered more of a philosophy than a religion?
2. In what ways did Siddhartha Buddha seek to find life's meaning? In what ways do you see people today searching for meaning?
3. What is your reaction to the Four Noble Truths and the Eightfold Path? What do you see as the positives and negatives of this view of suffering?
4. Review the theology of Buddhism. Why do you think many Westerners find these beliefs appealing?
5. What are the similarities and differences between Hindu theology and Buddhist theology?
6. What did the author mean by the statement, "Fundamentally, Buddhism is an ethical religion?"
7. Which bridge do you see as the most compelling one for the Buddhist? Why? How will you use it?

Chapter Five

CONFUCIANISM

THERE IS NO DOUBT that Confucius is *the* religious figure of importance in China. His influence was not only religious; it was political and practical as well. Politically, Confucius promoted an ethic that would harmonize all human relationships, especially in the government. That ethic had practical application in its support of family relationships. Even today the influence of Confucius remains strong in that nation; in fact, one cannot really understand the Chinese people without understanding Confucianism. This chapter will detail who Confucius was, summarize his teachings, and suggest ways to reach the Chinese Confucianist with the gospel.

Confucius lies at the very center of Chinese culture. Philosopher Lin Yutang has observed:

> To Western readers Confucius is chiefly known as a wise man speaking in aphorisms, five moral axioms, which hardly suffices to explain the depth of influence of Confucius. Without a deeper unity of belief or system of thought, no mere collection of aphorisms could dominate a nation's history as Confucius has dominated China.[1]

The core idea of Confucianism is the concept of virtue, of right living. More than any other major world religion, Confucianism is an attempt to provide systematic order to all human relationships. The Confucian worldview considers justice and happiness for both individuals and for society the highest goals to achieve.

CONFUCIANISM: ITS HISTORY

Life of Confucius

His real name was K'ung Fu-tzu, and he was born in 551 B.C. His father died when he was three, leaving the family poor. At a young age, Confucius cultivated his lifelong love of poetry and immersed himself in the historical traditions of China. According to the autobiographical summary in his *Analects,* at fifteen he determined to be a scholar. Confucius married at age nineteen, and a year later his only son was born. The government placed him in charge of the state granaries and of public lands in his province. The state also appointed him magistrate of his province and later minister of works and minister of justice.

Confucius never stopped studying the ancient works of China. In fact, he became both an authority on Chinese antiquity and a teacher in addition to his governmental duties. Increasingly, his interest shifted to reforming the government and the society. This concern forced him to reflect on the nature of political authority. What makes a good ruler? His writings and his teachings reflect this desire for reform.[2]

The Influence of Ancient China

The China of Confucius's time was one of political instability, plague, and famine. The ruling dynasty—the Chou dynasty—was in decline and could no longer control the entire country. Religiously, China was an aggregate of animism, polytheism, and ancestral worship. Confucius took the ancient teachings of China and reformulated them into a coherent ethical system of thought.

What were some of these ancient ideas that captivated Confucius and which he attempted to synthesize? First, the core of the Chinese religious conviction is the belief that the world of man and the world of nature are inseparable and interdependent. Beyond that interdependence lies the Eternal Order of the universe, called the *Tao* (pronounced "Dow"). Tao means road, way, or path, but to the Chinese it is the cosmic principle responsible for the harmony and order of nature. Because of the orderliness and cosmic harmony of the Tao, the individual must always seek to conform himself to that orderliness and harmony. Therefore, the natural world is the greatest reflection of the orderliness of the Tao. As Laurence G. Thompson argues, the Tao "might be likened to the Laws of Nature, or better to Nature itself. And whether taken as Being or as Nonbeing, or as the Principle in all particular things, it is in any case *never* conceived as Deity."[3]

The second principle is *Shang Ti.* Shang means "upper" and Ti means "ruler." This "ruler on high" was an ancestral figure type, located in the higher regions of the sky. Later in history, Shang Ti was thought to reside in "heaven" (or the Chinese term *T'ien*).[4]

The third principle is the *Yin-Yang* precept. The Yin-Yang is traced back to the oldest Chinese classic, *The I Ching (Book of Change),* and is depicted as a symbol found in Western jewelry today (a circle with two "eyes" separated by an S-like figure). In ancient Chinese history, people believed that all natural phenomena operated in accord with and were subject to the control of the Eternal Order, or Tao, which functioned in an interaction of opposing forces of Yin and Yang. The following chart summarizes these opposites, which, when combined, produce order and harmony.

Yang	Yin
Heaven	Earth
Masculine	Feminine
Active	Passive
Warm	Cold
Dry	Wet
Bright	Dark
Positive	Negative

Not only is everything in nature either Yin or Yang, but this principle affects everything in life. In the unseen spirit world, there are good spirits (Yang) and evil spirits (Yin). An elaborate system of pseudoscience developed within Chinese culture to control all parts of nature. The Yin-Yang principle carried over into the ethical world too. Yang is identified with virtue and Yin with vice.[5]

A final principle was that of *divination,* discerning will and direction from mysterious practices. Thompson[6] argues that Chinese divination is motivated by the desire to understand the operations of the natural and supernatural forces in nature, so that one's actions would be in accord with those forces and produce good results. One of the best examples of this type of divination is *feng-shui,* which means "wind and water." When choosing the best site to build a home, for example, people use *feng-shui* to guarantee wealth, prosperity, and honor to those who dwell there.

Divination was also used to keep in touch with deceased family members and help them in the afterlife. The practice of ancestor worship is one specific distinguishing characteristic of the Chinese family, even today. Ancestor worship reinforced the cohesion of the family and its lineage. It was likewise the one universal religious institution throughout China, connecting everyone to family and community. The Chinese have believed for thousands of years that the soul survives death and that there is ongoing contact between the dead and the living. The living family

members offer sacrifices and other forms of divination to make the ancestors happy in hopes of receiving their blessing.

The Confucian Texts

The main texts of Confucianism, which form the basis for this faith, have
come to us through the disciples of Confucius. Their recollections and
interpretations are found in the *Four Books:*[7]

1. The *Analects* (the "Lun Yu"), a collection of the sayings of
Confucius and some of his disciples. Though often fragmentary and
perplexing, it is the most nearly contemporary document of Confucius
we have, with verbatim quotations from the master himself.

2. The *Great Learning* ("Ta Hsueh") dates from a century and a half
after Confucius's death and thematically focuses on the ordering of society through the individual's self-cultivation. Originally developed as the
basis of education for the "ideal man" in classical Chinese education, it
was the first text studied.

3. The *Doctrine of the Mean* ("Chung Yung") is an excellent exposition of the philosophical presuppositions of Confucianism and relates
human nature to the underlying moral order of the universe.

4. The *Book of Mencius*, dating from the third century B.C., is a collection of the writings and sayings of the most original of the early
Confucian thinkers. Mencius has been called "the St. Paul to Confucius."

CONFUCIANISM AS A WORLDVIEW: ITS
THEOLOGY AND ITS ETHICS

God: Confucius's teaching on heaven and God is not religious;
Confucius did not see God as personal and infinite. He once said,
"Absorption in the study of the supernatural is most harmful."[8]
Confucianism is a humanistic, this-worldly, rational, ethical teaching
that has dominated the thought and action of the Chinese people for cen-
turies.

Humanity: Confucius taught that humans are born essentially, innately,
and morally good. How is a human to cultivate this innate goodness? For
Confucius it meant following the Tao ("the way") to become the "ideal
(or superior) man" ("chun-tzu"). As intrinsic goodness is cultivated, it over-
flows into the common life to serve the state and all humans.

The Confucian concept of the ideal man encompasses five major
virtues and five major social relationships. The five virtues are (compared
to the parts of a tree):

- *Jen*—Mutual benevolence, the will to seek the good of others (the root)
- *Yi*—Righteousness by justice (the trunk)
- *Li*—Propriety or reverence (the branches)
- *Chih*—Wisdom (the flower)
- *Hsin*—Faithfulness/Faith (the fruit)[9]

The ideal man is the embodiment of *Jen* (pronounced "ren"), which is the internal motivation to fulfill the other virtues. Because one is benevolent, one will manifest justice (*Yi*) and propriety (*Li*) in external relationships so that wisdom (*Chih*) and faithfulness (*Hsin*) will be the dominant character traits. Confucius wrote, "Desiring to sustain oneself, one sustains others; desiring to develop oneself, one develops others."[10] For that reason, the ideal man will always follow the Doctrine of the Mean: "Not to do to others what you do not wish yourself."

For Confucianism, there are five major social relationships demonstrating that the ideal man relates well to his family and extends his virtues to society at large. Those cardinal relationships and corresponding virtues look like this:

Relationship	Virtue
sovereign to subject	faithful loyalty
father to son	filial piety
elder to younger brother	fraternity
husband to wife	fidelity
friend to friend	friendly reciprocity

The family is the basic unit of society, and the ideal man recognizes that. He also understands that the ideal society is one in which all citizens know their proper place and their respective virtues.[11]

Because man is innately good, Confucius envisioned a utopian society where the ruler would benevolently rule as he followed the Doctrine of the Mean, seeking to become an ideal man. His subordinates would each seek to become the ideal man as well. This trickle-down ethic would have this effect:

First, extend to the utmost their knowledge in the investigation of things (antiquity). As a result knowledge will be complete which will in turn cause thoughts to become sincere. With thoughts sincere, the heart will be rectified. With the heart right, the person will be cultivated. With the person cultivated, the family will be regulated. With the family regulated, the government will be right and the whole empire will be made tranquil and happy.[12]

If Confucius is correct that humans are predisposed to goodness, his scheme is possible. If humans are not predisposed to goodness, his scheme collapses into meaningless individual autonomy.

Ancestor Worship: In many ways, the basic religion of China remains ancestor worship. The teachings of Confucius gave ethical meaning to this practice. Because his ethical system begins with the family, he consistently taught that parents must be treated with total respect. He instructed children to stay close to parents, especially when they became elderly. Love for parents is a lifetime commitment that continues even after their death. For Confucius, the most pious acts included repairing and keeping the ancestral temples orderly, carefully arranging the sacrificial vessels, the regalia, and the heirlooms of the family, and presenting appropriate sacrifices to them.[13]

Heaven: According to the Doctrine of the Mean, Confucius taught that the truths handed down from the ancients "harmonize with the divine order which governs the revolutions of the seasons in the Heaven above and . . . fit in with the moral design which is to be seen in physical nature upon the Earth below."[14] It seems that Confucius believed that his teaching had heaven's sanction and carried eternal significance because the teaching had its origin in the moral order of the world. However, there is no sense in the Confucian worldview of the personal God to whom Christians pray and relate. Heaven in Confucius's mind is not where a sovereign personal God dwells. Heaven is a divine principle synonymous with the eternal order of things. Heaven manifests the Tao of the universe.

The Cult of Confucius: The elevation and worship of Confucius began between the second and first centuries B.C. when the emperors honored him as a great sage and began to worship and make sacrifices at his grave. (One emperor sacrificed an ox, a sheep, and a pig.) By the second century A.D., readings, prayers, and gifts of money and silk were added to the sacrifices at the grave. In A.D. 630 the Chinese emperor issued a decree obliging every governor of China to erect a state temple to Confucius in which regular sacrifices to him were ordered. About a hundred years later, another emperor placed images of Confucius in the great hall of the state temples.[15]

In the beginning of the twentieth century, the Manchu rulers wanted to make Confucianism the main religion of China. Dr. Sun Yat-sen

(1866-1925), founder of the Chinese republic, continued to revere Confucius and tie his teaching to the new nation. Chiang Kai-shek centered his leadership of the Chinese Nationalists (now living in Taiwan) on the revised teachings of Confucius. Despite Mao Tse-tung's (1893-1976) attempt to destroy Confucianism and replace it with communism, it is evident since his death that many Chinese people continue to affirm the basic tenets of Confucianism.[16]

BUILDING BRIDGES TO THE CONFUCIANIST

Bridge #1

The Chinese ideal for society and for personal peace and happiness is to achieve order and harmony. There is an intense search for harmony in human relationships in Chinese thinking. The problem for the Chinese worldview so deeply rooted in the ancient texts including Confucianism is that it searches for order and harmony without any personal God, the author of such order and harmony. Christianity is likewise interested in the order and harmony of the family and society. That love for order and harmony is rooted in the personal, transcendent, and infinite Creator. For the Christian, right actions—a concept extremely important to the Chinese—are attained by aligning oneself with God's revealed righteousness in Jesus Christ.

Bridge #2

The Chinese worldview, rooted in the ancient texts and Confucianism, focuses strongly on the family. Confucius taught the perpetual respect and honor for parents and ancestors. The impact of the extended family is central to understanding the Chinese mind. Christianity affirms the critical importance of the family too—the first institution God created (see Gen. 2). The New Testament teachings of order, structure, love respect, and honor within the family are fundamental to Christianity (see Eph. 5:22ff.). Both the Christian and the Confucian worldview embrace the importance of family, and it can be common ground between them.

Bridge #3

The Confucian worldview has a high regard for personal and social ethics, the foundation of the Confucian system. The five major virtues and the five major relationships emphasize this point. The Doctrine of the Mean in Confucianism is identical to the teaching of Jesus (Matt. 7:12). Christians must therefore live authentic lives. Ethical commitment to honesty, truth, and justice are important to the Chinese and are valuable to Christians because they reflect the attributes of almighty God. This commonality of interest in personal and social ethics can provide a powerful and compelling bridge to share the truth about Jesus.

The entire Chinese way of life is now being challenged. Materialism, pluralism, Western culture, and the abandonment of ideological communism have left a spiritual and moral vacuum among the Chinese people. We have a fantastic opportunity to reach out to these people, located on every continent, with the truth of Jesus Christ. Rural life in mainland China is quickly fading as the urban centers grow and adapt to a quasi-capitalism. The Christian church in China is growing and with it the opportunity to confront the Chinese with the claims of Christ.

FOR FURTHER DISCUSSION

1. Why was Confucius more than simply a wise man with profound sayings?
2. Explain the relationship between the ideas of Tao and Yin-Yang. Is this view of order and harmony consistent with a Christian view of the world? Why or why not?
3. Imagine that God and heaven were merely impersonal principles. How would you feel? How would this affect your daily life and faith?
4. In what ways is the theology of Confucianism similar to the theology of naturalism (chapter 2)?
5. What is the Bible's concept of an ideal human being? How does this differ from the Confucian concept of the ideal man?
6. Debate this statement by Confucius about one's internal motivation to virtue: "Desiring to sustain oneself, one sustains others."
7. Name some additional bridges that could be used to reach Confucianists.

Chapter Six

SHINTOISM

WHEN MILITANT NATIONALISTS ruled Japan during the first half of the twentieth century, Shintoism was the official state religion of the country. It venerated the uniqueness of Japanese culture and bestowed divinity on the emperor. Soldiers who gave their lives for their country were quasi-deities, their souls honored in Shinto shrines, especially the large Yasukuni Shrine near the Imperial Palace in Tokyo. For many Japanese people, state Shintoism and military imperialism were inextricably linked. After World War II, Emperor Hirohito renounced his divinity, Shinto lost its official protection, and the new Constitution upheld the principle of church-state separation. However, Shintoism retains a special defining power in Japanese civilization.

According to Shintoism, Japan's national character was formed before history was recorded. When Japan was born, the emperor was already a high priest and head of state. He was a descendant in an unbroken line from the sun-goddess Amaterasu. The imperial family, therefore, cannot be separated from Japanese mythology. The myths chronicle the birth of Japan. The emperor is sacred because his blood ties go back to the gods who created the nation. Shintoism provides Japan with the spiritual culture central to its identity. For that reason when Emperor Hirohito died in 1989, the funeral ceremony contained all the trappings of Shintoism. As the ancient Shinto rituals were performed, national and international leaders gathered at the Grand Shrine at Ise in central Japan. Today Shintoism still defines the "who" and "what" of the Japanese people and their culture.[1]

About 90 percent of the people of Japan identify themselves as Shinto followers, although about 75 percent of that 90 percent also identify themselves as Buddhists. (Less than 1 percent of Japan is Christian.) For many in Japan, there is no conflict in saying they belong to both religions. We have already discussed Buddhism; what exactly is Shintoism? What are its distinctives? Although ancient, why does it still define Japanese civilization?

SHINTOISM: ITS HISTORY

The term "Shinto" is derived from the Chinese *shentao*, meaning "the way of the higher spirits or gods." To understand Shintoism, one must understand the concept of *kami*; Shinto is the way of kami. The term captures the transcendent element that affects all nature and life. Kami includes the various deities of heaven and earth, all forms of life—human, animal, and vegetable—as well as all things dreaded and revered. Kami refers to beings that possess sacred power or superior potency, filled with charismatic power. Kami is the single most important aspect of Japanese Shintoism.[2]

The origin of the doctrine of kami is rooted deep in Japanese history. Part of Japanese mythology recounts that Japan was once peopled exclusively with kami. The early Japanese regarded the whole of nature—mountains, lakes, trees, sea, and ground—as having kami powers. Shinto belief thus expresses a religious faith about Japan and its past. The customs of prehistoric Japan were the way followed by kami, the beings from whom the Japanese people are descended.[3]

The introduction of Buddhism and Confucianism into Japan, largely during the A.D. 700s, changed Shinto beliefs. These influences resulted in the systematized Shintoism that became a national religion. The ethics of Confucius introduced a new moral character into the kami and into religious practices as well. The Japanese adopted ancestor worship as a part of kami worship, stressing the important influence of genealogical descent of the kami. Confucian thought also influenced the social stratification of society into a ruling class and a common class. Buddhism became a religion of the upper class while the common people held to the veneration of their regional kami.[4]

In A.D. 710, the Japanese capital was moved from Yamato to Nara, beginning the Nara and Heian Periods of Japanese history (710-1191). Using the newly acquired Chinese writing skills, court scribes began to record the oral traditions of the Shinto mythologies. There are four major writings of importance. The *Kojiki* ("Chronicle of Ancient Events"), completed in 712, is the major history of mythology explaining the origin of the cosmos, the Japanese islands, the people, and the divine descendence of the emperor. The *Fudo-Ki* (713) is a topographical record that lists all the shrines and the oral tradition behind the kami manifestations that occurred at each shrine. The *Nihonshiki* ("Chronicles of Japan"), completed in 720, is a historical account of the ruling court from Japan's beginning. Finally, the *Engi-shiki* (927) is a compendium of Shinto traditions consisting of fifty parts. The most important is the *Norito*, the model for prayers at the Shinto shrines. [5]

It was also during the Nara and Heian periods that the government used these various writings to tie the nation and the official court to the past mythology of the ancient kami veneration. Finally, during these periods the government used the term "Shinto," which was defined as "the kami way."

By the 1100s, a mixture of Shinto and Buddhist practices had developed. The government began to build Shinto and Buddhist shrines side by side. The royal court put its stamp of approval upon Buddhism but also maintained the distinctive Shinto faith and practice. New Buddhist schools emerged that stressed the coexistence of Shinto and Buddhism in Buddhist terms. This mixture of Shinto and Buddhist beliefs and practices continued for several centuries.[6]

In 1868 the religious climate of Japan changed dramatically. Emperor Meiji made Shinto the state religion and ordered the elimination of Buddhism. The ancient view of the divine origin and authority of the emperor was again promoted within a state Shinto system consisting of government-sponsored programs. World War II shattered the unique Japanese faith in the inviolability and divine origin of their island, people, and emperor. Shintoism and Buddhism survive in Japan today, but the mythological mysticism of Shintoism has lost some of its former power.[7]

SHINTOISM AS A WORLDVIEW: ITS THEOLOGY AND ETHICS

In Japanese religious history, Shintoism is unique to the Japanese islands. Shinto refers to the traditional practices that originated in Japan and developed mainly among the Japanese people. There are no clearly defined doctrines, codes of behavior, specific canon, nor a specific founder of the faith.

In analyzing Shintoism, it is necessary to define the six major types:

1. *Domestic Shinto.* This type refers to the rituals performed at homes rather than at communal shrines. In the homes there are *kami-dana*, or "god-shelves," on which are placed memorial tablets with the names of long-honored ancestors or perhaps a patron deity of the household written on them. Ancestor worship plays a significant role in domestic Shinto.

2. *Folk Shinto.* This type encompasses local Shinto varieties found throughout the Japanese islands.

3. *Imperial Household Shinto*. This includes the special rites followed by the Imperial family at shrines within the Imperial Palace.

4. *State Shinto*. Historically, this was the most important and influential type of Shintoism. It was a government-fostered program of patriotic rites conducted from the 1860s through 1945 at the national shrines. Observed at the more than 110,000 national shrines existing before World War II, the ceremonies were to cultivate national patriotism and "the spirit of ancient Japan." The American occupation of Japan after the war ended the compulsory aspects of state Shintoism. Many of the state shrines were abolished or fell into disuse.

5. *Shrine Shinto*. Supported by private funds and voluntary gifts, many of these 110,000 shrines were rebuilt or renovated. Shrine Shinto refers to the core of traditional religious practices centered in rites related to these various shrines.

6. *Sect Shinto*. Various sectarian or religious Shintoists have emerged in the modern history of Japan. They vary widely in their importance, but each relates to Shinto beliefs and practices in some way.[8]

Kami: Since the concept of kami is so central to Shintoism, it is necessary to define this clearly. It is an abstract term; the English word *god* is not accurate. The basic idea of kami is "above" or "superior." Anything awe-inspiring may be "kamified" (e.g., the sun, wind, thunder, mountains). Today, kami refers to spiritual beings, mythological entities of ancient times, natural phenomena, physical objects of worship, or ancestral spirits.[9]

Creation: Shintoists recognize a creation of heaven and earth as a spontaneous generation of an original trio of kami deities. The first Japanese emperor was an offspring of the gods. The Japanese islands are also a special creation of the gods.[10]

Ethics: There is no written ethical code in Shintoism nor are there clearly defined standards in the Shinto faith. There are no absolutes; rather good is associated with beauty, conformity, excellence, nobility, and so on. Human beings are viewed as innately good, but purification rites are required if a person is defiled through contact with blood, sickness, or death. The purification is purely external; there is no reference to internal cleansing from sin as in Christianity or Judaism.[11]

Worship: Shinto worship focuses on certain rites or traditional practices at the various shrines, whether in the home or at the regional or national shrines. Here the kami or symbolic representations of the kami are enshrined. The shrine is the center of Shinto worship and supplies an abode for the kami. There are no images to worship in the shrine; kami may be known or unknown by the worshiper. Each part of Japan has a shrine dedicated to the local kami. Worship involves purification to rid oneself of impurities before approaching the kami.

There are also offerings to the kami, which include rice, water, salt, fish, or other foods. At communal shrines, the worshiper often gives money. Prayers are an aspect of worship, but they are often not verbal; rather, they might involve a sense of communion with the kami. Worship involves the sacred meal. Here the worshiper fellowships with the kami with whom the meal is symbolically shared. Finally, worship includes festivals and ceremonies. Every shrine has a festival day in which the entire community joins in celebration. Festivals consist of eating, drinking, dancing, and entertainment. Most shrine festivals are no longer celebrated in Japan, but there are two exceptions. During the fall, the Harvest Festival is overseen by the emperor, and twice a year the Great Purification Ceremony takes place to cleanse the nation of its impurities.[12]

BUILDING BRIDGES TO THE SHINTOIST

When one views Japan today, one sees a nation undergoing intense transition. World War II destroyed state Shintoism, but the other types mentioned continue. Overall, Shintoism is declining; emperor worship is dead and Buddhism lacks appeal to the typical Japanese person today. There remains the strong emphasis on the family and communal commitment. The nation is also economically prosperous. Corporate success in the urban areas appears to be the basic goal of the individual. In rural Japan, Shintoism lingers, but its power is declining. Many parts of Japanese civilization reflect a religious vacuum.

Christianity has a most negative reputation in Japan. It was brought to Japan in 1549 by Francis Xavier, but it has not grown successfully. It was banned until the mid-1840s. Today less than 1 percent of the Japanese population affirms Christianity.

Bridge #1

Shintoism promotes the importance of the family and the community; so does Christianity. Both see the family as strategic to the larger civilization. Both understand the importance of honor and respect in family relationships and in the larger community.

Bridge #2

Because Shintoism is highly pragmatic, it is important to stress the practical benefits of Christianity. Christianity provides a reason for existence.

Because the Japanese appreciate the importance of community, a lov-ing, committed, friendly church can provide a strong, loving, and com-mitted fellowship. An authentic, functioning New Testament church can be appealing to the Japanese.

Bridge #3

Because honor is such a core value of Shintoism, Christianity offers the basis for honoring all human beings—they are made in the image of God. This concept is somewhat close to the idea of kami and can be a strong connecting point for Christianity.

Japanese Shinto culture is very difficult to penetrate. Part of this dif-ficulty is due to the fact that Shinto worship does not promote morality and ethics. The Japanese Shinto culture has no religious or philosophi-cal basis. This deficiency is heightened by the materialism and prosper-ity of modern Japanese culture. There is a real spiritual vacuum within Japanese society today. The country is Western in its economic orienta-tion and increasingly in its cultural orientation.

From the outside, Japanese culture is heavily influenced by American pop culture and by the materialism that goes with it. Yet Japan keeps the traditions of Shintoism, although with decreasing commitment by many of the young people. So for this next generation there may be an open-ness to Christianity that has never characterized Japan. Shintoism no longer works and Western culture and materialism do not provide the organizing purpose and center for civilization. Japanese civilization is very vulnerable right now. Perhaps God will use this unique moment to pour out His Holy Spirit. Let us pray and work toward that end.

FOR FURTHER DISCUSSION

1. Define "Shinto" and "kami." Why are these important to Shintoism?
2. How did Emperor Meiji change Shintoism as he aligned the religion more with the state?
3. Describe the following types of Shintoism:
   - Domestic Shinto
   - State Shintoism
   - Shrine Shintoism
4. How did the Japanese defeat in World War II change Shintoism? How does this change underscore the problems with viewing nations and humans as divine?
5. Summarize the following aspects of the Shinto worldview:
   - creation

- ethics
- worship

6. Discuss the dangers of a society based on material prosperity. What is the best way to penetrate this type of culture with the gospel? Spend time praying for the spiritual state of Shintoists.

7. The author suggests three bridges we as Christians can build to reach the Japanese Shintoist. Name some possible additional bridges to Shintoism.

Chapter Seven

JUDAISM

IN JUNE 1987 the Reverend Bailey Smith, former president of the Southern Baptist Convention, audaciously declared that "God Almighty doesn't hear the prayer of a Jew," resulting in a veritable firestorm of criticism from both Christians and Jews. But Smith's comments reflect the tension Christians often feel when confronting Judaism. Christianity was born out of Judaism. Jesus and Paul, for example, were both Jews. But the fundamental difference separating the Christian from the Jew today remains the Messiahship of Jesus: Christians believe He is the Messiah; Jews do not. This gap between the two is seemingly insurmountable.

That gap between Christians and Jews over Jesus is compounded by the realities of history. The early church, clearly Jewish, was successful in reaching out to Gentiles, which in turn led to the landmark ruling of the Jerusalem Council (Acts 15). That decision in A.D. 49 released Gentile converts from the necessity of circumcision and adherence to the Mosaic law. By championing the cause of Gentile freedom from Jewish rituals and regulations, Paul and other apostolic leaders in effect produced a new community of believers. Could Jew and Gentile Christian live harmoniously together? As the second century dawned, this harmony became more problematic. Another point of contention between Jew and Christian (both Gentile and Jewish Christians) involved moving worship on the Sabbath to the Lord's Day.

Finally, the growing persecution of Jews widened the split between Christian and Jew. During the two early Jewish revolts against Rome (A.D. 66-73 and 132-135), Jewish Christians refused to fight, compromising both their allegiance to the Jewish community and their identity with the early Jewish state. Further, the destruction of Jerusalem in A.D. 70 and the disappearance of all major Jewish sects but the Pharisees forced a reformulation of Judaism. Rabbinic Judaism, as the new form came to be called, emerged as a separate religion from Christianity, and the deep-seated rivalry between synagogue and church developed. That institutional split remains today.[1]

The tearing away from Jewish roots resulted in the church defining itself largely in non-Jewish terminology. The term "Christianity" is an obvious example, for it gives singular focus to Jesus as the Christ (Greek) or the Messiah (Hebrew). The name of Christianity's holy book, the Bible, is a Greek term, a signal that this new faith was stepping away from Judaism. In addition, by the third century the early church had taken on an increasingly anti-Jewish tone. The posture of early Christian writings was decidedly against the synagogue system. Whereas one Gentile nation after another responded positively to the Christian message, Jews continued to cling stubbornly to their ancestral faith. The later leaders of the church taught that the unfaithfulness of the Jewish people resulted in a collective guilt that made them subject to the permanent curse of God. As church history progressed, contempt grew for the Jews and Judaism.

In the fourth century, when Emperor Constantine made Christianity a legitimate religion of Rome, Jews experienced a further wave of discrimination and persecution. They lost many of their legal rights, including being expelled from Jerusalem. In 339 it was considered a criminal offense to convert to Judaism.

During the medieval period (A.D. 500 to 1500), Jews were largely excluded from Christian culture. Therefore, Jews often avoided the Christian culture in Europe by living in secluded parts of the cities. Jews engaged in one major profession—money-lending. Deprived of basic liberties and ostracized from the culture, Jews were required to wear a distinctive hat or to sew a patch on their clothing. The Christian culture blamed Jews for many social wrongs but especially of being "Christ-killers." During the 1490s, the Spanish Inquisition persecuted Jews and eventually ordered them to leave Spain. Because they were not permitted to enter Western Europe, they fled to North Africa, Morocco, and the Eastern Mediterranean.

This ruthless persecution of Jews across Europe, including most viciously in czarist Russia, caused over two million to flee to America. But the Holocaust stands as the unparalleled embodiment of anti-Semitism's horror. The final solution of the Nazis involved concentration camps, gas chambers, and crematoriums. Between 1933, when Hitler came to power, and the end of World War II (1945), some six million Jews were exterminated. Wherever Jews are today, a vestige of anti-Semitism remains.[2]

JUDAISM: ITS HISTORY

In a world of more than 6.2 billion people, there are only 17 million Jews. Yet their impact on world history and on religious truth has been profound. The history of Judaism is the Old Testament. Jews are called "Hebrews," from Eber mentioned in Genesis 10:21. They are also descended from one of Noah's sons, Shem, from which the term "Semitic" originates. But Abraham is the true father of the Jewish people.

Abraham, a descendant of Shem (Gen. 11:10-28), lived in Mesopotamia, in the town of Ur around 2000 B.C. According to Genesis 12:1-7, the true God spoke to him and instructed him to leave Ur and go to a land that He would give him. God made (literally "cut") a covenant with Abraham, promising him that he would be the father of an entire nation of peoples, whose numbers would compare with the sand of the seashore and the stars of the sky. In addition, in Abraham all of the nations would be blessed. Finally, God promised Abraham and his descendants land—the land of Palestine (Gen. 12:8; 17:8). In essence, the covenant promise was land, seed, and blessing.

Abraham's son Isaac was the covenant son promised by God. He was born when Abraham was 100 years old, but, when Isaac was a teenager, God asked Abraham to sacrifice the boy to Him on Mount Moriah. In obedience Abraham took his son and was prepared to offer him back to God when God intervened, providing a ram as a substitutionary sacrifice. This test of Abraham's faith proved that he loved God and obeyed Him (Gen. 22). Isaac's covenant son was Jacob, who had twelve sons, the founders of what would become the twelve tribes of Israel (Jacob's covenant name, according to Gen. 32).

One of Jacob's sons, Joseph, was hated by his bothers, sold into slavery, and ended up as prime minister in the Egyptian government. In that role, Joseph provided food for his brothers and their families, bringing them to Egypt in the land of Goshen, in the Nile Delta region (Gen. 37—50). Israel grew into such a formidable nation that the pharaoh of Egypt enslaved them (Ex. 1).

Moses, himself a Hebrew but raised in the pharaoh's court, became the "deliverer" of the Israelites from their 400 years of slavery in Egypt. In confronting the pharaoh, Moses declared that the God of Israel was the true God, and He would prove it. That proof was the ten plagues against Egypt, each one directed at a specific Egyptian god. As a result of God's war on the Egyptian gods, the pharaoh allowed the Israelites to leave, carrying much of the wealth of Egypt with them (Ex. 5—14).

To Moses God had revealed Himself as the great "I AM THAT I AM," the self-sufficient, self-existent Being of the universe (Ex. 3:14). Moses, a highly educated and brilliant man, recorded the early history of the

Israelites in the first five books of the Old Testament (called the Torah or the Pentateuch). In that history, Genesis 1—11 declares that God created the physical world, cursed it for its sinful rebellion, and scattered the peoples throughout the world. He promised that He would redeem His creation through the "seed of the woman" (Gen. 3:15).

Under Moses' understudy, Joshua, the Israelites conquered the land of Palestine (Canaan), which God had promised to Abraham (recorded in the book of Joshua). Then they organized the land administratively in a decentralized manner (see the book of Judges). After the failure of the Judges, the people demanded a king like the surrounding nations. God granted that request, and after the reign of Saul, David became the king of Israel (about 1000 B.C.).

Under David Israel became a great nation. He consolidated his power, vanquished Israel's enemies, and made Jerusalem the capital city. David desired to build a mighty temple dedicated to the God of Israel, but because he was a man of war, God prohibited it. Instead, God promised David an eternal dynasty, throne, and kingdom (2 Sam. 7:16). From that covenant promise comes the promise of an anointed one, or Messiah, from God.

After David's son Solomon built the temple and established Israel as a wealthy military power, the kingdom of Israel split apart as a result of sin and rebellion; Israel was the northern kingdom, and Judah was in the south. After Solomon, Israel was ruled by a series of kings who did not honor God; only a few God-honoring kings came to power in Judah. God warned both Israel and Judah of impending judgment through his prophets (most of those warnings are recorded in the major prophets [e.g., Isaiah, Jeremiah, etc.] and the minor prophets [e.g., Joel, Amos, Hosea, etc.] in the Old Testament). As He said He would, God judged Israel for its idolatry and disobedience first through its conquest by Assyria in 722 B.C. The people of Israel were taken from the land in the north and relocated, never to return as a united people to their land. God judged Judah for its idolatry and disobedience in 586 B.C. Nebuchadnezzar of Babylonia successfully conquered the nation, destroyed the temple, and took most of the people back to Babylonia. (These events are recorded in the biblical books of 1 and 2 Kings and 1 and 2 Chronicles.)

The Jews of the Babylonian exile returned to their land seventy years later (recorded in Ezra and Nehemiah) and rebuilt the wall and the temple. They remained in their land until they rebelled against Roman occupation in A.D. 66. The Roman Empire responded savagely. Over the next four years, and especially during the siege of Jerusalem in A.D. 70, thousands of Jews were slaughtered (many by crucifixion), the city was razed, the temple was destroyed, and the remaining Jews were dispersed throughout the world. Their sacrificial system, their priestly worship, and their identity as a people with a nation ended.

After the return from the Babylonian exile, various sects of Judaism emerged. Each had a distinctive emphasis, and each played a role in the development of Judaism.

The Sadducees. Originally a party of aristocratic, wealthy leaders, the Sadducees accommodated their beliefs to the changing culture of Judea. They separated themselves from popular teaching and focused on the rational, easily defined teaching of the Torah only ("The Books of Moses"). They rejected the popular belief in angels and bodily resurrection, and they embraced the rationalism of Greco-Roman culture.

The Pharisees. The Pharisees consisted of the scribes, the rabbis, and most of the priesthood of Judaism. They adhered to the oral tradition that accompanied the Torah, the expositions, interpretations, and commentaries of the scribes and rabbis. Pharisees embraced the doctrine of the bodily resurrection, the last judgment of God at the end of history, and devotion to God's law. They scrupulously studied the Scriptures and rabbinic "tradition," stressing moral obedience, ceremonial purity, prayers, fasting, and the giving of alms to the poor. They were the legalists of Jewish society.

The Essenes. Although other parties emerged in Judaism at this time (e.g., the Herodians, who accommodated to Rome's rule, and the Zealots, revolutionaries who desired to overthrow Rome), the Essenes withdrew from Judean society to prepare for Messiah's coming. They lived in monastic seclusion where they fasted and prayed, following ceremonial rituals. The Essenes were the Jewish group that inhabited Qumran, where the famous Dead Sea Scrolls were discovered decades ago.[3]

JUDAISM AS A WORLDVIEW: ITS THEOLOGY AND ETHICS

With the destruction of the temple, the sacrificial system, and the priests in A.D. 70, the focal point of Judaism was the Law. The entire body of written and oral tradition of Judaism is known as "Torah," which "represents to the Jew the whole mystery and tangible expression of God."[4] The debates, discussions, and decisions of scholars and rabbis on the meaning of Torah were eventually compiled into a monumental work called the "Talmud," which aids the Jew in making the connection between theology and life.

Throughout Jewish history, there has been little focus on articulating a creed or confession of belief. The most significant attempt to do so was that of the twelfth century Jewish teacher, Moses Maimonides, who listed thirteen articles. This list remains a part of the Authorized Prayer Book.[5]

1. Belief in the existence of a Creator and Providence.
2. Belief in His unity.
3. Belief in His incorporeality [i.e., not of flesh and blood].
4. Belief in His eternity.
5. Belief that to Him alone is worship due.
6. Belief in the words of the prophets.
7. Belief that Moses was the greatest of all prophets.
8. Belief in the revelation of the Lord to Moses at Sinai.
9. Belief in the immutability of the revealed Law.
10. Belief that God is omniscient.
11. Belief in retribution in this world and the hereafter.
12. Belief in the coming of the Messiah.
13. Belief in the resurrection of the dead.

God: The theological center of Judaism is Deuteronomy 6:4-5: "The LORD (Yahweh) is our God (Elohim); the LORD is one." Jews are to love Him with heart, soul, and strength. God is transcendent (beyond the physical world) and is the Creator of all that exists. He is a God of righteousness, holiness, justice, and love. He deserves singular worship and devotion. He creates humans in His image, which becomes the basis for the value and worth of all humans. Jews teach that God's revelation to humanity in the Old Testament (OT) is how we as creatures know about Him and understand Him.

The Scriptures: Judaism looks at Scripture differently than Christianity. The Old Testament books remain the center of Jewish Scripture. In fact, between A.D. 69 to 90 a group of Jewish scholars, students, and rabbis gathered in Jamnia, Israel, to finalize what books exactly were in the Old Testament canon. They agreed to group the OT into the Torah (the first five books of the OT), the Prophets (the history books of Joshua, Judges, 1 and 2 Samuel, and 1 and 2 Kings; and the major and minor prophets), and the Miscellaneous books (comprising the rest of the OT books). For most Jews, this is the canon. However, over the history of Judaism other books of importance were added.

About A.D. 200 the Mishnah was added, which includes about 4,000 precepts of rabbinic law. About A.D. 500 the Mishnah was combined with the
Halakah (oral tradition of the Jewish people with instructions for daily
living) and the Haggadah (multiple synagogue homilies) to form the
Talmud, a work of some thirty-six volumes.

For Orthodox Jews, not only is the Torah their daily guide for life, but
so is the Talmud. They seek to bring their lives into meticulous conformity with both the Torah and the Talmud. Eating procedures are
very important to the Orthodox Jew. Pork and shellfish are forbidden in
their diet. Animals that are slaughtered for food must be done so in a special "kosher" manner, certified as such by rabbis. Further, Orthodox Jews
refrain from working, traveling, using the phone, touching money, or
even posing for pictures on the Sabbath. These are just a few of the
multiple restrictions detailed in the Talmud.

Conservative and Reform Jews have departed significantly from
Orthodox Jewry. Conservative Jews are more lenient in their interpretations of the Law, and Reform Jews teach that principles are more important than Jewish practices. In fact, Reform Jews rarely observe dietary
or Sabbath restrictions.[6]

Jewish Customs and Festivals: Within contemporary Judaism, there is widespread agreement
on one thing—observance of the Sabbath. For the Jew, the Sabbath begins at sundown on
Friday night and continues until sundown Saturday. In Orthodox and some Conservative Jewish
homes, as the sun is setting on Friday, the mother (traditionally) lights the designated candles
and gives the blessing: "Blessed are Thou, O Lord our God, King of the Universe, Who has
sanctified us by Thy laws and commanded us to kindle the Sabbath light." The father then blesses
the wine, and everyone takes a sip before the father slices the Sabbath bread.

After the Sabbath dinner, Conservative and Reform families go to
the synagogue. For the Orthodox Jew, the main service is on Saturday
morning; Orthodox and most Conservatives attend another Saturday
service that afternoon.[7]

Judaism has other High Holy Days. Among them are Rosh Hashana
(the Jewish New Year celebrated in September or October) and Yom
Kippur, the Day of Atonement. These Holy Days are characterized by
repentance, prayer, and acts of kindness toward others. This period of
self-examination results in open confession and a commitment to abstain
from these sins in the year to come. Although the Day of Atonement is
wrapped around the OT sacrifice of the lamb that atoned for (covered)
sin, the idea of substitutionary sacrifice is lost in much of modern
Judaism.[8]

Another significant Jewish High Holy Day is Passover, celebrated approximately the same time as the Christian Easter. Preceded by the Feast of Unleavened Bread (where all leaven is removed from the home), Passover begins with the question from the youngest son, "Why is this night different from all other nights?" An older family member answers, "We were slaves unto pharaoh in Egypt and the Eternal God led us from there with mighty hand." The Passover meal uses a roast shank bone to remind the family of the lamb that was slain and whose blood was sprinkled on the doorposts in Egypt so that the angel of death would recognize Jewish homes and "pass over" them. Today the Passover celebration includes not only prayers and special foods but also games for the children.[9]

When a Jewish boy reaches the age of thirteen, he becomes a "Son of the Commandment (or Covenant)," called a *Barmitzvah*, and is called up for the reading of the Torah on the Sabbath following his birthday. On that occasion, he recites the words: "Blessed are Thou, O Lord our God, King of the Universe, who has chosen us from all peoples, and has given us Thy Torah." Today in some Jewish synagogues, girls go through a similar ceremony called a *Batmitzvah*.[10]

The Messiah: For Jews of the Conservative and Reform perspective, the belief in a coming Messiah who will deliver Israel and bring about the consummation of history is no longer viable. Indeed, for many Jews the rebirth of the modern state of Israel in 1948 is now directly associated with the idea of Messiah. For one of the founders of that state, David Ben Gurion, the Messianic vision is centralized in the establishment of the state: "The ingathering of the exiles, the return of the Jewish people to their land, is the beginning of the realization of the Messianic vision."[11]

This mixing of political and religious ideas is central to understanding Judaism, Messiah, and the modern state of Israel. Thomas Friedman[12] argues that there are four distinct groups of Jews within modern Israel (and the world). The first and largest is the secular and nonobservant Jews who built the modern state of Israel. Many of them are secular Zionists who came to Israel in part as a rebellion against their grandfathers and Orthodox Judaism. For these secular Jews, being in the land, erecting a modern society and army, and observing the Jewish holidays as national holidays all substitute for religious observance and faith.

The second group is the religious Zionists, who are traditional or modern Orthodox Jews who fully support the secular Zionist state but insist it is not a substitute for the synagogue. The creation of the Jewish state is a religious, "messianic" event.

The third group is the religious or messianic Zionists who see the rebirth of the Jewish state as the first stage in a process that will culminate with the coming of the Messiah. The state is the necessary instrument for bringing the Messiah. Every inch of the land of Israel must be settled, and all defense and foreign policies are devoted to this end.

The final group is the ultra-Orthodox, non-Zionist Jews who do not regard the Jewish state as important. Only when the personal Messiah returns, and the rule of Jewish law is complete will the true Jewish state be created.[13]

Therefore, Jews today reject the teaching that Jesus is the Messiah. Except among the ultra-Orthodox and some messianic Zionists, the idea of a personal Messiah who will return to bring about a kingdom of peace, righteousness, and justice is foreign. The Messiah idea is either politicized and associated with the modern state of Israel or rejected as an aspect of an antiquated belief of a dead form of Judaism.

BUILDING BRIDGES TO JUDAISM

Because there is so much historical connection between Judaism and Christianity, the only significant bridge is Jesus. As mentioned above, most Jews reject the teaching that Jesus is the Messiah. The Christian must build the case that He indeed is Messiah. How can that be accomplished?

First, it is important to connect key New Testament (NT) passages with key Old Testament prophecies. Some examples include clear NT references to Jesus as the Messiah (or Christ)—see Matthew 16:16; 26:63-65; Luke 24:26; John 8:28. Also, when King Herod wanted to know where the Christ would be born, his advisors quoted Micah 5:1-3 for the answer—Bethlehem, the very city where Jesus was born. Matthew connects Isaiah's prophecy of 7:14 with the birth of Jesus (Matt. 1:23). Zechariah 9:9 clearly states that Messiah will come humbly, riding on a donkey into Jerusalem. That is what Jesus did on Palm Sunday (Matt. 21:4). Most study Bibles have charts that demonstrate the dozens of OT prophecies Jesus fulfilled. They can be helpful resources.

Several of those OT-NT connections include:[14]

Thirty pieces of silver	Zech. 11:12	Matt. 26:14, 15
Betrayal of a friend	Ps. 55:12-14	Matt. 26:49, 50
Hit, spit upon	Isa. 50:6	Matt. 26:6, 7
Silent before accusers	Isa. 53:7	Matt. 27:12, 14
Wounded, beaten	Isa. 53:5	Matt. 27:26, 29
Hands and feet pierced	Ps. 22:16	Luke 23:33
Crucified with thieves	Isa. 53:12	Mark 15:27, 28
Forsaken cry	Ps. 22:1	Matt. 27:46

Given gall and vinegar	Ps. 69:21	John 19:28, 29
Bones not broken	Ps. 34:20	John 19:33, 36
Buried in a rich man's tomb	Isa. 53:9	Matt. 27:57-60

Second, the OT passage of Isaiah 53 is central to Judaism. This passage is one of the servant passages of Isaiah. Consider Isaiah's depiction of the "servant" of God as despised, rejected, sorrowful, and full of grief (v. 3). Jesus is described throughout the Gospels in the same language.

Isaiah likewise describes the Messiah's redemptive ministry as a substitutionary one: being buried in a tomb other than his own and dying an unimaginably gruesome death. All of these prophetic statements accurately predicted what actually happened to Jesus at the time of His crucifixion. Careful study and presentation of the connections between the suffering servant of Isaiah 53 and Jesus can be powerful for the Jewish seeker after truth.

The question, then, for the adherent to Judaism is: What will you do with Jesus? As C. S. Lewis said, He is either a liar, a lunatic, or the Lord. The New Testament builds the case for Jesus as the crucified Messiah prophesied in the Old Testament. Believing this central truth is not only a rational act based on reasonable evidence, but it is also the work of the Holy Spirit of God. Our task, whether we are speaking with a Jew, a Shinto, Buddhist, or Hindu, is to faithfully declare the truth. The response of the hearer is God's business.

FOR FURTHER DISCUSSION

1. What is your reaction to the controversial statement: "God Almighty doesn't hear the prayer of a Jew?" What lessons can Christians learn from the history of the relationship between Jews and Christians?
2. Which Jewish historical figure do you most admire? Why? In what ways was he important to both the Jewish and the Christian faith?
3. What spiritual lessons can we learn by examining the fall of Israel to Assyria in 722 B.C. and the fall of Judah to Babylonia in 586 B.C.?
4. Identify the distinctives of each of the sects of Judaism listed below. In what ways does this knowledge deepen your understanding of Matthew 22:15-40 and other passages like it?
   • Sadducees
   • Pharisees
   • Essenes

5. How might you use one or more of the Jewish customs and festivals as bridges to share the light of the gospel with Jews?

6. How would your approach to witnessing differ, depending on whether a Jew is Orthodox, Conservative, or Reform?

7. Summarize the various beliefs of Jewish groups about Messiah. Write a prayer asking God to open the eyes of Jews to accept Jesus as the Messiah.

Chapter Eight

ISLAM

THE MORNING OF September 11, 2001, forever changed the United States and the world. Muslim terrorists targeted a vital center of America's economic power (the World Trade Center), its military power (the Pentagon), and, although the plane crashed, presumably its political power (the White House or the Capitol). The United States is still dealing with the ramifications of that horrific event. Americans remain perplexed about the faith of Islam. How could a religion like Islam motivate young men to commandeer airplanes and fly them into buildings? How could a worldview like this produce such fanaticism? Is such fanaticism typical or an exception? Our world is complex, and its worldviews are complex, but there is probably no worldview currently more important than Islam.

As a term, "Islam" means suffering (for Allah, or God) and "Muslim" is one who suffers (for Allah, or God). Islam is a religion of remarkable discipline and rigor. It promotes a works-righteousness view of salvation that instructs the worshiper on how to merit the favor of Allah. How did this worldview develop?

ISLAM: ITS HISTORY

The founding and early history of Islam revolves around the prophet Muhammad (A.D. 570-632). Muhammad was born about 570. Because he lost his father near the time of his birth and because his mother died when he was six, Muhammad was cared for briefly by his grandfather and later by his uncle, Abu Talib. Abu Talib was a merchant; so Muhammad traveled extensively with him in the thriving caravan network that wound through Arabia, Syria, then into India and northern Africa. No doubt it was these journeys that first exposed Muhammad to Christianity and Judaism. Although none of these contacts were with orthodox representatives of either faith, a deepening conviction about the truth of monotheism resulted.

According to Muslim tradition, the year 610 changed Muhammad and consequently the world. On the seventeenth night of the month of Ramadan, Muhammad was in solitary meditation in a cave at the foot of Mount Hira, near the city of Mecca, when he suddenly saw a vision. The angel Gabriel commanded him to "recite." Not understanding what he was to recite, Muhammad heard Gabriel exclaim that he was the prophet of God (Allah). Muhammad's newfound monotheism was controversial among the polytheistic tribes of Mecca. Resistance from Mecca intensified, and his life was in danger.

According to Muslim tradition, Allah confirmed Muhammad's prophethood in 620, miraculously bringing him at night to Jerusalem. There he conversed with Jesus, Moses, and Abraham, and there he and Gabriel were taken by a ladder to the seventh heaven. (Muslims believe that the Dome of the Rock is built on the site of this ascension). Still his monotheistic message was rejected by his people.

Muhammad continued to condemn the paganism of the polytheistic Arabian tribes. In Mecca there was a massive stone shrine called the Ka'bah, which attracted pilgrims from all over Arabia. Fifty feet high and nearly forty feet square, it housed one idol for each day of the year. Some said it had been built by Adam and Eve after their expulsion from the Garden of Eden. Others claimed that Abraham and Ishmael had built it. Arabian pilgrims came to kiss or touch the smooth black stone that glistened in the southeastern corner of the city.

So severe was Muhammad's persecution that he took his wife and small group of followers and fled to Medina, about 250 miles north of Mecca. For the Muslim this momentous event, called the "Hijra," is year 1 in the Muslim calendar. While in Medina, Muhammad found acceptance and began to build his army of Islam. He had become a military leader!

Eight years after the Hijra, Muhammad and his army of 10,000 reentered Mecca in triumph. Thronged by his followers, the sixty-two-year-old commander led a glorious pilgrimage to the Ka'bah, now the focal point of Islamic worship. There in 632, he announced the perfection of a new religion—the worship of Allah. Before he died, Muhammad established complete domination over the Arabian peninsula.[1]

What was Muhammad's relationship with the early Christians and the Jews? He was not really familiar with Christianity, nor the Bible.

The Qur'an, the 114 chapters of the archangel Gabriel's revelations to Muhammad, refutes Christian claims that Jesus died on the cross, that He was God's Son, and that God is triune. Likewise, the Qur'an alludes to other beliefs that are demonstrably false—that Mary was a sister of Aaron and Moses and that she was part of the Trinity. So Muhammad denied Jesus' deity, His atoning death on the cross, and the Trinitarian nature of God.[2]

Despite such error and misunderstanding of Christianity, Muhammad vigorously taught that he and his teachings were heirs to both Judaism and Christianity—those he called "peoples of the book." For that reason, Muhammad decreed that Christians and Jews were to receive protection under Muslim rule. He extended personal hospitality to Christians, but less to Jews. In fact, as Dr. Pat Cate demonstrates, when one evaluates the chapters of the Qur'an chronologically, a clear progression exists confirming hostility toward Jews and Christians.[3] During his early years in Mecca, Muhammad confirmed his basic allegiance with Jews and Christians. However, after the flight to Medina, he turned radically against them and developed his teachings about *jihad* (to be discussed later).

After Muhammad's death, Islam spread rapidly. In fact, in only a hundred years (632-732) it swept across the rest of Arabia, Palestine, all of northern Africa, and into Spain, only to be stopped in France. Why did it spread so quickly? The military vacuum left by the collapse of western Rome and the *jihad*, or holy war, proclaimed by the Qur'an help to explain the swift conquest. Huge territories, once dominated by Christianity, were lost, many of which have never been recovered to this day.

Muhammad had designated no successor to take up his cause. His followers had to decide the manner of the succession—was it to be based on heredity or on loyalty to Muhammad? The successors could not come to an agreement, which caused a fatal division in Islam that has never healed. According to the Sunni sect (the Traditionalists), the Medinans selected an aging member from Muhammad's tribe, Abu Bakr, Muhammad's father-in-law. But, according to the Shiah sect (partisans of Ali), the prophet's cousin and son-in-law was the designated successor—Ali ibn Abi Talib. For the sake of unity, Ali ultimately deferred to Abu Bakr, but Islam today remains divided between the Sunnis and the Shiites.

The remaining history of Islam can be summarized in the following manner:

• After the first four caliphates (rulers/followers of Muhammad), the Umayyad tribe gained political control of Islam and formed a dynasty that lasted from 661-750. It was the Umayyads that spread Islam across northern Africa and into Spain. Islam remained militant and militaristic during this period.

• The next dynasty, the Abbasids, followed after a successful revolt against the Umayyads. This dynasty lasted from 750 to 1055 and was characterized by peace, not war. Its political center was Baghdad, and the Abbasid courts were filled with luxury and wealth that resulted from prolific trade policies. The Abbasid dynasty is considered the high water mark of Islamic culture.

• In the 1050s, the Seljuk Turks gained control of Islam. Coming from central Asia, the Turks were brutal and aggressive and destroyed the peaceful court of the Abbasids. They denied Christians access to the Holy Land, which sparked the Crusades (1096-1200s), an attempt by Christian Europe to drive the Muslims out.

• The Ottoman Turks succeeded their cousins, the Seljuk Turks, and conquered the eastern empire centered in Istanbul (1454) and invaded Europe. Much of central and southern Europe fell under Muslim control as a result.

• The modern period of Islamic history (much of the twentieth century) is characterized by nationalism mixing with Islam in the emergence of modern Islamic nation states such as Egypt, Iran, Turkey, Saudi Arabia, Kuwait, and Iraq. Although Islam continues to expand as a faith, it is wrapped up in the larger geopolitical issues of global trade in oil, terrorism, political alliances, and the larger Israeli-Palestinian conflict. As a faith, Islam is the fastest growing world religion; as a political/economic force in an age of terrorism, it is at the center of today's world events.

ISLAM AS A WORLDVIEW: ITS THEOLOGY AND ITS ETHICS

God: The Muslim concept of God is summed up in the name "Allah." A critical point for Islamic doctrine is the stress on Allah's unity of being. This dominates the Muslim's thinking about God and is expressed in the phrase, "There is no God but Allah." He is absolutely unique and inconceivable. An Islamic proverb says, "Whatever your mind may think of, God is not that!" A constant phrase repeated in Muslim prayers is "Allah akbar" (God is great). God is far greater than any thought humans can have of him. Allah is so great that he can do what he likes, even break his own laws.

In Islam, Allah has decreed all that will occur. He is the creator of all that is in heaven and on earth. His knowledge is perfect; his will is beyond challenge; and his power is irresistible. All of these attributes—omniscience, sovereignty, and omnipotence—are evident in his creation. Many pious Muslims carry a rosary that has ninety-nine beads, each one representing one of Allah's names. The one-hundredth name is unknown to humans; according to Muslim legend, only the camel knows it.

Allah's might and majesty are tempered with justice. He rewards and punishes; yet he is merciful, a guardian of his servants, defender of the orphan, guide of the wrongdoer, liberator from pain, friend of the poor, and ready-to-forgive master.[4]

Allah resides in the seventh heaven, far removed from his creation. He is unknowable, but he has chosen to make himself known through the holy books and through his prophets. The books include the Old and New Testaments, and the prophets include the prophets of the Old Testament and Jesus.

Angels and Evil Spirits: Allah is surrounded by angels—pure, sexless beings who worship and adore him. Angels also serve as messengers from Allah to his people and fight for the true Muslim believers. Some of them are known as the good "jinn," as the guardian angels of man, who not only guard humans but also keep records for the day of judgment. Other angels guard hell to insure that all who are condemned to go there, stay there.

The fear of evil spirits plays a prominent role in the lives of Muslims. They believe that the entire universe is inhabited by both good and bad jinn. Chief among the evil jinn is the devil or Satan. Once an angel, Allah expelled him from heaven for refusing to bow to Adam at Allah's command. Most Muslims believe in Satan and continually ask Allah for protection from him.

The Holy Books: Muslims maintain that Allah handed down 104 books, and of these, only four are most important. They believe that the Law was given to Moses; that the Psalms were given to David; that the Gospels were given to Jesus, and that the Qur'an was given to Muhammad. Muhammad made no claim that his teaching invalidated the Jewish and Christian Scriptures; rather he instructed both Christians and Jews to follow their respective teachings[5] and commanded Muslims to believe in and obey the Law and the Psalms.[6] He taught that the Gospels were sent to confirm and safeguard the Law, which served as guidance and light to those who fear Allah.[7] The Qur'an safeguards both the Law and the Gospels.[8]

The Prophets: Muslims believe that Allah sent 124,000 prophets and apostles, but that the three greatest prophets were Moses, Jesus, and Muhammad. Muhammad, the Qur'an teaches, is the last and the greatest prophet, for he proclaimed Allah's final revelation. The heart of his message was one of morality, a call to righteousness. That meant abandoning polytheism and paganism and submitting totally to the will of Allah. His message, however, also involved community. Islam would create a new fellowship based on loyalty to Allah and to one another. The old loyalties to clan, tribe, nation, and state would be set aside for loyalty to Allah. For that reason, even today, Muslims of all clans, tribes, and nations gather in Mecca. Islam refuses to separate church and state, and Islamic judges always respect the consensus of the community.[9]

The Day of Judgment: The inevitability of divine judgment permeates the Qur'an. In Sura 2, it is described as the Day of Gathering, when there will be a group in Paradise and one in the Fire. It teaches that Allah will take a scale and weigh the good and evil deeds of each person. If the good outweighs the bad—paradise; otherwise hell. But for Muslims, Allah is great and merciful, and Muhammad intercedes for them. The result is that Allah's decision on judgment is more related to his will than to his justice. The Qur'an offers little assurance on this matter of eternity.

The Pillars of Islamic Practice: Submission and obedience constitute the core of Islam. By good deeds, the Muslim expresses his commitment to Allah. The moral and ritual obligations of Muslims are summed up in the five pillars of Islam:

• *Pillar 1: The Witness.* To make the profession, "There is no God but Allah, and Muhammad is his prophet," is to become a Muslim. In uttering the first part, one submits to Allah; by uttering the second, one becomes an adherent of Islam. This profession is not to be taken lightly. It begins with an affirmation of Allah and his oneness. It continues with the means by which Allah reveals himself to humanity—through Muhammad.

• *Pillar 2: The Ritual Prayers.* Every devout Muslim performs the ritual prayers at least five times a day. There are the prayers of the morning, at midday, midway between midday and sunset, at sunset, and one hour after sunset. Ritual prayers mainly are praises to Allah and are always recited in Arabic.

In most Muslim countries, a spiritual leader, called a "muezzin," mounts the balcony of the minarets that dot Muslim city skylines and calls Muslims to prayer. The prayer is recited in any location a Muslim finds himself, although urban Muslims usually gather in the mosques.

All face the direction of Mecca when they pray—to remind them of the birthplace of their faith.

• *Pillar 3: The Paying of Alms.* Paying alms is giving back to Allah a portion of his bounty in order to avoid suffering in the next life and as a purification of what one retains materially. It is not voluntary, but is an obligation to gain favor with Allah.

• *Pillar 4: The Fast of Ramadan.* The fast of Ramadan is an obligatory duty for all Muslims (except the sick, pregnant women, travelers under certain conditions, and soldiers in combat). Because Muslims follow the lunar calendar, Ramadan lasts thirty days, and in each successive year it occurs about nine days earlier than the previous year. Each day the fast begins from the moment one awakes, and it lasts until sunset. The night is spent eating and drinking. During the day of the fast, the Qur'an prohibits eating, drinking, smoking, swallowing saliva, and sex. The fast is a debt owed to Allah, and it atones for sin, helps control passions, and merits favor with Allah.

• *Pillar 5: The Pilgrimage to Mecca.* This obligation to Allah is to be performed at least once during a Muslim's life. The pilgrimage is filled with ritualistic observances such as stopping at the well where Gabriel heard Hannah's plea for water, the place where Satan is believed to have been stoned, and kissing the sacred black stone of the Ka'bah.[10]

A Word About Jihad: The term *jihad* literally means "struggle" or "exertion." In the religious context it always involves a struggle against evil. That struggle can involve one of the heart, where the Muslim fights the evil of his nature, but it can also be a "jihad of the mouth," where the Muslim struggles against those who oppose Islam. The most controversial form of jihad is the "jihad of the sword."

Throughout the Qur'an there are calls to physical combat on behalf of Islam. In fact, this doctrine developed over time in Muhammad's teaching. In the Qur'an chapters that focus on his time in Mecca and even early Medina, the militancy of jihad is absent. However, as the opposition to Islam mounted, so did Muhammad's teaching that jihad is military force in the name of Allah. As the doctrine developed, Muhammad taught that those who sacrificed their lives in the battle for Allah were guaranteed admission to the highest level of heaven. Jihad became a violent military means of spreading the faith, and Allah was glorified through it. Historically, jihad became the heart of Islam's expansion. Today Islamic terrorists are trying to resurrect that militant, aggressive form of jihad.[11]

At the beginning of this chapter, I posed the question as to whether the fanaticism seen on September 11, 2001, is typical of Islam. Within the entire spectrum of Islam, such fanaticism is not typical (e.g., Egypt, Kuwait, Jordan, Saudi Arabia, Turkey, etc.). The vast majority of Muslims are not committed to fanatical jihad where killing civilians in terrorist attacks is a holy cause. However, to the followers of Osama bin Laden, al Qaeda, the Palestinian terrorists of Hamas, Hezbollah, and Islamic Jihad, fanatical jihad is becoming the norm. Many of these terrorists were radicalized in the war against the Soviet Union in Afghanistan during the 1980s. They defeated a superpower there, and now they believe they can do so against the United States, which they regard as corrupt, decadent, and ultimately weak. Such groups believe they can destroy Israel and the United States. Although small, such groups can wreak devastation, fear, and destruction on their enemies. Such fanaticism will not be easily defeated.

BUILDING BRIDGES TO THE MUSLIM

Charles R. Marsh, a pioneer missionary in Algeria, offers several guidelines for communicating the gospel to Muslims. Each is an effective bridge to Islam:

Bridge #1

Avoid condemning Islam or speaking in a derogatory manner about Muhammad. Instead of criticizing Islam outright, one must seek to understand it. This involves being a good listener. When speaking with a Muslim, it is generally wise to allow the Muslim to speak first. Courtesy, respect, and honor are important in Islamic culture.

Bridge #2

Remember that a Muslim is a believer in god. Islam is monotheistic, and Allah shares many of the same attributes as the true God of the Bible. This is the common ground upon which a relationship can be built.

Bridge #3

In the heart of every Muslim is the fear of Allah. The Qur'an teaches that every Muslim will someday stand before him. Most Muslims have anxiety that they are not doing enough to merit Allah's favor. The Christian must be able to communicate the critical concept of grace. For Christians, the fear of God is not based on terror; it is reverence and awe for the one with whom we have a personal relationship. This point is crucial for Muslims because they have no concept of a personal relationship with the living God.

Bridge #4

Most Muslims have a certain sense of sin, rooted largely in their failure to attain Allah's high standards. Islam gives no assurance of pardon for sin. Here is where the Christian message takes hold, for Jesus provided that assurance on Calvary's cross.

Bridge #5

Make use of the truth that Muslims know to lead them to the whole truth about God's Word. Muslims already know that God is light and that in Him there is no darkness at all. They know Jesus is the son of Mary and that one of His titles is the Word of God. They know that Jesus will soon return to reign. They know that humans must be pure to approach God. Once a relationship is established, the Word of God can be used to corroborate what Islam teaches and provide further instruction regarding the true nature of Christianity.

Bridge #6

Because the Qur'an rejects God as Trinitarian, it is difficult for Muslims to grasp the deity of Jesus. For that reason, once a relationship of trust is established, it is imperative to focus on the deity of Jesus, perhaps using such verses as Matthew 3:16,17; 17:5; 28:19; John 10:30; 14:6; 8:58; Romans 8:26-27; 1 Peter 1:2.

Muslims also stumble over Jesus as the Son of God because often they teach that God cohabited with Mary to produce Jesus. What we as Christians must do is demonstrate that Jesus' sonship describes His relationship to the other members of the Godhead; sonship is not proof that He had a point of origin or beginning. Jesus is the manifestation of the unseen God (see Heb. 1:1-3 and Col. 1:15-20).[12]

Islam is one of the most difficult religions to penetrate with the gospel. For that reason, the establishment of a relationship with Muslims is imperative. Once trust and confidence are present, the Holy Spirit will have the freedom to move in the hearts of Muslims through us. We must know Islam, and we must be willing to spend time with those who follow it.

FOR FURTHER DISCUSSION

1. What insights do the definitions for "Islam" and "Muslim" give you into the Islamic faith?
2. What was impressive or not so impressive to you about Muhammad and his founding of Islam?

3. After a review of Islam's history, what new perspectives have you gained about this religion and its wide influence? What do you predict will be the influence of Islam in the future?
4. What inconsistencies do you see with the Muslim affirmation of both the Gospels and the Qur'an? How might this be used as a bridge to Muslims?
5. Compare and contrast the five pillars of Islamic practice with Christian disciplines. In what ways are the motivations for the disciplines different?
6. How would your faith be affected if you accepted the Muslim belief that God was unpredictable and unknowable in a personal way?
7. In what practical, respectful ways could you demonstrate your personal relationship with God to a Muslim friend? Develop friendships with Muslims and begin to build your bridges to their lives.

Chapter Nine

THE NEW AGE
MOVEMENT

PERHAPS NO OTHER modern figure personifies the New Age world-view better than Shirley MacLaine, the Hollywood actress. In 1987, based on her book *Out on a Limb*, her life story was told on an ABC miniseries. That TV series legitimized the New Age worldview and presented it in a popular format so that millions could view a woman transformed by New Age teachings. Listen to Shirley MacLaine describe her worldview:

> Regardless of how I looked at the riddle of life, it always came down to one thing: personal identity, personal reality. Having complete dominion and understanding of myself was the answer to harmony, balance, and peace. . . .
>
> If I created my own reality, then—on some level and dimension I didn't understand—I had created everything I saw, heard, touched, smelled, tasted; everything I loved, hated, revered, abhorred; every-thing I responded to or that responded to me. Then I created every-thing I knew. I was therefore responsible for all there was in my reality. . . . I was my own universe. Did that mean I had created God and I had created life and death? . . .
>
> Was this what was meant by the statement I AM THAT I AM?[1]

In MacLaine's comments we see major themes associated with the New Age worldview: Self defines reality; self is all that really matters; self is in effect God; self is the center of everything. At first glance, this worldview seems utterly bizarre; yet today it appeals to millions of peo-ple in Western civilization.

The New Age Movement (NAM) is virtually impossible to define. It has no central leader and no major texts that specify its cardinal tenets. There is no geographical center to the movement and there is no consensus of theology or agenda. It is an amorphous movement that perplexes many and yet energizes so many more. Can we determine its history and unravel its powerful appeal?

THE HISTORY OF THE NEW AGE MOVEMENT

Although New Age thinking is rooted deeply in ideas associated with Eastern pantheism, occult groups of the nineteenth century, and other mystical movements, the 1960s appear to be the decisive decade for the formation of the NAM. First, the 1960s witnessed the first major change in immigration laws, where laws that excluded people coming from the East were repealed and large numbers of Asians poured into America, including countless teachers of Eastern religions such as Buddhism and Hinduism. Gradually those ideas mixed with Western thought to produce the hybrid called the New Age. Furthermore, popular music groups, especially the Beatles, sought out Eastern gurus as they pursued truth and life's purpose. Many of these Eastern gurus came to America and gathered large numbers of followers.[2]

New Age thinking comes essentially out of a fusion of Eastern and Western belief systems. It combines the Western naturalist commitment to the Darwinian hypothesis, which sees natural selection as the key to explaining all forms of life, and Eastern thought, which rejects reason as the sole means to understanding the world. There is a spiritual realm beyond the physical, but that realm is discernible only through means that raise human consciousness. As that level of consciousness is reached, the NAM teaches, the next stage of human evolution will be upon us. This strange fusion of ideas produces the optimistic, energized dynamic of the New Age.[3]

Second, in 1968 Carlos Castaneda published the first of four novels called *The Teaching of Don Juan: The Yagui Way of Knowledge,* a book that stressed South American sorcery as the key to a "New Consciousness." This concept, New Consciousness, entered the vocabulary of the West as a popular phrase and goal for life. Its impact on the college community was especially decisive.

Third, the discipline of psychology was transformed into a hotbed of New Age thinking. Psychologists such as Abraham Maslow, Carl Rogers, and Rollo May refocused much of popular psychology from dealing with pathology to helping people develop through a more transcendental and humanistic approach. For example, Maslow talked much about "self-actualization" as the goal of popular psychological thinking and counseling. Maslow's self-actualized human was a truly satisfied, fulfilled human, essentially "full of self." This new approach to psychology "was a psychology that glorified self. It pronounced people's impulses essentially good, affirmed the unfathomable depths of human potential, and held out personal growth as an individual's highest goal."[4] As Douglas Groothius comments, "Human experience is thus the center and source of meaning and is valuable apart from any dependence on or subservience to a higher power."[5]

Fourth, the growing influence of Eastern thinking and popular psychology's emphasis on the human potential combined to transform almost all disciplines of human knowledge and professional practice. James Sire details the impact of this synthesis of Eastern thought and human potential psychology:

• Within the fields of psychology and psychiatry, there was a new openness to using drugs to determine the purpose and meaning of life. Some researchers in these fields used LSD and other mind-altering drugs to foster "cosmic unity" and "consciousness." In addition, some psychologists and psychiatrists began to study biofeedback of alpha and beta waves as a means to producing altered states of consciousness.

• In the fields of sociology and cultural history, the NAM was legitimized through the works of Theodore Rozak, George Leonard, and William Irwin Thompson. Each of these respectable scholars took NAM ideas and worked them into their disciplines, thereby gaining increased acceptability for the NAM.

• In anthropology, the works of Carlos Castaneda (previously mentioned) have been decisive in introducing thousands of college students to the teaching of the NAM. Castaneda spent years studying sorcery and the use of psychedelic drugs to alter consciousness among members of Latin American Indian culture. His works are now standard NAM books.

• Remarkably, even in the sciences NAM thinking is prevalent. There are now popular NAM interpretations of physics and biology in the works of Gary Zukav and Lewis Thomas.

• In the fields of popularized medicine and health there is an abundance of evidence that NAM is defining the future of these fields. Acupuncture, Rolfing, psychic healing, kinesiology, and therapeutic touch are only a few of the NAM practices mainstreamed in the West today.

• In politics, the most important area of influence has been in the environmental arena. Groups that are politically active and lobby for NAM goals are the Sierra Club and the Green Party in Germany. Such organizations are pervasive and extraordinarily powerful in Western Europe, where they actually define much of the political agenda.

• In science fiction, one sees significant NAM influence. Arthur Clarke's book and Stanley Kubrick's movie *2001* (1968) conclude with the dawning of a New Age child—"the Star-Child." Robert A. Heinlein's *Stranger in a Strange Land* (1961) was for years an underground classic in the NAM. The works of Philip K. Dick are currently the most important vehicle for NAM thought in this genre of writing.

• In Hollywood movies we see the most powerful communication of NAM ideas. Arguably, the most significant example is the highly popular and ongoing Star Wars series by George Lucas. The Force is the divine power guiding the world, and the goal of each human is to be in touch with the good side of the Force. Yoda is the NAM guru of the original trilogy of the Star Wars series.

• In athletics, sports, and personal exercise programs, NAM practices and ideas are prominent. Kung fu, judo, karate, and aikido are martial arts programs rooted in Eastern techniques that may involve altered states of consciousness. Professional baseball, basketball, and football players are increasingly involved in meditative programs like yoga that relax them and enhance their powers of concentration.[6]

The influence of the NAM is extensive, touching nearly every facet of our culture. NAM ideas enable the modern person to keep all of the Western naturalistic ideas associated with Darwin and modernity and yet add a spiritually satisfying dimension to life. This curious mix of East and West in the NAM is no longer a fad; it is a part of our world—it is mainstreamed. What was once the "lunatic fringe" is now an acceptable worldview option. What is its theology, and how does that theology impact ethics?

THE NEW AGE: ITS THEOLOGY AND ITS ETHICS

God: At the heart of NAM theology is pantheism, which holds that everything and everyone is God. God is an impersonal, undifferentiated force or principle, not separate nor distinct from the physical world. Humans must raise their consciousness to understand that they are God. This point manifests the governing principle of the NAM, namely that self is the prime reality. Self defines and names reality, which we see in the comments by Shirley MacLaine that opened this chapter. She questions whether she "had created God" and "had created life and death."[7]

How does the NAM raise consciousness so that humans can realize that they are indeed God? A myriad of "doors" to open this level of consciousness are suggested by the NAM. Among them are certain drugs, meditation, trances, biofeedback, ritualized dance, certain kinds of music, channeling (a form of séance), using crystals, etc. Each of these "doors" enables human beings to come to terms with the truth that they are indeed "God" and that they know no dimensions of any kind. Listen to Shirley MacLaine: "I was learning to recognize the invisible dimension where there are no measurements possible. In fact, it is the dimension of no-height, no-width, no-breadth, and no-mass, and as a matter of further fact, no-time. It is the dimension of the spirit."[8]

James Sire explains further: "When the self perceives itself to be at one with the cosmos, it is at one with it. Self-realization, then, is the realization that self and the cosmos are not only of a piece but are the same piece."[9] This statement defines the ultimate goal of the NAM, which is summarized as "cosmic consciousness."

Jesus: For the NAM, Jesus is not the one true God. He is not the Savior, but a spiritual model, a guru, and as some state, "an ascended master." He was a New Ager who achieved "cosmic consciousness" and "rose" into a higher spiritual realm of consciousness. That is the nature of his "resurrection." For the NAM, to speak of Jesus as God is not difficult, but to speak of Him as the unique, one true God, whose death and resurrection were substitutionary for human sin, is ludicrous. He is a spiritual guru, not the Savior.

Sin: The concept of sin as the Bible defines it is a foreign concept to the NAM. They see sin as the absence of enlightenment, of cosmic consciousness. There is no need for an atonement for human sin; rather, there is the need for proper methods to raise that consciousness.

Most NAM members believe in reincarnation. However, unlike Hinduism, which regards reincarnation as a curse and a horrific cycle that must be broken, the NAM regards reincarnation as a more positive part of the cosmic cycle of evolution, where the human race achieves the higher stage of cosmic consciousness. Once that realization occurs, ultimate consciousness is attained, and reincarnation ends. There will then be mass enlightenment and greater human unity. As Gruss elaborates, "This unity will transcend the individual and social self-centeredness that has created the present crises in the environment, world hunger, international relations, racism, etc."[10] Humans will have attained the "Age of Aquarius."

Ethics—Good and Evil: As epitomized in the Star Wars trilogies of movies, the NAM sees both good and evil as part of the Force. The NAM does not make clear distinctions between good and evil, right and wrong. Further, what makes it more difficult is that the self for the NAM is really sovereign, the center of all things. Self creates its own reality. The result is that self defines good and evil, with the end being no ethical absolutes. For example, in Shirley MacLaine's first NAM book, *Out on a Limb,* and the subsequent ABC television program, she justifies an adulterous affair with a member of the British Parliament by claiming that they were lovers in another life. So they run along the seashore of England screaming, "I am God. I am God."[11] With self defining reality, anything can ultimately be justified as acceptable. There are simply no ethical absolutes to guide human behavior. It is self living out its own conscious reality.

In conclusion, Douglas Groothuis analyzes the NAM as a "counterfeit religion." Several of its unifying ideas can be distilled into a basic worldview, which Groothuis summarizes in nine doctrines:

1. Evolutionary Optimism: A Counterfeit Kingdom. [Christians look to Christ's return for the kingdom.]
2. Monism: A Counterfeit Cosmos. [All is not one (monism). God created a world filled with diversity and plurality.]
3. Pantheism: A Counterfeit God and Humanity. [God is personal, and humans are not divine.]
4. Transformation of Consciousness: Counterfeit Conversion. [True conversion is not the realization of one's deity through one of the NAM "doors."]
5. Create Your Own Reality: Counterfeit Morality. [Biblical morality is grounded in the moral character of a personal God and His moral will revealed in Scripture.]
6. Unlimited Human Potential: Counterfeit Miracles. [Humans are limited by sin, depravity, and finiteness.]
7. Spirit Contact: Counterfeit Revelations. [Occult practices associated with the NAM open humans to contact with demonic powers, not the true God.]
8. Masters from Above: Counterfeit Angels. [Claims of UFO and extraterrestrial sightings validate NAM teachings about self and consciousness, all clearly contradicted by Scripture.]
9. Religious Syncretism: Counterfeit Religion. The NAM is a mixture of Eastern mysticism, occult practices, and Western humanism. [Both the Old and New Testaments condemn syncretism because it destroys the uniqueness of Jesus and the gospel (John 14:6 and Acts 4:12.)][12]

BUILDING BRIDGES TO THE NEW AGE MOVEMENT

In an "Open Letter to the New Agers," former New Age advocate Randall Baer invites members of the NAM to consider Jesus Christ:

> I testify to you, in love and compassion, that what I found when I accepted Jesus as my Lord and personal Savior opened my eyes to seeing truth in a totally different way, a much grander way than anything I ever knew in the New Age. What I have experienced as a Christian *far* surpasses even the most incredible, mind-blowing mystical experiences I had as a New Ager.[13]

Christians need to understand the complexities of the NAM but also be willing to reach out to NAM advocates.

Bridge #1

The most important place to start is to build relationships with NAM advocates. Members of the NAM are seeking something that thrills and awes, but many have also found that nothing really satisfies. Mystical experiences, rituals, and other fantastic elements of the New Age ultimately do not bring the satisfaction and fulfillment that all seek. Therefore, the authenticity and genuineness of the Christian life can speak volumes to a person embracing NAM. If they see the fruit of the Spirit (Gal. 5:22-23) and the Beatitudes of Jesus (Matt. 5:1-16) lived out, God's Spirit can use this supernatural life to attract them to genuine faith in Christ.

Bridge #2

Because the NAM stresses so heavily the sovereignty of self, it is imperative to press the point that self acting out its own desires and wants naturally results in the abandonment of all ethical standards and absolutes. If self is in the driver's seat in all areas and is satisfied, then who sets the boundaries for life? Who or what determines right and wrong? The result is moral and ethical anarchy, and no one who is intellectually honest can accept that. This remains one of the most vulnerable aspects of NAM thinking.[14]

Bridge #3

A third area to focus on with the NAM is the realm of the spirit world. For the person centered in the NAM, the world is filled with the supernatural, the spiritual, and the angelic. As Sire argues, "The New Age has reopened a door closed since Christianity drove out the demons from the woods, desacralized the natural world and generally took a dim view of excessive interest in the affairs of Satan's kingdom of fallen angels. Now they are back, knocking on university dorm-room doors, sneaking around psychology laboratories and chilling the spines of Ouija players."[15] As NAM advocates open themselves to this spirit world, there will be consequences, including demon possession, power, and occult activities. As Christians, we know that God is far more powerful than the spirit world, for He is its Creator. Deuteronomy 18:9-14 clearly prohibits any form of dabbling in the occult world, practices so central to the NAM. Jesus cast out numerous demons and offered freedom to millions. We must be ready to declare the truth about the occult world but also to offer the freedom that Jesus Christ brings from such enslavement. The fact is unmistakable: The NAM is a worldview deeply influenced by the occult.

Bridge #4

The NAM movement defines truth in a self-centered manner. Sire maintains that in the NAM "there is no critique of anyone's ideas or anyone's experience. Every system is equally valid; it must only pass the test of experience; and experience is private."[16] The end result is that in the NAM people can only know what they experience. But that rarely satisfies anyone. History has shown us that just experiencing all the facets of life, even those fantastic ones of the NAM, does not produce fulfillment or bring purpose. Jesus said that He had come that we might have life and have it more abundantly (John 10:10). As Christians, our task is both to live and to declare with our words that abundant life. If we have established a genuine relationship of trust and confidence with a member of the NAM, God can use our lives to point them to life's meaning and purpose, not in the mysticism of the NAM, but in Jesus Christ.

FOR FURTHER DISCUSSION

1. What is your reaction to Shirley MacLaine's New Age worldview? Which other worldviews studied so far in this text are similar?
2. The author suggests that the 1960s were critical to the popularization of New Age ideas. Explain some of the developments of the 1960s.
3. Where have you personally seen reflections of New Age ideas in the following areas?
    - psychology
    - anthropology

- medicine
- athletics
- Hollywood movies
4. List a Scripture verse or passage that contradicts each of the New Age ideas about:
   - God
   - Jesus
   - sin
   - angels
   - good and evil
5. Which parts of New Age theology are reminiscent of Buddhist and Hindu views?
6. Write a letter to a New Age friend, incorporating several evangelistic bridges.

Chapter Ten

THE JEHOVAH'S WITNESS, CHRISTIAN SCIENCE, AND MORMON WORLDVIEWS

HISTORICALLY, THE United States of America has been a deeply religious nation, especially in its commitment to Protestant evangelicalism. In many ways this commitment to evangelicalism has meshed well with the political culture of America with its emphasis on liberty, personal responsibility, and individualism. This shared consensus has provided the basis for the nation's ethics and values for most of its history. Ironically, this freedom has also spawned major cults that today are growing in numbers and challenging this consensus and even the limits of what freedom of religion in America means.

This chapter seeks to summarize and analyze three of these cults—the Jehovah's Witnesses, Christian Science, and Mormonism. Obviously in a book this size, a comprehensive summary and analysis are not possible. What is possible are salient summaries that stress the history and then the similarities and distinctives of each cult. A discussion on how to reach each cult with the truth of the gospel will end this chapter.

First of all, the term "cult" needs defining. Theologian Anthony Hoekema offers perhaps the best set of distinctives:

1. An Extra-Scriptural Source of Authority;
2. The Denial of Justification by Faith Alone;
3. The Devaluation of Jesus Christ and His Uniqueness;
4. The Group as the Exclusive Community of the Saved.[1]

With these four distinctives in mind, we shall examine three major cults born in nineteenth-century America.

THE HISTORY OF THE JEHOVAH'S WITNESSES, CHRISTIAN SCIENCE, AND MORMON CULTS

Jehovah's Witnesses

The founder of this cult was Charles Taze Russell (1852-1916). Heavily influenced by Seventh Day Adventism in his early years, Russell broke with the Adventists and began publishing his own magazine, *Zion's Watchtower and Herald of Christ's Presence.* In 1884 he founded the Zion Watchtower Tract Society. A voluminous writer, Russell's most important work was a seven-volume series titled *Studies in the Scriptures,* published over the period from 1886 to 1904. Because he was a man of questionable character and ethics, Russell has been disowned by modern-day Jehovah's Witnesses.

Russell was succeeded in 1917 by Joseph Franklin Rutherford. Rutherford gained absolute control over the Watchtower Society, and in 1931, following Isaiah 43:10, he renamed the movement Jehovah's Witnesses. He also denounced all organized religions and fostered a tone of hostility toward Christianity. Rutherford built on the teachings of Russell and became an even more prolific writer.

Nathan Homer Knorr followed Rutherford, and under his leadership the Jehovah's Witnesses stressed intense training for their disciples. The image of the movement changed. It became more respectable and highly organized. The movement's training of its layman and its leaders took place in what are known today as Kingdom Halls.

Why are Jehovah's Witnesses so aggressive and energetic? Because of their eschatology (doctrine of the end times). As Boa demonstrates, Witnesses teach that Christ's second coming has already occurred. It involved three stages: in 1874, Christ came to the "upper air" and later caught up the apostles and dead members of the 144,000, who will be immortal; in 1914 Christ ended the times of the Gentiles and began to reign; in 1918 He came to the spiritual temple and began the judgment of the nations. Witnesses now eagerly await the imminent battle of Armageddon in which Jesus will lead Jehovah's forces to defeat evil. Only faithful Witnesses will escape death in this battle,[2] and only those who earn their place among the Witnesses through their door-to-door work are the "saved."

In the Witnesses door-to-door ministry, their most effective tools are their publications—*The Watchtower* and *Awake!*, the two predominant ones. Included in *The Watchtower* are doctrinal treatises and historical reviews of how the Witness movement developed. The other major publication of the Society is *The New World Translation of the Holy Scriptures*, completed in 1960. Hoekema writes of this "translation" that it "is by no means an objective rendering of the sacred text into modern English, but is a biased translation in which many of the peculiar teachings of the Watchtower Society are smuggled into the text of the Bible itself."[3] Witnesses are aggressive and passionate in their use of this translation.

Christian Science

The founder of Christian Science was Mary Baker Eddy. Born in 1821, Eddy was raised by strict Congregationalist parents, and her youth was characterized by various illnesses and spinal problems. Her first husband, George Washington Glover, died of yellow fever, which along with the birth of her son a few months later, affected her emotionally and mentally. These difficulties continued into her second marriage to Daniel M. Patterson, which later ended in divorce.

During her marriage to Patterson, she traveled to Portland, Maine, where she was healed of her spinal problems by "Dr." P. P. Quimby, who had developed a system of mental healing that he called "The Science of Health" or "Christian Science." Seemingly cured by his techniques, Mary Baker Glover Patterson became an ardent disciple of his teaching and incorporated much of his work into her book *Science and Health* (1875). In later years, she denied her dependence on Quimby, but in reality she took his ideas and assimilated them into her religious convictions.

On February 1, 1866, she fell on an icy sidewalk and was, she claims, given only three days to live. On the third day, she read Matthew 9:2, after which she was miraculously healed. This she dates as the beginning of her discovery of Christian Science. Although this story remains highly suspect, it marks the beginning of this cult.

In 1877 she married Asa Eddy and became Mary Baker Glover Patterson Eddy. The rest of her life she devoted to teaching the principles of Christian Science, which she systematized in her text *Science and Health*. She formed the official organization called The Christian Scientists, which was incorporated in 1879 as Church of Christ, Scientist, with the mother church located in Boston.

The Christian Science movement grew significantly over the next decades, marking more than 200,000 members by 1900. Mary Baker Eddy was the undisputed authority over the church, even claiming to be Christ's successor. She died in 1910 at the age of eighty-nine, leaving an estate valued at $3 million.[4]

As Boa makes clear, Mary Baker Eddy was not well educated, and "she knew nothing about philosophy, logic, theology, Hebrew, Greek, or biblical history."[5] The earliest editions of her work are filled with grammatical errors, later corrected. Her work is also saturated with repetition, jargon, and rambling sentences. "The material is disjointed and far removed from any logical sequence."[6]

To promote its worldview, the Christian Science movement has published the rather prestigious *Christian Science Monitor* newspaper. But changes and increased competition in the newspaper industry have made the newspaper unprofitable. The Christian Science leadership also experimented with operating a cable news channel, a magazine, and a Boston radio station.[7] Today the church publishes the following:

• *Christian Science Quarterly,* weekly Bible lessons that combine the Bible and the works of Eddy in *Science and Health* into a weekly study format

• *The Christian Science Journal,* which offers instructive articles and "verified" reports of Christian healing and the work of the "divine Principle"

• *Christian Science Sentinel*, which comments on world events and trends and relates them to Christian Science principles

• *The Christian Science Monitor*, a scaled-down newspaper published internationally. [For a review of these publications see the church Web site at www.tfccs.com]

Today the Christian Science movement continues to maintain Reading Rooms in major cities across the nation. Each Room is filled with the works of Mrs. Eddy and other related literature. Church membership has plummeted in the last few decades, with only about 2,400 churches presently in the movement.

Mormonism

Of the three cults discussed in this chapter, Mormonism is by far the largest and fastest growing, with as many as ten million adherents worldwide. Its founder, Joseph Smith, Jr., was born December 23, 1805, in Sharon, Vermont. From an early age, Joseph was greatly influenced by his father, who curiously spent a great deal of time searching for buried treasure using unorthodox and often occult methods. Joseph Smith's life changed in 1820 when he supposedly received a vision from God the Father and the Son, who told him that all other religions were an abomination, but that he was the prophet to bring restoration.

In 1823 another vision from the angel Moroni further solidified

Smith's charge from God. The angel informed him that he would uncover a number of golden plates that needed translating. Smith discovered these plates, inscribed with what he called "reformed Egyptian hieroglyphics," outside Palmyra, New York. He was able to translate them with a huge pair of spectacles that he called the "Urim and Thummim." According to his story, between 1827 and 1829, he "translated" the plates, and in 1830 published *The Book of Mormon*. The plates were purportedly taken to heaven by Moroni.

In 1829, Smith founded the Church of Jesus Christ of Latter-Day Saints. After a few relocations, Smith finally brought his religious headquarters to Illinois where Mormons built the city of Nauvoo and Smith instituted the practice of polygamy. When Smith and his brother Hyrum tried to destroy a local newspaper office because of its stand against the Mormons, they were arrested and jailed in Carthage, Illinois. Tragically, an angry mob stormed the prison, and on June 27, 1844, shot and killed the two brothers, making them martyrs. The leadership mantle passed to Brigham Young, the First President and prophet of the church.

Under Young's leadership, the Mormons relocated to Salt Lake City in July 1847. There they settled and built their unique brand of religion. In the face of U.S. governmental regulations, Mormon leaders eventually abolished polygamy as a doctrine.

Today the Mormons are a highly structured and organized religion. Led by a First President, a Council of Twelve Apostles, and a Council of Seventy, the church also has bishops, counselors, and teachers at all levels. Further, virtually all Mormon males serve as deacons and elders. Males over twelve years old are also members of the Mormon priesthood of Aaron or Melchizedek. Because they regard themselves as the true church, Mormons refer to all non-Mormons as "Gentiles."[8]

For the Mormons, their scriptures define their faith. They regard scripture as the Bible, *The Book of Mormon*, *Doctrines and Covenants*, and *The Pearl of Great Price*. Ken Boa summarizes the content of *The Book of Mormon*, the most important of the Mormon texts:

> The *Book of Mormon*, which supposedly was written by several people from about 600 B.C. to A.D. 428, tells of the migration of an ancient people from the Tower of Babel to Central America. These people, known as the Jaredites, perished because of apostasy. A later migration occurred in 600 B.C. when a group of Jews were supposedly told by God to flee Jerusalem before the Babylonian captivity. These

Jews, led by Lehi and his son Nephi, crossed the Pacific Ocean and landed in South America. There they divided into two opposing nations, the Nephites and the Lamanites. . . .

The Nephites recorded prophecies about the coming of Christ, and after His resurrection Christ visited them in South America. He instituted communion, baptism, and the priesthood for the Nephites. Later they were annihilated in a battle with the Lamanites in A.D. 428. Before they were killed in battle, Mormon, the compiler of the divinely revealed *Book of Mormon,* and his son Moroni took the golden plates on which "the revelation" was recorded and buried them. These plates were uncovered 1,400 years later by Joseph Smith.[9]

How reliable is this "history?" Several key points demonstrate that *The Book of Mormon* is unreliable as a historic text:

1. There are no reliable witnesses who saw the plates Smith supposedly translated.

2. As Boa remarks, "Though *The Book of Mormon* was buried in A.D. 428, it contains about 25,000 words verbatim from the A.D. 1611 King James version of the Bible!"[10]

3. I recently visited the new Mormon temple in Omaha, Nebraska, where I live. During the tour, one guest asked why there is no archeological evidence for the historical claims of *The Book of Mormon.* Our guide could offer no answer, but the extensive claims of the book would necessitate some kind of evidence for these peoples. There is none.

4. There is absolutely no evidence of anything called "reformed Egyptian hieroglyphics."

Mormonism is a worldview that has generated passion and incredible growth. It has been an aggressive religion, expecting all teens to commit two years to self-funded missionary service. Also, the LDS leaders expect every Mormon to tithe 10 percent of all income; the result is that the LDS church is extremely wealthy, with assets of over $30 billion.[11] Mormons are also visibly active in politics and social causes that promote conservative values and ethics. They remain a powerful force in American culture.

JEHOVAH'S WITNESSES, CHRISTIAN SCIENCE, AND MORMONISM: THEOLOGY AND ETHICS

God: Each of these cults views God differently; so here is a summary of each perspective.

1. *Jehovah's Witnesses* reject God as Trinitarian. God is one (called Jehovah), and the first being he created was Jesus Christ, who then cre-

ated everything else. The Holy Spirit is an impersonal and active force of Jehovah.

2. *Christian Science* teaches that all matter is an illusion (as is sin, disease, and death) and that God is an impersonal principle of life, truth, intelligence, and spirit. God is "Divine Mind." The result is that God to the Christian Scientist is actually an impersonal, pantheistic force, thereby denying the Trinity and the deity of Christ.

3. *Mormonism* teaches that God the Father was once a man but became God. He has a physical body, as does his wife (the Heavenly Mother). Mormons deny the Trinity, arguing that the Father, Son, and Spirit are three separate gods. Mormons likewise teach that it is possible for all faithful Mormons to one day become gods too.

Jesus Christ: Each cult also has a different view of Jesus.

1. *Jehovah's Witnesses* teach that Jesus, while in heaven, was the archangel Michael, but that Jehovah, after creating him as Jesus Christ, made the physical universe through Him. He lived a perfect life on earth, and after dying on a stake (not a cross), He was resurrected as a spirit, and His body was destroyed. Jesus is "a god," not *the* God.

2. *Christian Science* teaches that Jesus was not God but lived the "Christ" (perfection) ideal. Because Christian Science teaches that all matter is an illusion, Jesus never became flesh and blood, never suffered for human sin on a cross, was not bodily resurrected, and is not coming again.

3. *Mormonism* teaches that Jesus is a separate god from the Father (Elohim) and is the spirit child of the Father and Mother in heaven. He is, therefore, the "elder brother" of all human spirit beings. His body was created through sexual union between Elohim and Mary. In fact, Mormonism teaches that Jesus was married, as a polygamist, to the two Marys and Martha. His death on Calvary's cross does not provide full atonement, but does guarantee resurrection for everyone.

Scripture: The Bible is important to each of these cults but is superseded or modified by other writings.

1. *Jehovah's Witnesses*—As mentioned in the historical review earlier, the writings of the founder and early leaders (Russell and Rutherford) are important foundational teachings of this cult. However, today Witnesses also depend on the *New World Translation of the Holy Scriptures* and their magazines, *The Watchtower* and *Awake!*, to guide their thinking about doctrine and theology. The result is that they teach that the Bible cannot be understood without the guidance of the Zion Watchtower Society.

2. *Christian Science*—There is no question that Christian Science interprets the Bible through the works of Mary Baker Eddy, specifically *Science and Health, with Key to the Scriptures,* which is their real source of authority. Indeed, Eddy claimed that she was inspired by a direct revelation from God when she wrote *Science and Health,* considering it equal with the Bible. Boa reveals that she "believed she was the woman of Revelation 12 because she was being given the 'key to the Scriptures'."[12]

3. *Mormonism*—Without question, Mormons equate *The Book of Mormon: Another Testament of Jesus Christ* with the Bible; in fact, they regard it as more authoritative. The Book of Mormon is complemented by other texts, the *Pearl of Great Price* and *Doctrines and Covenants.*

Salvation: The similarity of these three cults is that each, in very different ways, promotes a works-righteousness view of salvation.

1. *Jehovah's Witnesses*—The first step is to be baptized as a Jehovah's Witness. But their core teaching is that followers merit everlasting life through door-to-door promotion of Witness beliefs. However, eternal life in heaven is limited to 144,000 "anointed ones" who have already been chosen by Jehovah. The remaining Witnesses who merit Jehovah's favor through their works will spend eternity on the rejuvenated earth, not in heaven.

2. *Christian Science*—Since humanity is not in a fallen state and because sin is an illusion, there is no real need for a savior. "Salvation" is thus mental deliverance from the error propagated by the illusions of the physical world—sickness, death, and evil. Christian Scientists seek that higher level of spiritual awareness that Mary Baker Eddy promised in her books. Victory over suffering and pain brings that spiritual awareness.

Mormonism—The LDS church actually defines "salvation" as an exaltation to godhood, which can only be earned through obedience to LDS leaders, Mormon baptism, tithing, marriage (which they believe is eternal), and secret temple rituals. Using 1 Corinthians 15:29, the LDS church also teaches that present-day Mormons can be vicariously baptized for their ancestors, who will then be "saved." For that reason, Mormons spend a great deal of time studying their family's genealogy so that they can be baptized in their place.[13]

BUILDING BRIDGES TO THE CULTS

Because there is so much complexity in dealing with these three different cults, here are three basic bridges that we can build to reach their followers with the gospel of Jesus Christ.

Bridge #1

Each one of these cults has a strong commitment to the spiritual realm beyond the physical. Each believes it is possible to connect with this spiritual world through the specific activities of the believer. As Bible-centered Christians, we believe that as well, but we must explain clearly that a relationship with God is possible only through Jesus Christ (John 14:6). In effect, as we build a relationship with cult members, we must keep coming back to Jesus—He is the only Way! Through our lifestyle and our words, we can demonstrate that truth. Jehovah's Witnesses, Christian Scientists, and Mormons all believe in a spiritual world, but they simply do not have certainty on how to get there.

Bridge #2

Each one of these cults also believes in the Bible. Each cult reads the Bible but through the lens of cult beliefs. Each has other books to explain what the Bible teaches. The Bible is not enough for them. We must be ready to demonstrate an apologetic for the Bible as the unique Word of God. We must also be prepared to use God's Word to demonstrate the deity of Jesus, the unique saving work of Jesus, and the clear understanding that salvation is through faith in Jesus, not through works. It is important to keep the focus on God's Word, not on their books. If they do not want to discuss the Bible, then do not get engaged in a conversation about their written works unless you have adequately studied them. Remember, it is not your job to change a cult member; that is God's business. Your job is to be a faithful witness of the truth revealed in the Bible.

Bridge #3

As with Christianity, each one of these cults calls for an intense commitment. Few Mormons joined the LDS church because they were drawn initially to *The Book of Mormon.* Few Christian Scientists joined Christian Science because they were drawn to Eddy's *Science and Health.* Jehovah's Witnesses initially drawn to the Zion Watchtower Society didn't join because they read the *New World Translation.* The appeal of the cults is quite simple. Each cult meets basic human needs: the need to belong, to have fellowship, to have a sense of identity and purpose, to be affirmed as a person, to have answers for life's enduring problems. Also many join one of the cults because of the need for authority and certainty in their lives. In most cults, there is little ambiguity.

Therefore, we must not only be willing to demonstrate the trustworthiness of the Bible and the uniqueness of Jesus Christ, but also the authenticity and genuineness of biblical Christianity. The fruit of the Spirit (Gal. 5:22-23) are powerful manifestations of that authenticity. Christians must also show the same intense commitment to Jesus and to truth that cultists show to their ideology. We have the answers, and we have the truth. The supernatural nature of our "walk" must match the power of our words.

In Acts 17:16-34, the apostle Paul met the Athenian philosophers on their own turf. He recognized their spiritual need, recognized their religiosity, and recognized their quest for truth; but he demonstrated the inadequacy of all of these by pointing them correctly to Jesus. That must be our methodology as we seek to build bridges to the cults.[14]

FOR FURTHER DISCUSSION

1. Identify common themes in the characteristics and history of the three cults of this chapter.
2. What has been your experience or what observations can you make related to members of these three cults?
3. Name reasons why the Bible is more reliable than the supplemental holy books of each cult.
4. How does each cult studied in this chapter view the following:
    • God
    • Jesus
    • salvation
5. What are some key points from the chapter that you will keep in mind the next time you talk to a member of one of these cults?
6. Why is it important to stay focused on Jesus and the Bible when witnessing to cult members?

Chapter Eleven

ROMAN CATHOLICISM, PROTESTANTISM, AND EASTERN ORTHODOXY: WHAT'S THE DIFFERENCE?

TODAY WHEN SOMEONE uses the term "Christian" to describe their religious convictions or worship preferences, it is no longer clear what that means. There is Roman Catholic Christianity, Eastern Orthodox Christianity with its multifaceted liturgy and divisions (Greek, Russian, Serbian, etc.), and Protestant Christianity with its many denominational structures and worship styles. How do we evaluate and understand these various expressions of Christianity? What aspects do they have in common? Where do the doctrinal differences lie?

The way to answer these questions is to understand the historical background and development of each one. This chapter will trace this development, stressing the historical and doctrinal differences of each and concluding with bridges to Eastern Orthodoxy and Roman Catholicism. Since both traditions are expressions of Christianity, the bridges will not necessarily be for evangelistic purposes, as in previous chapters. Rather, they will give some points of connection, or commonalities, between Protestants, Roman Catholics, and Eastern Orthodox Christians and some points for dialogue about the differences, including places for mutual learning. The goal is to build relationships centered on biblical truth with Christian individuals from different traditions. Because I am an evangelical Protestant, I am evaluating Orthodoxy and Catholicism from that perspective.

By way of introduction, it is imperative to remember how much Vatican II changed the Roman Catholic church. Called initially by Pope John XXIII, Vatican II was a Council of 2,500 bishops who met in four sessions from 1962 through 1965. In effect, this Council reconciled Catholicism with the modern world. It permitted the Mass to be said in the language of the people instead of only in Latin. It endorsed a more positive attitude toward Protestants and Jews. Perhaps most important, it encouraged the laity to study Scripture for themselves under a priest's guidance and to play a greater role in the church. Finally, it insisted on the necessity of religious liberty, especially on issues of conscience. The result nearly forty years later is that Catholicism is actually a spectrum, with those who affirm the traditional Latin-oriented Mass and historic Catholicism on the one end and evangelical/charismatic/Pentecostal Catholics on the other. This chapter recognizes this diversity within the church but focuses its theological analysis on the official statements of theology within that church.

THE HISTORY OF CHRISTIANITY: CATHOLICISM, ORTHODOXY, AND THE ORIGIN OF PROTESTANTISM

The Origins of Roman Catholicism

The Christian church began on Pentecost when the Holy Spirit filled the nearly 120 believers gathered in Jerusalem. From there it spread to Judea, Samaria, and then to the uttermost parts of the earth (Acts 1:8). Organizationally, the church developed from a plurality of church leadership in the first century (e.g., Phil. 1:1), to a bishop having authority over several churches in the second century, to a hierarchical structure in the third and fourth centuries. By the fifth century, the church regarded the Bishop of Rome as the first among equals and the city of Rome as its geographical center. Through church councils (c.f., Nicea in 325, Chalcedon in 451, and others), the church agreed that the Bible taught that God is Trinitarian, Jesus is God, His death is a substitutionary one, and He is coming again.

Protestant church historians generally maintain that institutionalized Roman Catholicism began with Gregory's appointment as bishop of Rome in A.D. 590. Though he refused the title of pope, administratively, he organized the papal system of government that characterized the entire medieval period. Thus, all the major bishoprics of the West looked to him for guidance and leadership. He likewise standardized the liturgy and theology of the burgeoning Roman church. Doctrines such as the veneration of Mary, purgatory, an early form of transubstantiation, and praying to departed saints found their initial pronouncements in his writings.

Gregory also promoted missionary activity among the Germanic tribes who had conquered the western Roman Empire and now needed to hear the gospel. Gregory's zeal for missions led him to send dozens of monks to northern Europe, especially to England. Many in England came to Christ, and Canterbury became the English center of Catholicism. Bishop Gregory laid the foundation for the great edifice known as Roman Catholicism.

Two other factors contributed to the growing power and prestige of the Roman bishop. First, an early king of the Franks, Pepin the Short (741-768), granted the pope extensive land in central Italy—the Donation of Pepin—making the Catholic church a temporal and political power in Europe. Second, the Donation of Constantine allegedly gave power and authority to the Roman bishop when Constantine relocated his capital to the East. That document was later discovered to be a forgery. Both, however, solidified the power of the pope.

Missionary activity throughout Europe by Boniface (672-754), Columba (521-597), Patrick (ca. 389-461), and many others brought the areas under Germanic tribal domination into the Roman Catholic fold. The church became a civilizing force as these tribes converted to faith.

During the medieval period of church history (600-1500), a group of theologians called the scholastics systematized the body of critical Roman Catholic doctrine. Anselm (1033-1109) gave reasonable proofs for God's existence and compelling reasons for God as the self-existent, incorporeal, almighty, compassionate, just, and merciful one. In his book *Why the Godman?* Anselm also demonstrated the crucial interrelationship between the incarnation of God's Son and His atonement for sin.

The apex of scholastic theology, however, was reached with Thomas Aquinas. His life of scholarship forever shaped the direction of institutionalized Catholicism. In his *Summa Theologica*, he gave critical support to the distinctive doctrines of the Christian faith, including the attributes of God, the Resurrection, and *ex nihilo* creation. He also defended the veneration of Mary, purgatory, the seven holy sacraments through which God conveys grace, and the role of human merit in salvation—all distinctive Roman Catholic doctrines. Aquinas likewise gave a philosophical defense that the Communion elements at the prayer of consecration become, sacrificially, the actual body and blood of Christ (transubstantiation). Roman Catholicism not only had a distinct hierarchical structure with clear geographical support, but it now had a defining theology that was being defended.[1]

The Split between Western Catholicism and Eastern Orthodoxy

The division of the church between East and West is rooted deeply in church history. Early on, the church leaders noticed the difference and discrepancies that language presented. The Eastern church spoke and wrote Greek, while the West began to speak and write in Latin. This was perhaps the first sign of division within the church.

Several additional developments enhanced the separation that was clearly geographical and lingual. First, when Pepin made his donation of land in central Italy to the papacy in 756, the pope naturally fixed his attention more on the West, essentially ignoring the East. Second, Pepin's son Charlemagne came to Rome and on Christmas Day, 800, was formally crowned Holy Roman Emperor by Pope Leo III. This act symbolized the division of East and West.

A doctrinal development further intensified the East-West division. The issue centered on the question: Who sent the Holy Spirit—the Father or the Father and the Son? The great fifth-century theologian Augustine (354-430) argued strongly that the Spirit was sent ("proceeded from") both the Father and the Son. In 589, at a Western council that met in Toledo, Spain, Western theologians added to the Nicene Creed of 381 the language that the Spirit proceeded from the Father and the Son (in Latin *filioque*, which means "and from the Son"). This controversy is hence called the *filioque* controversy. The Eastern theologians strongly protested this addition.

Another theological controversy separating East and West was the dating of Easter. During the first several centuries of the church, Eastern Christians celebrated Easter on Passover. The West always celebrated Easter on a Sunday. At the 325 Council of Nicea, the Eastern practice was condemned, thereby marking another divergence.

Other historical developments magnified the East-West split. First, in 858 Pope Nicholas reversed the appointment of Photius as the Eastern patriarch of Constantinople. Eastern Christians regarded this as yet another encroachment upon their autonomy. Second, in 876 an Eastern church synod in Constantinople (modern-day Istanbul) condemned the Western pope for his increasing political activities as a secular ruler of Italian land and for his failure to correct what they called the heresy of the *filioque* clause. This synod symbolized the entire East's rejection of the pope's claim of universal jurisdiction over the church.

The most noticeable break, or what came to be known as the Great Schism, happened in 1054. On June 16th of that year, Pope Leo IX excommunicated Orthodox Patriarch Michael Cerularius for "trying to humiliate and crush the holy catholic and apostolic church." The patri-arch then excommunicated Pope Leo. This mutual excommunication marks the formal break between Eastern and Western Christianity that has lasted to this day.[2]

The hostility and split were further intensified when, during the 1204 crusade, the crusaders sacked and pillaged Constantinople on Good Friday. So horrific and inexcusable was this event that the break between Eastern and Western Christianity was final and complete.

Islam also had a devastating effect on the Eastern church. Major centers of the Eastern church—Jerusalem, Antioch, and Alexandria—fell into Muslim hands, and after the eighth century theological development in these areas ceased. Therefore, leadership of the Eastern church gravi-tated to Constantinople's patriarch. When that city fell to the Muslim Ottoman Turks in 1453, leadership passed to the Russian Orthodox patriarch, who declared that Moscow would be the "Third Rome," after historic Rome and Constantinople. Today, in effect, there are thirteen self-governing and independent churches in Eastern Orthodoxy, each with its own leader—either a patriarch, archbishop, or metropolitan.

The Split Between Western Catholicism and Protestant Christianity
The Roman Catholic church experienced a crisis of authority during the fourteenth and fifteenth centuries. Upheaval within and remarkable pressures from without undermined its credibility and legitimacy. Several developments heightened this crisis:

• From 1309-1378, due to political and religious controversies, there were in effect two popes, one in Rome and one in Avignon, France. Attempts to settle this unacceptable situation further divided church leaders and harmed the church's leadership.

• In addition, the church was racked by corruption and fraud. Clergy bought and sold offices (simony). Immorality among church leaders who professed celibacy elevated the crisis of confidence. The church likewise spent a fortune acquiring thousands of relics for its cathedrals and paying for them with the sale of forgiveness (indulgences). The church thus became an object of ridicule and satire in pamphlets and books readily available due to the invention of the printing press.

• In the fourteenth and fifteenth centuries, mystics such as the Brethren of Common Life, rejecting the scholastic coldness and legal-ism of the church, emphasized obedience, holiness, and simplicity through meditation, confession of sin, and the imitation of Christ.

• Availability of the Word of God further undermined the church. John

Wycliffe (ca. 1329-1384) believed that the Bible was the final authority for the believer and that each believer should have an opportunity to read it. He and his followers translated the Latin Vulgate into English.

• Finally, modern nation-states challenged the church for supremacy, and the voyages of discovery made the earth appear smaller. Further, the Renaissance of northern Italy caused many to abandon Catholicism in favor of the glories of ancient Greece and Rome.

Into the volatile sixteenth century stepped Martin Luther (1483-1546). After his education in law and theology, he accepted a teaching position at a small university at Wittenberg, Germany. There he challenged the church on its sale of indulgences. On October 31, 1517, he nailed his Ninety-five Theses for debate to the Castle Church door at Wittenberg. Those theses and subsequent events set off a firestorm within the church that led to his excommunication and the formation of the Lutheran church. Among many other things, Luther and his followers rejected the dogma of transubstantiation, argued for the sole authority of Scripture, and advocated justification by faith alone.

Luther's followers increased, and at the German Imperial Diet at Speyer in 1529, those who dissented due to the church's clampdown on religious renewal were called "Protestants." That name has since characterized all religious groups during the Reformation that left the Catholic church. Throughout the Holy Roman Empire, towns removed religious statues, abolished the Mass, and forced priests from churches. The Reformation had become political as well as religious.

In Switzerland two major leaders emerged to lay the foundation for the Reformed tradition—Ulrich Zwingli (1484-1531) and John Calvin (1509-1564). Each married, demonstrating like Luther that spiritual leadership did not demand celibacy. Zwingli died young, but Calvin's influence extended to the Presbyterian John Knox (1514-1572), the Dutch Reformation, the English Reformation, and the Pilgrims and Puritans who would take Protestantism to North America. Because Calvin believed so strongly in the sovereignty of God, he held that God was directly involved in all aspects of the drama of salvation, including predestination and election. Today Calvinism is found in historic Presbyterianism, Reformed faiths, and some Baptist groups.

Anabaptism was another influential aspect of the Protestant Reformation. As a term, *anabaptist* means "to again baptize." As a movement, Anabaptism stressed believer's baptism, as opposed to infant baptism. But the term also refers to widely diverse groups of Reformers, many of whom embraced quite radical social, political, economic, and religious views. The most respectable Anabaptist groups included the Swiss Brethren, the Mennonites, and the Amish. Other distinctives of Anabaptism include a commitment to the gathered church concept as opposed to the state church. Therefore, many called for the separation of church and state. Many also advocated the position of nonresistance and even pacifism.

In Britain and America other Protestant denominational groups developed. In the mid-to-late 1700s the Methodists, under John Wesley, broke from the state-supported Anglican church and preached revival throughout England and America. The Baptists, who stressed believer's baptism, spread across America. They followed the teachings of John Arminius, which stressed human free will and the importance of trusting Christ for salvation. In America the Black church, originating out of the slave religion of the South, grew and began to organize into denominations as early as 1816.

In early twentieth-century America, the Pentecostal movement was born. This movement, first institutionalized in the Assembly of God churches in 1916, emphasized the spiritual gifts of healing and speaking in tongues. It evolved through the century in many ways, each facet stressing one or more of the sign gifts. In Asia, Latin America, Africa, and the United States it remains a formidable Protestant and Catholic force in the church today.

Since Protestantism broke from the Catholic church through the sixteenth century Reformation, it has continued to fragment and divide. Today denominationalism is the chief characteristic of the multiple expressions of Protestant Christianity.[3]

ROMAN CATHOLICISM AND EASTERN ORTHODOXY: THEOLOGY AND ETHICS

Roman Catholicism

Theologically, the Roman Catholic church has consistently held to the historical and biblical view of the Trinity—God as Father, Son, and Holy Spirit. Equally, the church has defended the deity of Jesus Christ and His virgin birth. However, Catholics and Protestants have differed in several areas.

Scripture: The official position of the Roman Catholic church is that "Sacred Tradition and Sacred Scripture" are equal sources of authority for the Christian. The church is entrusted with the transmission and interpretation of these two authorities, and it declares what that revelation from God says and means. Tradition for the Roman Catholic refers to the external dogmatic authority that resides in the teaching "magisterium of the church" as expressed in the primacy and infallibility of the papacy. "Both Scripture and Tradition must be accepted and honored with equal sentiments of devotion and reverence."[4]

Mary: The Catholic church teaches that Mary is the "mother of God," who was immaculately conceived (that is born without original sin) and instead of dying, was bodily taken to heaven (the Assumption of Mary). Therefore, the church teaches that "the Holy Mother of God, the new Eve, Mother of the Church, continues in heaven to exercise her maternal role on behalf of the members of Christ."[5]

Sacraments: The Catholic church teaches that there are seven grace-conveying sacraments—baptism, confirmation, the Eucharist (or Communion), penance, Extreme Unction (last rites), holy orders, and marriage. Although the church baptizes adults when they convert to Catholicism, it practices infant baptism to cleanse the child of original sin. The church also teaches baptismal regeneration (i.e., that baptism is necessary for salvation). For the church, the Eucharist centers on transubstantiation. Catholics believe that during the prayer of consecration made by the priest, the bread and the wine literally become the body and blood of Jesus. Each time the Mass is said, Jesus is sacrificially present in the elements.[6]

Salvation: For the Roman Catholic church, salvation is more of a process than an event—a line not a point. That process begins with infant baptism and is nourished throughout life by the sacraments. The church teaches that after baptism the believer will continue to sin. However, there are two categories of sin: (1) *Mortal sin,* which can cause a person to lose sanctifying grace and thereby separates the person from God. Forgiveness for mortal sin can come only through confession to a priest or an act of repentance. (2) *Venial sins* are less serious and do not take away grace. They are removed by simple acts of repentance.

The church teaches that faith is merely the beginning of salvation, for the believer must work throughout life to complete the process begun by faith. The faithful Catholic must follow the sacraments regularly. If he or she neglects the sacraments, or if mortal or venial sins are committed, and there is no confession, then the believer who dies in this condition will spend time in purgatory. In purgatory, believers can receive temporal punishment for sin that then purifies them for heaven.[7]

Eastern Orthodoxy

Daniel Clendenin describes a typical Orthodox worship service: "The near absence of chairs or pews, dim lighting, head coverings for most women, icons and frescoes covering almost every inch of space on the walls and ceiling, a massive and ornate iconostasis separating the priest and the worshipers, the smoky smell of incense and hundreds of candles burning in memory of the dead, the priest resplendent in his ornate vestments and enormous beard, and worshipers repeatedly prostrating themselves, kissing the icons, and making the sign of the cross."[8] What are the beliefs of Orthodoxy that produce a worship service often so foreign to Western Protestants?

The Church: Eastern Orthodoxy teaches that it is the one true church on earth, tracing its origins back to the apostolic church in unbroken succession. The implication of this position is that both Catholics and Protestants have departed from the true church and the true faith.

The Sacraments: As with the Roman Catholic church, Eastern Orthodoxy affirms the seven sacraments through which God transmits both saving and sanctifying grace. Baptism, however, is the primary sacrament, for "everything in the church flows out of the waters of baptism: the remission of sin and life eternal."[9] Orthodoxy practices infant baptism, immersing the child three times, by which the infant is "born again" and wholly cleansed from all sin. Immediately following baptism is the rite of "chrismation." The priest anoints the child with a special ointment, making the sign of the cross on various parts of the body, symbolizing the gift and seal of the Holy Spirit.

Like Catholicism, Orthodoxy teaches the sacrificial presence of Jesus in the Communion elements, but Orthodoxy rejects transubstantiation, simply affirming the mystery of the sacrament. Orthodoxy also administers Communion to infants.

Icons: Probably the most unusual aspect of Orthodoxy for the Protestant is the centrality of icons during worship. At baptism the believer often receives an icon of the saint whose name he or she takes; at marriage the fathers of the couple bless them with icons; and at death the icon precedes the burial procession. Icons are flat images of Christ, Mary, or a saint. These usually take the form of wooden pictures painted in oils and are often ornately decorated with brilliant colors.

The icons are central to Orthodoxy because they are of equal benefit and mutually revelatory with the written Word. Icons are not idols or vile images. They are types, figures, and shadows of the truths of Christianity. What the Bible proclaims in words, the icon proclaims in color. For the

THE TRUTH ABOUT WORLDVIEWS

Eastern Orthodox Christian, icons demonstrate the humanity of Jesus, which is the key to His incarnation. The icons of Jesus demonstrate that He is God and man together in one person localized in space-time history. Icons thus teach a profound truth of Christianity.

Theosis: One of the most difficult Orthodox doctrines to understand is that of "theosis" (deification). Orthodoxy teaches that "As human beings we each have this one unique calling, to achieve Theosis. In other words, we each are destined to become a god; to be like God Himself, to be united with Him. . . . (2 Pet. 1:4). This is the purpose of your life . . . to become just like God, a true God."[10] For Orthodoxy, this astonishing doctrine does not mean that humans become or join the essence of God (as in pantheism); rather humans remain distinctly human by nature "but participate in God by divine energies or grace. At no point, even when deified, is our humanity diminished or destroyed."[11] Synonyms for this Orthodox teaching might be transformation, co-mingling, assimilation, or an "influx of the divine."[12]

Scripture: For the Protestant, Scripture is the final authority. For the Roman Catholic, both Scripture and tradition have authority. However, for the Eastern Orthodox, theological authority is internal, coming from the Spirit Who speaks to believers through tradition. For Orthodoxy, the papacy is not the guardian of truth, the "whole people of God is the protector of apostolic tradition."[13] As Clendenin argues, "tradition is the life of the Spirit in the church, who alone is the ultimate criterion of truth."[14] For that reason, since the Bible is the unique expression of that tradition, it is elevated, incensed, kissed, and given a place of honor in various processions. However, tradition also includes the historic church councils and the early church fathers and their writings. Orthodox believers never approach Scripture without filtering it through the grid provided by the councils and the fathers. They are all complementary in the Spirit's witness to truth.

Other Differences with Roman Catholicism

Where the Catholic church affirms purgatory, Orthodoxy repudiates this belief. Where the Catholic church demands celibacy of all its clergy, Orthodoxy permits clergy below the office of bishop to marry. Where the Catholic church affirms the Bishop of Rome (the pope) as head of the church, Orthodoxy repudiates that teaching. Orthodoxy mandates its clergy wear beards, while that is not an issue in Catholicism.

Roman Catholicism and Eastern Orthodoxy strongly agree on the foundational doctrine of the Trinitarian godhead. But when it comes to almost all other manifestations of faith and practice, they differ, often considerably. Both of these Christian traditions also differ rather radically from historic Protestantism. Building any bridges between the three expressions is challenging. However, a focus on the commonalities between all three expressions, a respectful yet firm dialogue about the differences, and a humility and openness to learn from each other are essential for building mutually beneficial, cooperative, and respectful relationships with individuals from all three traditions.

BUILDING BRIDGES TO ROMAN CATHOLICS AND EASTERN ORTHODOXY

Bridge #1

Both Roman Catholicism and Eastern Orthodoxy affirm a belief in the Trinitarian God. Each believe that God is one essence of three persons—Father, Son, and Holy Spirit. Agreement on this truth becomes a central starting point for both appreciating and understanding each Christian tradition. This agreement is also the starting point in building relationships with Christians from different traditions.

Bridge #2

Both Catholicism and Orthodoxy affirm the deity and redemptive work of Jesus Christ to save humankind from sin. They agree with Protestantism's emphasis on the centrality of the cross for Christianity. There can be no stronger connection than this! The incarnation, crucifixion, resurrection, and glorification of our King of Kings and Lord of Lords is the common heartbeat of every Christian church. This connection should never be minimized.

Bridge #3

All three expressions of Christianity share a common historic tradition. In fact, both Catholicism and Orthodoxy often have a greater respect for church history and the Christian tradition that has developed through history than evangelical Protestants. Evangelical Protestants often have the conviction that they are the first ones to discover truths from Scripture, when in reality most truths have been discovered before, probably during the first few hundred years of church history. This respect for and acknowledgment of the Christian historic tradition is an important link between all expressions of Christianity. We are all on common ground here, a fact that evangelical Protestants especially need to recognize.

Bridge #4

Fourth, Scripture is held in high regard in both Catholicism and Orthodoxy. Although there is disagreement as to the level of authority placed on Scripture, each tradition honors Scripture and accepts it as a reliable source of Christian doctrine and practice. This is an important starting place in framing discussions centered on biblical truth.

POINTS FOR DIALOGUE AND MUTUAL LEARNING

Although there are several commonalities between the three expressions of Christianity, there are also many differences that cannot be minimized. First, one of the major doctrinal differences is the understanding of exactly how salvation occurs. Protestant teaching is that justification (i.e., salvation) is solely by faith. Both Catholicism and Orthodoxy teach that human works, usually through the sacraments, are needed to, in the end, merit God's favor. It is therefore justification by faith plus human works. This belief contradicts the entire book of Galatians and the simplicity of teaching in Ephesians 2:8-9. Justification by faith alone was the central message of the Reformation and remains the major difference between biblical Protestant Christianity and Catholicism and Orthodoxy.

However, on the other hand, Protestants would benefit from placing more value on good works. Justification is immediate, but sanctification is a lifelong process. Although works do not merit God's favor, sometimes Protestants minimize works so much that their spirituality becomes lazy and is only "fire insurance" for staying out of hell. Good works should be held in high regard as the fruits and proof of salvation.

A second area of dialogue is church tradition. Catholics and Orthodox Christians emphasize tradition while Protestants often minimize it. For Protestants, an increased appreciation of the Christian historic tradition would provide an accurate understanding of the complexities and richness of historic Christianity. As we understand the diversity and the contributions many individuals and groups have made to the church, we become more tolerant and appreciative of groups with which we may personally disagree. Such humility can be a real growth point for us as evangelical Protestants. It likewise provides a basis for very meaningful dialogue between evangelical Protestants, Catholics, and Orthodoxy. Hopefully that dialogue will also help the Catholic and Orthodox Christian see that historical tradition is not to be idolized, but is a source of help in solving the difficulties of the present. We can learn from the past, but we are not frozen in the past. Catholicism and Ortho-doxy need to learn that truth.

The Catholic and Orthodox expressions of Christianity are difficult for the Protestant evangelical to understand and identify with. We certainly can learn from them, but God can use us to emphasize the truth to them that their faith is centered in the person of Jesus and His finished work on Calvary's cross. Appropriating that finished work by faith is how justification occurs. For many Catholic and Orthodox Christians, their allegiance to tradition has kept them from seeing that central truth.

FOR FURTHER DISCUSSION

1. What new perspectives have you gained about each of the Christian traditions from a review of its history? What do you see as low points and high points in these histories?
2. What historical events and figures do you see as most important in shaping current church traditions and practices today?
3. Summarize the theological differences between Catholicism and Protestantism about the following:
   • Scripture
   • Mary
   • salvation
   • sacraments
4. What was most interesting or surprising to you about Eastern Orthodoxy? Explain the meaning behind icons and the doctrine of Theosis.
5. Summarize the different views of each of the three groups on Scripture and tradition. How might Scripture be used as a bridge?
6. Where do you see your need to learn from other Christian traditions? What bridge or bridges will you use as you seek to form Bible-based relationships with your Catholic and Orthodox friends?

Chapter Twelve

CHRISTIANITY AS A WORLDVIEW

CHRISTIANITY IS NOT ONLY a personal relationship with the living God through faith in Jesus Christ; it is a worldview. It is an entire way of thinking, covering not only theology, but how to think about ethics, history, science, literature—about everything. Because God has revealed Himself verbally in the Bible, Christians have the answers to the most penetrating questions of life. James W. Sire suggests that there are seven such basic questions, similar to the worldview questions we have been seeking to answer throughout this book:

1. What is prime reality—the really real?
2. What is the nature of external reality, i.e., outside of ourselves?
3. What is a human being?
4. What happens to a person at death?
5. Why is it possible to know anything at all?
6. How do we know what is right and wrong?
7. What is the meaning of history?

Human beings must come to terms with these questions at some time during their life. Sire argues that to discover one's worldview is a "significant step toward self-awareness, self-knowledge, and self-understanding."[1]

This book has been a brief survey of the major worldviews currently dominant in our world today. Each worldview has a significant portion of humanity convinced that it is the legitimate worldview. After reviewing briefly the history and theology of each and how to build bridges to each, I am concluding the book with a rigorous presentation of genuine biblical Christianity as a worldview. By the phrase "genuine biblical Christianity," I mean the faith clearly revealed in God's Word, the Bible, and which has been validated through human history.

God: Biblical Christianity views God as He is revealed in the Bible; one of those central truths is the doctrine of the Trinity. It separates biblical Christianity from all other worldviews.

The Bible teaches in Deuteronomy 6:4 that God is one; yet from the New Testament it is clear that this one God consists of three persons—Father, Son, and Holy Spirit. The church has always affirmed this doctrine as orthodox, but wrestling with its theological and philosophical implications has always been a challenge. Especially in the early church, this struggle often produced heresy, and it continues to do so today (e.g., the Jehovah's Witnesses and Mormonism).

The ancient church of the third and fourth centuries was plagued with false teaching that challenged the deity of Jesus and the Holy Spirit, whether it was the teachings of Arius (who denied Jesus' deity) or the Pneumatomachians, who believed that the Son and the Spirit were subordinate to the Father. In order to preserve the oneness of God, others argued that Jesus was a man who was *adopted* as the Son of God; thus He was not eternally the Son. Others contended there was one God who revealed Himself in one of three modes—Father, Son, and Spirit.

The critical question has always been, "What does Scripture teach?" More specifically, what precise, descriptive words will guard against heresy when it comes to the relationship between the Father, Son, and Spirit? The biblical teaching on God as Trinity argues that we must always separate the terms *essence* and *person;* they are not synonyms. *Essence* is what makes God, God. Attributes such as omnipotence, omnipresence, and omniscience are encompassed here. *Person* is a term that defines the distinctions within that one essence. Thus we can correctly say "God the Father," "God the Son," and "God the Holy Spirit," while maintaining that they are one and inseparable in being. Yet the difference between each can be grounded only in relational and functional differences. Any language that results in the Son's or Spirit's subordination to the Father is simply unacceptable.

Thus, by definition, the Trinity is one God of three persons whose difference is relational and functional, not essential. We do not have three gods or three modes of God; we have one God. Ephesians 1:1-14 illustrates this truth quite well—the Father chooses, the Son redeems, the Spirit seals (see also 2 Cor. 13:14; 1 Pet. 1:2). Each member of the Godhead is intimately involved in the drama of salvation. We thus can join Paul and praise the Trinitarian God of grace.[2]

God is also revealed in Scripture as the creator and sustainer of all life. As prime reality, God creates *ex nihilo* and then sustains all that He creates (see Gen. 1—2; Col. 1:15-20). He is a God of truth (John 14:6), and His revelation (i.e., the written Word) is truth (John 17:17).

He is a personal God who seeks intimacy and fellowship with His crea-tures (see the Psalms, 1 John and John 4). Atheism, pantheism, or polytheism are not viable options for understanding God as the prime reality.

Jesus: Without question, the defining issue of biblical Christianity is Jesus Christ. Only a Jesus who is truly God and truly man can provide complete salvation for humanity. He must be fully human to be our substitute, and He must be fully God to be our perfect substitute. For that reason biblical Christianity has always taught that Jesus is both God and man—the Godman.

Since He is both God and man in one person, how does His deity and His humanity relate to each other? Both natures are joined in a miraculous way so that neither is damaged, diminished, or impaired. He is, then, an undiminished deity plus perfect humanity united in one person, without any confusion of the two natures. In that absolute sense, He is the Godman! Therefore, when describing Jesus, any choice of words that diminishes His deity or His humanity (e.g., Mormonism and Jehovah's Witnesses) is incorrect and heretical. A complete salvation demands it; faith in the Godman, Jesus Christ, procures it.[3]

Salvation: Biblical Christianity declares that humans are born sin-ners and inherit the guilt and corruption of Adam, for when Adam sinned, all sinned (Rom. 5:12). Therefore, the fundamental problem of the human race is not political, social, economic, or psychological; it is spiritual. Following the apostle Paul's articulation in Romans and Galatians of the human problem of sin, the Bible gives the solution as the free-grace gospel of Jesus Christ. God's grace is thus absolutely essential for human salvation, and that grace is magnified in Jesus.

How does one appropriate God's grace in Jesus? Only by faith in His finished work on Calvary's cross. Because God is just and holy, He demands payment for sin. Further, any human action or work to merit God's favor in salvation is inadequate—all human righteousness is as "filthy rags" (Isa. 64:6). The situation, therefore, appears hopeless. Because of this hopeless human condition and because of His love, God sent the second Person of the Trinity to add a human nature to His divine nature and die on the cross as our substitute (Isa. 52:13—53:12; John 3:16). God's just demands are thus met and we appropriate that fin-ished work through faith (Eph. 2:8-9). We then become His children by adoption into His family with all the rights, benefits, and privileges intact (Gal. 4:1-7).

For that reason, any worldview that adds something to faith contradicts biblical teaching. Every worldview covered in this book, whether the major world religions or the cults, declares that human works in some form are necessary to merit the favor of deity. God's Word is very clear that no human work can merit salvation. In terms of salvation, any teaching that adds to or substitutes for the finished work of Jesus Christ, the apostle Paul calls "another gospel" (Gal. 1:6-7) and is regarded as heretical.

Ethics: This book has demonstrated that ethical human behavior is tied to worldview. Whether one worships the gods of the world religions or the heretical gods of the cults, worldview determines ethical behavior. The thesis of this section is that biblical Christianity roots ethics in God's moral law as revealed in His Word.

Erwin Lutzer makes this compelling argument: "If naturalism is false and if theism is true, and therefore God is responsible for all that is, then revelation is possible. And if revelation is possible, then absolute standards are possible, should the Deity choose to make them known."[4]

Has God chosen to make such standards known? The resounding answer of biblical Christianity is yes. He has chosen to reveal Himself in His Son (Heb. 1:1-4), through His creation (Ps. 19; Rom. 1:18ff.), and through His Word (Ps. 119; 2 Tim. 3:16; 2 Pet. 1:21), and we know about the Son through the Word. These propositional truths form the basis for ethical absolutes.

What are these propositional truths that constitute the Christian ethical framework?

1. *God's moral revelation in His Word is an expression of His own nature.* He is holy, and therefore He insists that His human creatures also meet that standard. If they do not, judgment results. Hence, the vital nature of Jesus' substitutionary atonement. Appropriating that atoning work by faith makes the human holy in God's eyes, and thus acceptable to God. The same argument can be made about God's ethical standards of truth, beauty, love, life, and sexuality.

2. *God's moral and ethical system consists of more than external conformity to His moral code; it centers on conformity with internal issues of motivation and personal attitudes.* Jesus' teaching in the Sermon on the Mount presses this point. The ethical standard prohibiting adultery involves more than simply the external act; it also involves lusting with the heart after someone (Matt. 5:27-28). The prohibition of murder involves more than the external act; it includes bitterness, hatred, and anger in the heart (Matt. 5:21-22).

3. *God provides the absolute criteria for determining the value of human*

beings. Because physical, economic, mental, and social/cultural criteria are all arbitrary and relative, they are inadequate for assigning value to humans. God created humans in His image (Gen. 1:26ff.) and established His absolute criteria for their value. Being made in the image of God means that humans *resemble* God. Like God, humans possess self-consciousness, self-will, and moral responsibility. What humans lost in the Fall (Gen. 3) was righteousness, holiness, and knowledge; these are renewed in Christians as they are being conformed to the image of Christ. Being in God's image also means that humans *represent* God. God's purpose in creating human beings is functional (Gen. 1:26-27). Humans have the responsibility of dominion over creation and of being fruitful and multiplying. Humans represent God as His stewards over His world. This concept is emphasized in Genesis 2 and reiterated in Psalms 8 and 110. Humans are God's vice-regents over all creation with power to control, regulate, and harness its potential. The Fall did not abolish this stewardship. Instead, Satan is the usurper and enemy of humans in their dominion status. Man lives out of harmony with himself and with nature. Created to rule, humans find that the crown has fallen from their brows.[5]

History: Biblical Christianity offers an approach to history rooted in God's revelation. Past historical perspectives offer little help today. The ancient Greeks adhered to a cyclical philosophy of history that saw past events as a series of repetitive cycles—the old adage that history repeats itself. The religions of Hinduism, Buddhism, and the amorphous New Age Movement, with their common emphasis on reincarnation, all view history similarly. The common element among them all is an absence of hope, meaning, and purpose.

Other approaches to history are inadequate as well. The eighteenth-century Enlightenment saw history through the grid of progress. The Scientific Revolution of the preceding century and the certainty of constructing a science of man created an optimism about humanity that viewed human perfectibility as imminent. Destroyed by the carnage of the twentieth century (two World Wars and the Holocaust), the view of progress is no longer viable. Modern existentialism or postmodernism offer no meaning to history except individual autonomy and choice.

Biblical Christianity's approach, rooted in God's revelation, gives hope and solid confidence for the future. This approach has four essential aspects:

First, the Bible calls for a worldview that rejects the cyclical model of history. The ancient Hebrews saw history as a line with a beginning, a middle, and an end. Creation marked the initiation of history with God creating the universe *ex nihilo*. The Old Testament records God revealing Himself to men and women through many means, while the New Testament demonstrated His power and purposes through miracles and signs. The greatest revelation, the incarnation of Jesus Christ, bifurcates history, and when He returns, Christ will bring history to an end. For the Christian, then, history is linear, has purpose and meaning, and is filled with hope.

Second, the Christian approach to history is a commitment to God's sovereignty. Daniel 4:17, 25 affirms in the message to King Nebuchadnezzar that God rules in the affairs of men, seeking the counsel of no one. The Old Testament also declares that God's sovereignty entails overruling the evil deeds of men so that His purposes are attained. The narrative of Joseph details God's providence over his life—"the Lord was with Joseph"—despite the evil intents of Potiphar's wife and of Joseph's brothers. God's purpose was to preserve life, and Joseph was His means of doing that. Furthermore, God's sovereignty extends to the counsel that rulers receive. Second Samuel 17:14 demonstrates that God thwarted the counsel of Absalom's adviser, Ahithophel, to secure the safety of David's retreat from Absalom.

The crucifixion of Jesus Christ constitutes the foremost New Testament example of God's sovereignty in the face of evil. Acts 4:27-28 depicts this monstrous evil as under God's sovereign control: "For truly in this city there were gathered together against Your holy servant Jesus, whom You anointed, both Herod and Pontius Pilate, along with the Gentiles and the peoples of Israel, to do whatever Your hand and Your purpose predestined to occur."

A third element in the Christian approach to history is that God uses pagan nations to accomplish His ends. When Jeremiah warned Judah that God was about to judge them for their spiritual adultery, he shows God summoning Nebuchadnezzar, "My servant," to be the instrument of His judgment. In Jeremiah 27:7 God declares, "all the nations shall serve him, and his son, and his grandson, until the time of his own land comes." When Isaiah prophesied of the coming liberation of the exiles from captivity, he prophetically named the Persian ruler Cyrus as the one to effect that liberation. God said of Cyrus, "He is My shepherd! And he will perform all My desire . . . Whom I have taken by the right hand, to subdue nations before him, and to loose the loins of kings" (Isa. 44:28—45:1). Thus the Bible strips away the surface of history and reveals the transcendent sovereign God moving history His way.

Finally, the Christian approach to history focuses on the principle of justice that pervades God's character and subsequently His history. When He uses a pagan nation to accomplish His ends, as He did in choosing Babylon to judge Judah, His justice demands that that nation likewise be judged. In Jeremiah 50:29 God calls for the nations to align against Babylon: "Repay her according to her work; according to all that she has done, so do to her; for she has become arrogant against the LORD, against the Holy One of Israel." When the nation God has raised up accomplishes His purposes, He judges that nation righteously and justly. Just as an individual cannot sin with impunity, the same is true for a nation.

It is rare today to approach world events with the certainty of Jeremiah revealing God's workings with Babylon and Judah, but we can gain a principle that produces confidence and certainty: God stands above the line of history as sovereign. Our assurance is that He controls all that occurs on that line for His glorious purposes. There is no geographical refuge that can guarantee such security. It comes only from faith and trust in the sovereign God of history.

Genuine biblical Christianity is a holistic worldview that provides the answers to the key questions of life. It is under severe attack today within Western civilization. Both the postmodern and the secular mind-set see biblical Christianity as the only major Western worldview articulating and defending absolutes. In that sense, biblical Christianity is the enemy of pluralism and relativism. This book has offered a clear articulation of its major tenets and its distinctives in this pluralistic world. Because our Lord has commanded it and because the fate of billions depends on it, biblical Christianity must be defended with love, and it must be championed with courage and boldness.

FOR FURTHER DISCUSSION

1. Describe a time in your life when you began wrestling with one or more of the penetrating worldview questions. What was your approach to finding answers?
2. What new insights have you gleaned from this chapter about God, Jesus, or salvation?
3. In what ways does an in-depth understanding of the Christian worldview strengthen your faith?
4. Discuss what you would say to a Mormon in defense of the Trinity.
5. What characteristics of the biblical Christian worldview distinguish it from all other worldviews presented in this book?

6. What are the three major ethical points that characterize biblical Christianity? Give reasons for the superiority of the Christian ethical system.
7. How does a Christian approach to history impact your daily life?
8. What are the key learnings you will take with you from this book? How will your life and faith be different as a result of this study?

NOTES

CHAPTER 1: POSTMODERNISM

1. Jeffrey L. Sheler, "Faith in America," *US News and World Report* (May 6, 2002), 40.
2. Ibid., 42.
3. Ibid., 42-43.
4. Ibid., 43.
5. *Time* (October 13, 1997), 81.
6. Millard Erickson, *Postmodernizing the Faith* (Grand Rapids: Baker, 1998), 16-17.
7. Stanley Grenz, "Postmodernism and the Future of Evangelical Theology: *Star Trek* and the Next Generation," *Evangelical Review of Theology* 18:2 (October 1994), 325.
8. Alister McGrath, *A Passion for Truth* (Downers Grove, Ill.: InterVarsity, 1996), 186.
9. Cited by John Leo, "Professors Who See No Evil," *US News and World Report* (July 22, 2002), 14.
10. Ibid., 14.
11. Alister McGrath, *Intellectuals Don't Need God and Other Modern Myths* (Grand Rapids: Zondervan, 1993), 28.
12. Ken Boa, *Cults, World Religions and You* (Wheaton, Ill.: Victor Books, 1981), 10-14.

CHAPTER 2: NATURALISM

1. James Davison Hunter, *Culture Wars* (New York: Basic Books, 1991).
2. Cited by James P. Eckman in *Exploring Church History* (Wheaton, Ill.: Crossway Books/ETA, 2002), 72.
3. This survey of the Enlightenment is taken from ibid., 71-74.
4. Ibid., 93-94.
5. Ian S. Markham, ed., *A World Religions Reader,* 2nd ed. (Malden, Mass.: Blackwell, 2000), 240.
6. Paul Kurtz, ed., *The Humanist Manifesto I and II* (Buffalo: Prometheus Books, 1973), 8.
7. Quoted in James Sire, *The Universe Next Door: A Basic Worldview Catalog,* 3rd ed. (Downers Grove, Ill.: InterVarsity, 1997), 63.
8. Ibid., 65-66.
9. Paul Kurtz, ed., *The Humanist Manifesto I and II* (Buffalo: Prometheus Books, 1973), 16.
10. Ibid., 17.
11. Ibid.
12. See Fritz Ridenour, *So What's the Difference?* (Glendale, Calif.: Regal Books, 1967), 118-29.
13. Kurtz, *Humanist Manifesto I and II,* 17.

CHAPTER 3: HINDUISM

1. Percival Spear, *India, Pakistan, and the West* (Oxford: Oxford University Press, 1958), 57.
2. This summary of the Hindu texts is taken from Arthur J. Dalavai, "A Critical Appraisal of and Christian Approach to Philosophical Hinduism," Th.D. dissertation (Dallas Theological Seminary, 1977), 85-103.
3. This survey of Hindu history is taken from Geoffrey Parrinder, ed., *World Religions: From Ancient History to the Present* (Bicester, England: Hamlyn, 1971), 192-238 and John B. Noss, *Man's Religions,* 6th ed. (New York: Macmillan, 1980), 72-94, 177-219.
4. Upanishads, I, 34.
5. Taken from Michael J. Longden, "Some Prominent Doctrines of Divinity, Man, and Salvation in Hinduism," Unpublished Master's thesis (Dallas Theological Seminary, 1974), 46.
6. Malcolm Pitt, *Introducing Hinduism* (New York: Friendship Press, 1955), 21.
7. These definitions were drawn from Noss's book, *Man's Religions,* 88-92.
8. Sir Norman Anderson, ed., *The World's Religions* (Grand Rapids: Eerdmans, 1950), 148.
9. This explanation of reincarnation is based on Robert A. Morey, *Reincarnation and Christianity* (Minneapolis: Bethany Fellowship, 1980), 11-21.
10. This review of the bridges and barriers to Hinduism comes from Dalavai, "A Critical Appraisal of and Christian Approach to Philosophical Hinduism," 125-37.

CHAPTER 4: BUDDHISM

1. Richard A. Gard, *Buddhism* (Englewood Cliffs, N. J.: Prentice-Hall, 1961), 13.
2. David Bentley Taylor, "Buddhism," in *The World's Religions,* ed. Sir Norman Anderson (Grand Rapids: Eerdmans, 1950), 178.
3. Richard Robinson and Willard Johnson, *The Buddhist Religion* (Belmont, Calif.: Dickinson), 14.
4. John B. Noss, *Man's Religions,* 6th ed. (New York: Macmillan, 1980), 106-09.
5. Ibid., 109-10.
6. W. St. Clair-Tisdall, *The Noble Eightfold Path* (London: Elliot Stock, 1903), 181.
7. Fritz Ridenour, *So What's the Difference?* (Glendale, Calif.: Regal, 1967), 106-09; Noss, *Man's Religions,* 175.
8. Noss, *Man's Religions,* 113; Subhadra Bhikshu, *A Buddhist Catechism* (London: George Redway, 1890), 43-45.
9. Ridenour, *So What's the Difference?* 109-10.
10. This summary of the two sects of Buddhism is based on Ridenour, *So What's the Difference?* 110-11.
11. Noss, *Man's Religions,* 114-15.
12. Ibid., 118.
13. Ibid., 122.
14. Bhikshu, *A Buddhist Catechism,* 35.
15. Ibid., 58-59.

CHAPTER 5: CONFUCIANISM

1. Lin Yutang, ed., *The Wisdom of Confucius* (New York: Random House, 1938), 5.
2. John B. Noss, *Man's Religions,* 6th ed. (New York: Macmillan, 1980), 266-68.

3. Laurence G. Thompson, *Chinese Religion: An Introduction,* 2nd ed. (Encino, Calif.: Dickerson, 1975), 6.

4. Ibid., 5.

5. Ian S. Markham, ed., *A World Religions Reader,* 2nd ed. (Malden, Mass.: Blackwell, 2000), 160.

6. Thompson, *Chinese Religion: An Introduction,* 19.

7. See Noss, *Man's Religions,* 269-70.

8. Ibid., 278.

9. Ibid., 271.

10. James Legge, *Confucian Analects* (Oxford: Oxford University Press, 1892), VI:28.

11. Enoch Wan, "The Confucian Ethic and the Chinese Cultural Attitudes Toward Work," *Crux* 24:3 (September 1988), 2.

12. James Hastings, ed., *The Encyclopedia of Religion and Ethics* (New York: Scribner's, 1965), 16.

13. Noss, *Man's Religions,* 279.

14. Ibid.

15. Ibid., 296-300.

16. Markham, *A World Religions Reader,* 187.

CHAPTER 6: SHINTOISM

1. Ian Buruma, "After Hirohito," *The New York Times Magazine* (May 28, 1989), 29, 52-57.

2. Ian S. Markham, ed., *A World Religions Reader,* 2nd ed. (Malden, Mass.: Blackwell, 2000), 201.

3. John B. Noss, *Man's Religions,* 6th ed. (New York: Macmillan, 1980), 302-03.

4. Ibid., 304; Joseph M. Kitagawa, *Religion in Japanese History* (New York: Columbia, 1966), 28, 34, 38.

5. Noss, *Man's Religions,* 304-05; Kitagawa, *Religion in Japanese History,* 30.

6. Kitagawa, *Religion in Japanese History,* 34, 38, 57-59; Noss, *Man's Religions,* 161-63.

7. Noss, *Man's Religions,* 311-12.

8. Clark Offner, "Shinto," in *The World's Religions,* ed. Sir Norman Anderson (Grand Rapids: Eerdmans, 1950), 192, 312, 321, 325.

9. Ibid., 193-94.

10. Noss, *Man's Religions,* 305-06.

11. Offner, "Shinto," 198-99.

12. Ibid., 199-200.

CHAPTER 7: JUDAISM

1. Marvin R. Wilson, "A History of Contempt," *Christianity Today* (October 7, 1988), 60.

2. Ibid., 61-65.

3. See John B. Noss, *Man's Religions,* 6th ed. (New York: Macmillan, 1980), 391-94.

4. Sir Norman Anderson, ed., *The World's Religions* (Grand Rapids: Eerdmans, 1950), 55.

5. Authorized Prayer Book, 56-57.

6. Fritz Ridenour, *So What's the Difference?* (Glendale, Calif.: Regal, 1967), 71-72.

7. Ibid., 72-73.

8. Anderson, *The World's Religions*, 63-64.
9. Ibid., 74; Ridenour, *So What's the Difference?* 73.
10. Anderson, *The World's Religions*, 67.
11. Ibid., 63.
12. Thomas Friedman, *From Beirut to Jerusalem* (New York: Doubleday, 1989).
13. Ibid., 285-87.
14. Ridenour, *So What's the Difference?* 78.

CHAPTER 8: ISLAM

1. For this historical review, see James A. Beverley, "Muhammad amid the Faiths," *Christian History* (22:2), 10-15 and "Islam: A Christian Perspective," a pamphlet of InterAct Ministries, n.d.
2. Beverley, "Muhammad amid the Faiths," 13.
3. Patrick O. Cate, *Understanding and Responding to Islam* (Dallas: Dallas Theological Seminary, 2001), 12-14.
4. Qur'an, 11:52.
5. Ibid., 5:72.73.
6. Ibid., 3:78.
7. Ibid., 5:48.
8. Ibid., 5:52.
9. For this survey of the teaching of Islam, see George Fry and James King, *A Survey of the Muslim Faith* (Grand Rapids: Baker, 1979), 40-65.
10. This review of the pillars is summarized in Beverley, "Muhammad amid the Faiths," 14-15.
11. See Mateen A. Elass, "Four Jihads," *Christian History* (21:2), 35-38.
12. This section has summarized the entire book by Charles R. Marsh, *Share Your Faith with a Muslim* (Chicago: Moody, 1975).

CHAPTER 9: THE NEW AGE MOVEMENT

1. Shirley MacLaine, *It's All in the Playing* (New York: Bantam, 1987), 191-93.
2. Edmund C. Gruss, *Cults and the Occult* (Phillipsburg, N.J.: Presbyterian and Reformed, 1994), 204-06.
3. James Sire, *The Universe Next Door: A Basic Worldview Catalog* (Downers Grove, Ill.: InterVarsity, 1988), 165-67.
4. Gruss, *Cults and the Occult*, 205.
5. Douglas Groothius, *Unmasking the New Age* (Downers Grove, Ill.: InterVarsity, 1986), 77-78.
6. Sire, *The Universe Next Door*, 161-65.
7. Ibid., 170-71.
8. Shirley MacLaine, *Dancing in the Light* (New York: Bantam, 1985), 309.
9. Sire, *The Universe Next Door*, 178.
10. Gruss, *Cults and the Occult*, 208.
11. Shirley MacLaine, *Out on a Limb* (New York: Bantam, 1983), 140-50.
12. Groothius, *Unmasking the New Age*, 20-31; Gruss, *Cults and the Occult*, 208-10.
13. Randall Baer, *Inside the New Age Nightmare* (Lafayette, La.: Huntington, 1989), 186 and Gruss, *Cults and the Occult*, 211.
14. See Sire, *The Universe Next Door*, 203.

15. Ibid., 204.
16. Ibid., 207.

CHAPTER 10: THE JEHOVAH'S WITNESS, CHRISTIAN SCIENCE, AND MORMON WORLDVIEWS

1. Anthony Hoekema, *The Four Major Cults* (Grand Rapids: Eerdmans, 1963), 378-403.
2. Ken Boa, *Cults, World Religions and You* (Wheaton, Ill.: Victor Books, 1981), 77-78.
3. Edmond C. Gruss, *Cults and the Occult* (Phillipsburg, N.J.: Presbyterian and Reformed, 1994), 17 and Hoekema, *The Four Major Cults,* 238-39.
4. For this historical summary, see Boa, *Cults, World Religions, and You,* 81-84.
5. Ibid., 84.
6. Ibid.
7. Gruss, *Cults and the Occult,* 57-58.
8. For this summary of Mormon history, see Boa, *Cults, World Religions, and You,* 64-68 and Gruss, *Cults and the Occult,* 29-37.
9. Boa, *Cults, World Religions, and You,* 67-68.
10. Ibid., 68.
11. *Time* (August 4, 1997), 54.
12. Boa, *Cults, World Religions, and You,* 84.
13. This section on cult theology was based on the chart titled "Christianity, Cults, and Religions" (Torrance, Calif.: Rose Publishing, 1994); Boa, *Cults, World Religions, and You,* 64-89; Gruss, *Cults and the Occult,* 12-65; Walter Martin, *The Kingdom of the Cults* (Minneapolis: Bethany Fellowship, 1977), 34-198.
14. See Ronald Enroth, "How Can You Reach a Cultist?" *Moody Monthly* (November 1987), 66-68.

CHAPTER 11: ROMAN CATHOLICISM, PROTESTANTISM, AND EASTERN ORTHODOXY: WHAT'S THE DIFFERENCE?

1. This summary of Catholicism is taken from James P. Eckman, *Exploring Church History* (Wheaton, Ill.: Crossway Books/ETA, 2002), 17-47.
2. For this historical survey see Daniel B. Clendenin, *Eastern Orthodox Christianity: A Western Perspective* (Grand Rapids: Baker, 1994), 454-55.
3. For this historic review of Protestantism, see Eckman, *Exploring Church History,* 49-57, 83-99.
4. Joseph Cardinal Ratzinger, *Catechism of the Catholic Church* (Liguori, Mo.: Liguori Press, 1994), 26.
5. Ibid., 251-52, 254.
6. Ibid., 312-25, 334-56.
7. Ibid., 288-92 and Fritz Ridenour, *So What's the Difference?* (Glendale, Calif.: Regal, 1967), 39-51.
8. Daniel Clendenin, "Why I'm Not Orthodox," *Christianity Today* (January 6, 1997), 35.
9. Ibid., 36-37.
10. Ibid., 120.
11. Ibid., 130.

12. Ibid., 131.
13. Ibid., 106-07.
14. Ibid., 107-08.

CHAPTER 12: CHRISTIANITY AS A WORLDVIEW

1. James W. Sire, *The Universe Next Door: A Basic Worldview Catalog* (Downers Grove, Ill.: InterVarsity, 1988), 17-18.
2. See James P. Eckman, *Exploring Church History* (Wheaton, Ill.: Crossway Books/ETA, 2002), 30-32.
3. Ibid., 32-35.
4. Erwin Lutzer, *The Necessity of Ethical Absolutes* (Dallas: Probe, 1981), 70.
5. This review of ethics is taken from James P. Eckman, *Biblical Ethics: Choosing Right in a World Gone Wrong* (Wheaton, Ill.: Crossway Books/ETA, 2004), 16-18.

BIBLIOGRAPHY

Dockery, David S. *The Challenge of Postmodernism: An Evangelical Engagement.* Wheaton, Ill.: BridgePoint, 1995.

Naugle, David K. *Worldview: The History of a Concept.* Grand Rapids: Eerdmans, 2002.

Sire, James W. *The Universe Next Door: A Basic Worldview Catalog,* 3rd ed. Downers Grove, Ill.: InterVarsity, 1997.

Veith, Gene Edward, Jr. *Postmodern Times: A Christian Guide to Contemporary Thought and Culture.* Wheaton, Ill.: Crossway Books, 1994.

WORLD RELIGIONS

Anderson, Sir Norman. *Christianity and World Religions.* Downers Grove, Ill.: InterVarsity, 1984. (Updated version of 1950 book.)

_____. *The World's Religions.* Grand Rapids: Eerdmans, 1950.

Boa, Kenneth. *Cults, World Religions and You.* Wheaton, Ill.: Victor Books, 1981.

Clendenin, Daniel B. *Eastern Orthodox Christianity: A Western Perspective.* Grand Rapids: Baker, 1994.

_____, ed. *Eastern Orthodox Theology: A Contemporary Reader.* Grand Rapids: Baker, 1995.

Markham, Ian S., ed. *A World Religions Reader,* 2nd ed. Oxford and Malden, Mass.: Blackwell, 2000.

Moucarry, Chawkat. *The Prophet and the Messiah: An Arab Christian's Perspective on Islam and Christianity.* Downers Grove, Ill.: InterVarsity, 2001.

Noss, John B. *Man's Religions.* 6th Edition. New York: Macmillan, 1980.

Parrinder, Geoffrey, ed. *World Religions from Ancient History to the Present.* Bicester, England: Hamlyn, 1971.

Ratzinger, Joseph Cardinal. *Catechism of the Catholic Church.* Liguori, Mo.: Liguori Press, 1994.

Zacharias, Ravi. *Jesus Among Other Gods.* Nashville: Nelson, 2000.

CULTS

Berry, Harold J. *Truth Twisters.* Lincoln, Neb.: Back to the Bible, 1987.

Gruss, Edmond C. *Cults and the Occult.* Phillipsburg, N.J.: Presbyterian and Reformed, 1994.

Martin, Walter R. *The Kingdom of the Cults.* Minneapolis: Bethany Fellowship, 1977.

Ridenour, Fritz. *So What's the Difference?* Glendale, Calif.: Regal, 1967.

OTHER RESOURCES

Lewis, C. S. *The Problem of Pain.* New York: Macmillan, 1962.

Yancey, Philip. *Where Is God When It Hurts?* Grand Rapids: Zondervan, 1977.

BOOK THREE:

BIBLICAL
ETHICS

CONTENTS

Chapter One

ETHICS: AN INTRODUCTION

IN MODERN CULTURE the terms *ethics* and *morals* are virtual synonyms. Quite frankly the confusion over the interchangeableness of these two terms is understandable, but it is wrong. From history we learn that the two words have different meanings. *Ethics* comes from the Greek word *ethos*, meaning a "stall" for horses, a place of stability and permanence. The word *morality* came from *mores*, which describes the shifting behavioral patterns of society.

Ethics is what is normative, absolute. It refers to a set of standards around which we organize our lives and from which we define our duties and obligations. It results in a set of imperatives that establishes acceptable behavior patterns. It is what people *ought* to do. By contrast, morality is more concerned with what people *do*. It describes what people are already doing, often regardless of any absolute set of standards.[1]

We now see the problem of the modern human condition. When ethics and morality are confused and mixed, the result is that the culture makes the norms. The standards become relativistic and changing. That which is the norm is identified with that which is the absolute. The absolute standards are destroyed by the fluid nature of the culture. Relativism triumphs over the absolute.

This is where modern culture is today. We determine the norm of human behavior through statistical studies, like the Kinsey report[2] did on human sexuality. Behavior the Bible condemns (e.g., adultery, homosexuality) is practiced widely, statistical analysis demonstrates. Therefore, since this behavior is widely practiced, that becomes society's norm and therefore its ethical standard. Ethics becomes a relativistic, floating set of patterns that determines our duty and obligation. Nothing is absolute, and nothing is forever. What the culture thought was nailed down is not. It is as fluid as a changing river.

The Bible will have none of this. The deep-seated conviction of the Christian is the proposition that God exists and that He has revealed Himself. That revelation is verbal and propositional; it is contained in the Bible. That revelation contains the absolute set of standards rooted in God's character and will. He knows what is best for us because He created us and He redeemed us. Therefore, His verbal revelation contains the absolute standard on which we base our lives and construct our duties and obligations to the family, the church, and the state.

To God ethics is not a set of fluid standards. It is a set of absolutes that reflects His character and defines human duty. He wants us to love Him and love our neighbor as ourselves. This twin injunction is a powerful example of duty to God and duty to other humans. It is an imperative for all humans. It constitutes a supernatural window into what is good, right, just, and perfect. As Erwin Lutzer has argued, "We must be willing to set aside temporarily the question of what actions *are* right or wrong to focus on a more basic question: What *makes* an action right or wrong?"[3] That is why God has the right to say to us, "Be holy for I am holy." He, the Creator, sets the standard against which we must measure all behavior.

WHY STUDY ETHICS?

There are several reasons for the study of ethics. Each is separate, and yet they overlap. The reasons I offer here are not exhaustive. Rather, they offer compelling evidence that the study of ethics is desperately needed in the church. Few Christians know how to think about the major cultural issues ripping apart our society. Instead, they often sit on the sidelines and allow non-Christians to dominate the discussion on abortion, human sexuality, the role of the state, issues of war, and the environment. Few seem ready to give a defense of the absolute standards of God's Word. This book gives Christians a starting point for thinking and acting on the basis of God's revelation. It enables believers to speak ethical truth to the culture.

The first reason for a study of ethics is that Western culture has relinquished any absolute framework for thinking about ethical standards. One powerful example of this is bioethics. Medical technology is moving so fast that ethical considerations usually are subsumed by the practical. But this is not right!

How should we think about the issue of using animal organs in human beings? Should we place a baboon's heart in a human being?

Should we place animal tissue in humans? Should we use the cells of an anencephalic baby in a human? Should we use *in vitro* fertilization to help infertile couples have a baby? Should we clone human beings? Should we use gender selection when parents want to choose whether to have a boy or girl?

All of these medical practices are being done or can be done. Does the Bible say anything about these issues? As later chapters in this book show, the Bible does speak to these questions and provides a set of standards and principles to guide humans in making these difficult decisions. Christians *must* be involved in this debate over bioethics (see chapter 6).

A second reason focuses on the "slippery slope" nature of so many ethical questions. Consider abortion. In 1973 when the Supreme Court ruled that a woman could have an abortion based on the implied right of privacy it said was in the United States Constitution, no one realized how powerful this doctrine would become. This implied right reframed the whole abortion issue. Now the culture no longer focuses on the rights of the baby; instead, the entire debate focuses on the rights of the woman to the total exclusion of the baby's rights (see chapter 4).

That same logic now informs the euthanasia debate. The discussion focuses on the right of the person to die with dignity. Doctor-assisted suicide is now sanctioned in some states using the implied right of privacy that formerly sanctioned the practice of abortion. A person who is ill and no longer desires to live, based on the implied right of privacy, can receive assistance from a doctor to commit suicide (see chapter 5).

Ethical issues feed on one another. The logic of one is used by the culture to frame the debate on the other. Christians must understand this process, or they will have no impact on the debates about life currently raging in our culture. The slippery slope nature of ethics without divine revelation explains why what was once unthinkable becomes debatable, and soon becomes culturally acceptable. We must come to terms with this aspect of humanistic ethics.

Third, Christians must understand the integrated nature of ethical issues. Most Christians do not know how to use the Bible to approach contemporary ethical issues. For many the Bible seems irrelevant. But this sad state of affairs cannot continue. Christians must learn to think biblically and Christianly about ethical concerns.

The Bible is God's Word. In 2 Timothy Paul argues that the Bible equips for every good work and is beneficial for correction, rebuking, and training in righteousness (3:16-17). Obviously, studying the Word is necessary for ethical decision-making. God's Word gives God's view of life and His absolute standards. One cannot assume that the baby growing in the mother's womb has no value to God. If He is the Creator, as the Bible declares Him, then life is of infinite value to Him. Humans, regardless of any discussion of rights, do not have permission to wantonly destroy life. To do so violates one of God's absolute standards rooted in His character. This process of discerning God's mind on an issue, developing a principle from it, and then reaching an ethical position is the process defended in this book. The Bible is not irrelevant to ethics. Instead, it is the foundation for ethics.

Fourth, many Christians know where they stand on certain ethical issues, but they cannot defend their positions. This book charts a biblical defense for each position presented. For example, most Christians believe that homosexuality is wrong. That is an ethical judgment. But why is it wrong? It is not much help to simply state, "The Bible says it is wrong." Perhaps a better defense is to root the ethical belief about human sexuality in the creation ordinance of God.

God created humanity in two grand streams—male and female. In Genesis 2 He makes clear that His design is that the male and female marry and "become one flesh." This solves the challenge of human loneliness and isolation that Adam experienced. Eve, as God's gift to the man, serves as his spiritual equal (both are in His image, Gen. 1:26-27) but yet his complement. This complementary relationship defines the basis of human sexuality, because men and women rule the creation as God's stewards and populate His planet. Human sexuality relates to the essence of human responsibility—ruling God's creation together as a complementary whole, male and female together (Gen. 1:26ff.). Whenever Jesus or Paul deals with marriage or human sexuality, each goes back to this creation ordinance of God (Matt. 19; 1 Cor. 7). Here we see God's ideal for human sexual relationships, and there is no room for homosexuality in this ordinance (see chapter 7).

Ethical decision-making is a part of everyday life. Christians must not only know what they believe, but they must likewise explain why. This book gives Christians a resource to define ethics as absolute standards that result in proper duty and obligation to God and fellow humans. The next chapter surveys the ethical options for Christians, defending the position of ethical absolutes as the only biblical option.

FOR FURTHER DISCUSSION

1. Summarize the difference between morality and ethics.
2. What is the result of the confusion of ethics and morality?
3. How does God's revelation impact the view of absolute ethics?
4. List and briefly explain the four reasons for a study of ethics.

Chapter Two

ETHICAL OPTIONS
FOR THE CHRISTIAN

THE THESIS OF this book is that ethics must be rooted in the proposition that ethical absolutes exist. Those absolutes are based on God's moral law revealed in His Word. God may be approached and His revelation understood through intellectual analysis. This claim is uniquely Christian and central to reconciliation with ethical absolutes. But before this absolute moral law is examined, the present culture's penchant for relativism needs discussion. This is necessary because relativistic ethical systems are inadequate moral guides. Why is this so?

CULTURAL RELATIVISM

Consider the option of cultural relativism. This view argues that whatever a cultural group approves of becomes right; whatever the group disapproves of is wrong. Since there are no fixed principles to guide developing moral codes, culture determines what is right and wrong. Every culture develops its own moral standards, and no other culture has the right to judge another's value system.

Consider the consequences of cultural relativism. The existence of varying cultural norms is undeniable. Whether these cultural differences ought to exist or whether all the moral viewpoints of the culture are equal must be settled by some other means. There simply must be something transcendent to settle these cultural differences. Furthermore, if culture decides the validity of moral behavior, we really cannot condemn any acceptable action within its own culture. For example, the Nazis were acting quite consistently within their cultural worldview. They believed Jews were a threat to their perfect Aryan race. Therefore, to rid European civilization of Jews was logically consistent within their cultural norms. Following cultural relativism, can Nazism be condemned?

Recent developments in higher education indicate another consequence of cultural relativism. Some students are unwilling to oppose great moral horrors (including human sacrifice, ethnic cleansing, and slavery) because they think no one has the right to criticize the moral views of another group or culture. Professor Robert Simon, who has been teaching philosophy for twenty years at Hamilton College in Clinton, New York, indicates that his students acknowledge the Holocaust occurred but cannot bring themselves to say that killing millions of people was wrong. Between 10 percent and 20 percent deplore what the Nazis did, but their disapproval is expressed as a matter of taste or personal preference, not of moral judgment. One student told Simon, "Of course I dislike the Nazis, but who is to say they are wrong?"

Another professor, Kay Haugaard of Pasadena College in California, wrote of a literature student who said of human sacrifice, "I really don't know. If it was a religion of long standing . . ." Haugaard was stunned that her student could not make a moral judgment. "This was a woman who wrote passionately of saving the whales, of concern for the rainforests, of her rescue and tender care of a stray dog."[1]

Cultural relativism can also lead to individual relativism. Truth in today's world is relegated to the individual or the group. What is true for one is not necessarily true for another. Truths for two different groups are equally valid, for they are equally based on personal outlook. The result of this ludicrous situation reminds one of the book of Judges: "Every man did what was right in his own eyes" (17:6). Individual relativism leads to social and ethical anarchy.

In the final analysis, cultural relativism propagates an unacceptable inconsistency. Denying the existence of all moral absolutes, the system wants to proclaim its own absolute—culture![2] The argument of the ethical relativist can be summarized in three propositions:

  • What is considered morally right and wrong varies from society to society, so that there are no universal moral standards held by all societies.

  • Whether or not it is right for an individual to act in a certain way depends on or is relative to the society to which he or she belongs.

  • Therefore, there are no absolute or objective moral standards that apply to all people everywhere and at all times.[3]

The fallacy of absolutizing culture is exposed the moment sin enters into the discussion. Because sin is rebellion against God, one should not expect to see consistency of moral standards across various cultures, despite near universal condemnation of murder and incest, for example. The struggle to enforce even the standards against murder and incest is further evidence of the human need for redemption. It does not invalidate the ethical absolutes revealed in God's Word.

SITUATION ETHICS

Another option is situation ethics, popularized by Joseph Fletcher.[4] The core of his argument centers on the elimination of absolute moral principles because they place themselves over people. The only absolute that can be affirmed is love. But how is this universal of love defined? For Fletcher it must be defined in a utilitarian sense. Any action that produces more pleasure and less pain, the greatest good for the greatest number, is the "loving" thing to do. In other words, as Lutzer echoes, the end justifies the means.[5] In its utilitarian understanding of "love," adultery or lying could be justified.

In Fletcher's world, if a husband is married to an invalid, it would be loving for him to have an adulterous affair with another woman because his needs cannot be met by his wife. It is likewise loving for a woman to have an abortion because an unwanted or unintended baby should never be born. But this is biblically indefensible. Who decides what is loving? Who determines the definition of the "greatest good"? You are back to a subjectivism, where each person ultimately decides on his or her own definition of "good" and "loving."

BEHAVIORISM

A third ethical option is a product of behavioral psychology. Whether it is through genetics or the environment, humans are products of forces beyond their control, this position argues. Therefore, moral values and ethical issues are simply the product of genetic makeup or of environmental factors. The result is that people are not responsible for personal behavior.

One of the greatest proponents of behaviorism was the late B. F. Skinner,[6] famed psychologist from Harvard. Following his work with pigeons, Skinner believed that he could modify the behavior of any human. He argued that ethics are entirely based on responses to the conditioning factors of the environment. Human freedom and dignity are outmoded concepts that must be discarded if the human race is to survive. Utilizing the manipulative and conditioning techniques so central to behaviorism, Skinner maintained that "man has yet to discover what man can do for man." We must be willing to surrender human freedom and jettison human dignity if the race is to survive.

The Bible will have none of this. It declares that humans are responsible for their actions (Rom. 1—3). Although a factor, a person's environment does not totally explain a person's actions. To excuse someone's actions as an exclusive product of environmental conditioning flies in the face of the biblical doctrine of sin. Humans, because they are in rebellion against God, are guilty of sin and in need of redemption. No one is ever going to stand before God and offer an acceptable behaviorist response to explain his or her sin.

A CASE FOR ETHICAL ABSOLUTES

Erwin Lutzer makes this compelling argument: "If naturalism is false and if theism is true, and therefore God is responsible for all that is, then revelation is possible. And if revelation is possible, absolute standards are possible, should the Deity choose to make them known."[7]

Has, then, God chosen to make them known? The resounding answer is yes. He has chosen to reveal Himself in His Son (Heb. 1:1-4), through His creation (Ps. 19; Rom. 1:18ff.), and through His Word (Ps. 119; 2 Tim. 3:16; 2 Pet. 1:21). We know about the Son through the Word. These propositional truths form the basis for ethical absolutes.

What are these propositional truths that constitute the ethical framework for the Christian?

1. *God's moral revelation in His Word is an expression of His own nature.* He is holy, and therefore He insists that His human creatures also meet that standard. If they do not, judgment results. Hence, the vital nature of Jesus' substitutionary atonement. Appropriating that atoning work by faith makes the human holy in God's sight. The same could be argued for ethical standards of truth, beauty, love, life, and sexuality.

2. *God's moral and ethical system consists of more than external conformity to His moral code; it centers on conformity with internal issues of motivation and personal attitudes.* Jesus' teaching in the Sermon on the Mount presses this point. The ethical standard of prohibiting adultery involves more than simply the external act; it also involves lusting with the heart after another person (Matt. 5:27-28). The ethical standard of prohibiting murder involves more than the external act; it also involves the standard of bitterness, hatred, and anger in the heart (Matt. 5:21-22).

3. *God provides the absolute criteria for determining the value of human beings.* Because physical, economic, mental, and social/cultural criteria are all arbitrary and relative, they are inadequate for assigning value to humans. For example, Francis Crick, the Nobel prize-winning biologist, has advocated legislation mandating that newborn babies would not

be considered legally alive until they were two days old and had been certified as healthy by medical examiners. Former Senator Charles Percy
of Illinois argued that abortion is a good deal for the taxpayer because it
is considerably cheaper than welfare. Winston L. Duke, a nuclear physi-
cist, stated that reason should define a human being as life that demonstrates self-awareness, volition, and rationality. Since some people do not
manifest these qualities, some are not human. Finally, Ashley Montagu,
a British anthropologist, believes that a baby is not born human. Instead,
it is born with a capacity for becoming human as he or she is molded
by social and cultural influences.[8]

God created humans in His image (Gen. 1:26ff.) and established
His absolute criteria for assigning value to human beings. Being in
the image of God means that humans resemble God. Humans possess self-consciousness, self-will, and moral responsibility, as does
God. What humans lost in the Fall (Gen. 3) was righteousness, holiness, and knowledge; these are renewed in the Christian as he or she
is conformed to the image of Christ. Theology calls these communi-
cable attributes (e.g., love, holiness, mercy, etc.) as they are present
and possible in humans.

Being in His image also means that humans represent God. God's
purpose in creating human beings in His image is functional (Gen.
1:26-27). Humans have the responsibility of dominion over creation and
of being fruitful and multiplying. Humans represent God as His stewards
over all creation. This concept is emphasized in Genesis 2 and reiterated in Psalms 8 and 110. Human beings are God's vice-regents over all
creation with power to control, regulate, and harness its potential. The
Fall did not abolish this stewardship. Instead, Satan is the usurper and
enemy of humans in this dominion status. Humans live out of harmony
with themselves and with nature. Created to rule, men and women find
that the crown has fallen from their brows.[9]

As Francis Schaeffer argued, "Unlike the evolutionary concept of
an impersonal beginning plus time plus chance, the Bible gives an
account of man's origin as a finite person made in God's image. . . ."[10]
Humans have personality, dignity, and value and are superbly unique.
Unlike the naturalistic worldview, where there is no qualitative difference between human and other life, the Bible declares the infinite
value of all humans. This proposition forms the basis for examining
all ethical issues that relate to life and provides the foundation for
Christians to uphold God's view of human beings in an increasingly
pagan culture.

FOR FURTHER DISCUSSION

1. Define and give a reasoned critique of the following ethical options:
   • cultural/ethical relativism
   • situation ethics
   • behaviorism
2. How does the proposition that God has revealed Himself relate to ethical absolutes?
3. What can we say about God's standard concerning the following:
   • The external and internal dimensions of moral/ethical behavior
   • The value of human life to God
   • The image-of-God concept
   • The created-person concept
4. On what basis can we say that humans are of infinite value to God? Explain.

Chapter Three

HOW SHOULD A CHRISTIAN RELATE TO CULTURE?

THE BIBLE WARNS against worldliness and the devastating consequences of following the world rather than Christ (James 4). From the Old Testament we see that the children of Israel got into big trouble when they imitated their pagan neighbors and brought their altars and images into the temple. Yet Christians are somehow to be in the world, but not of the world (John 17:14-18). Christians have been removed from the world's power at conversion (Gal. 6:14), and because the cross established a judicial separation between believers and the world, Christians are citizens of a new kingdom (Phil. 3:20). The Bible both discourages absolute physical separation from the people of the world (1 Cor. 5:9-10) and instructs believers to witness to this world (John 17:18), all the while avoiding the influence of the world (James 1:27; 1 Cor. 7:31; Rom. 12:2; 1 John 2:15). How does one resolve this tension?

This is a profoundly important question for those who hold to ethical absolutes. In a culture that is increasingly pagan and relativistic, how one "speaks" Christianity to the culture is critical. Should Christians separate from the culture and live in isolation? Should Christians seek to accommodate completely to the culture and seek to influence its institutions and values from the inside? Or should Christians try to transform the culture by seeking to control its institutions and claim each for Christ? Historical examples for each approach are readily available from church history and are present today in our world. The goal of this chapter is to examine and evaluate each model biblically.[1]

THE SEPARATIONAL MODEL

The separational model of relating to culture argues that Christians must withdraw from any involvement in the world. There is an antithesis between the kingdom of God and the kingdom of this world, and the choice is clear— withdraw. Clear biblical examples of this choice are Noah (whom God called out of the culture before He destroyed it), Abram (called to separate from pagan Mesopotamia), and Moses (called to separate from idolatrous Egypt). The New Testament buttresses this conviction with verses such as Matthew 6:24 ("No one can serve two masters. . . ."), 1 Peter 2:11, and 1 John 2:15. For this model, the church of Jesus Christ is a counterculture that lives by kingdom principles. She is to have nothing to do with this world.

One historical example of this model centers on the church before Constantine's critical decree in A.D. 313. During that time, Christians refused to serve in the Roman army, to participate in pagan entertainment, and to bow to Caesar as lord. Christians were antagonistic and separated from the culture and yet sought to win unbelievers to Christ.

Another historical example is Anabaptism, exemplified in the various Mennonite and Amish groups of the sixteenth century, many of whom continue today. For them there is an absolute antithesis between the kingdom of God and this world. This enmity necessitates a rejection of the church-state concept—the revolutionary center of their worldview. The church, in their view, is a free association of believers; there is no "established" state church. Religious liberty, nonresistance, often pacifism, and refusal to take vows and oaths separate these communities from their culture. Isolated and separate, these groups engage in social service to further Christ's kingdom on earth.

A final historical example was the Christian community movement in the 1960s, when Christian communes dotted the American and European religious landscape. Clearly countercultural, these groups believed that the church had become hopelessly secularized. Therefore, Christianity needed to get back to the book of Acts where resources were shared, lifestyles were simple, and believers were clearly separate from the hostile culture. This alternative way, rooted in a radical separation, would lead the church back to its roots and to revival.

How should we think about the separational model? In a culture that is increasingly pagan and antagonistic, Christianity offers some appealing options. This model stresses the "otherworldly" character of a genuinely biblical Christianity and calls people to recognize that "this world is not my home," as we often sing. After all, Jesus radically rejected the status quo of His culture and died as a result.

Yet this model has serious dangers that necessitate its rejection as a viable option. First, separatism can quickly lead to asceticism, a lifestyle of self-denial that ends up denying the goodness of God's creation. From

God's declaration in Genesis 1 that all of His creation is "good," to Paul's powerful affirmation that everything is created by God, and nothing is to be rejected (1 Tim. 4:4), the Bible condemns all tendencies toward an asceticism that denies creation's innate goodness.

Second, this model easily produces a dangerous sacred/secular dichotomy. The Bible clearly rejects the compartmentalization of life into things that are sacred and those that are secular. For the Christian, everything is sacred. Paul writes in 1 Corinthians 10:31 that the believer is to "do all to the glory of God." Finally, this model can lead to a complete withdrawal from culture, something clearly condemned in the Bible. In 1 Corinthians 5:9-11 Paul chastises the Corinthians for misunderstanding his admonition about disciplining the wayward brother. He says they incorrectly processed his teaching about not associating with sinners. The only way to completely avoid unbelievers, as they seemed to take Paul's instruction, was to die, and that is not what he had in mind. So the separational model is inadequate for the believer.

THE IDENTIFICATIONAL MODEL

Accommodation to the culture is the key word for this model—to live both in the kingdom of God and in the world. God works in the world both through the state and through the church. The believer, therefore, has a dual commitment to both. Identifying with, participating in, and working within all cultural institutions (e.g., business, government, law) is part of the mandate for the Christian. Christians are, therefore, to live both in the kingdom of God and the kingdom of this world.

Biblical examples of this model abound. Joseph rose to the top of ancient Egypt, serving as a sort of prime minister (Gen. 41:41-43). Similarly, Daniel played key political and advisory roles in the empires of both Babylon and Persia (Dan. 6:1-4). Jesus identified with the world, eating and drinking with tax collectors and assorted sinners. He clearly did not separate from the world, for He was a friend of Nicodemus and associated with key officials in the Roman army (e.g., the centurion). Finally, the book of Acts records apostles associating with the Ethiopian eunuch and Cornelius, another Roman official. Paul, in Romans 13:1-7, illustrates the role of the state as a clear sphere of God's work.

Historical examples are likewise numerous. After Constantine's decree in A.D. 313, the church-state dynamic changed. He restored church property. Bishops became equal with Roman officials. Over time the church became wealthy and powerful. Christianity became popular, the "in thing" for the empire. Complacency resulted. The church's power became political, and through the medieval period (A.D. 500-1500) it gained immense prestige and dominance. In fact, during the papacy of Innocent III (early 1200s), the church in effect ruled Western Europe.

Another example is modern civil religion, which sees the nation-state as ordained by God for a special redemptive mission. American religious leaders like Jonathan Edwards, Charles Finney, and Lyman Beecher believed that God chose America to be the savior of the world, a chosen people to accomplish redemptive purposes for all humanity. God's kingdom, they argued, would come first to America and then would spread through the rest of the world. Manifest Destiny, which defined American foreign policy in the pre-Civil War period, saw America's institutions as ideal, and God destined that those institutions be spread through North America. Such thinking had its origins in civil religion and partially explains the Mexican-American War (1846-1848) and other forms of expansionism. Similar arguments could be made about expansionism in the late nineteenth century, specifically the Spanish-American War of 1898.

As we evaluate the identificational model, its strengths are clear. It emphasizes the "this-worldly" character of the Christian life. There is much in this world that can and should be affirmed because it is ultimately good. This model calls people to recognize that there is importance and good in this world now. It likewise affirms that God is at work in and through the cultural institutions—the state, business, and even the arts. A Christian can identify and find benefit in each of these institutions.

However, the weaknesses of this model are glaring. Its principal danger is that it can lull the Christian into complacency, into blindness toward the influence of evil in the culture's institutions. Anyone involved in politics knows that it is the greatest test of one's faith to work in politics. Evil is always present, and the pressure to compromise one's convictions is ever present. This model can also lead to an uncritical acceptance of prevailing cultural practices and attitudes. Particularly in democracies where majority rule is so prevalent, pressures are strong to go with polling data as the basis for decision-making. The more Christians identify with the institutions, the more the institutions influence the Christian. Contemporary society is more permissive than that of the past, and the evangelical community is being affected by that permissiveness.

Finally, this model can lead to a loss of the church's prophetic stance. The church can almost become "married to the culture." A disastrous example comes from Nazi Germany. The church was crying, "better Hitler than Stalin," and uncritically embraced Hitler's state as a matter of expediency. The same happened in American culture, especially to justify the Mexican-American War and aspects of the Spanish-American War. This model has the danger, then, of producing a complacent and soft Christianity.

THE TRANSFORMATIONAL MODEL

This model takes the transforming power of Christ and applies it to culture. Despite the fallen nature of humanity and the subsequent curse on creation, Jesus' death, burial, and resurrection reversed the curse for both humans and culture. There is now hope of human release from the bondage to sin and for creation as well. This truth is the center of ancient Israel's hope that the world would be restored (Isa. 65) and of the New Testament's focus on Christ's redemptive work (Rom. 5:12-21). Romans 8:19-22 also emphasizes the complete remaking of creation from sin's curse. This hope is easily translated into an optimism about culture's transformation.

Historical examples of this model center on the transforming work of the gospel in a geographical area. During the Reformation, John Calvin's Geneva reflected this transforming power. Calvin taught the total lordship of Christ, that it extended to the state and to economics. Therefore, the government of Geneva experienced radical reform and pursued righteousness in making and enforcing its laws. Work to Calvin and Geneva was a God-ordained vocation, whatever its specific nature. The city, therefore, experienced a remarkable economic transformation as well. A similar process of change characterized the Puritan colony of Massachusetts Bay in the 1600s. The Puritans sought to bring all aspects of their culture into conformity with God's revelation. It was a great cultural transformation.

There is much to affirm in this model. It recognizes the gospel's power to change both individuals and their culture. It is common sense to expect that when a person trusts Christ, his or her lifestyle and culture will therefore change. Ultimately, nothing in culture is immune from the gospel's impact. Likewise, this model calls on Christians to recognize their responsibility to work toward the day when God's kingdom will come to earth and justice will rule (Amos 5:15, 24).

There are, however, several serious shortcomings with this model. The transformationist can neglect the radical nature of sin's devastation. Humans remain enslaved to sin, and even believers struggle daily with

its power. Scripture abounds with warnings about how subtle and powerful the enemies of the world, the flesh, and the devil really are. In addition, the transformational model can promote an unbiblical optimism, a
near utopianism. The Bible rejects such optimism apart from the return of
Jesus Christ. Humans, even those regenerated by faith, always struggle
with sin, and only when Jesus returns will the victory over evil be complete. Therefore the transformational model must also be rejected.

THE INCARNATIONAL MODEL

Robert Webber[2] proposes a synthesis of all three models as the best alternative. His proposal is modeled after Jesus, for He separated from the
evils of His culture, identified with its institutions and people, and yet
sought to transform it from the inside out. By adding humanity to His deity,
Jesus identified with the world in its social order—its people and its customs. The church is to do something similar. At bottom, this is the heart
of Christ's admonition that we are to be in the world but not of it. Yet Christ
separated Himself from the evil distortions of the created order. He had
nothing to do with the wrong use of wealth, social position, or political
power. Finally, through His death, burial, and resurrection, He broke the
power of sin and Satan and guaranteed the world's transformation when
He returns in glory and power. Similarly, the church is to move culture's
institutions toward genuine biblical righteousness, all the while antici-
pating Christ's final transforming work when He returns.

How does the believer live out Webber's incarnational model? First,
the Christian always lives with tension, the tension between what is
transformable and that from which he or she must separate. For example, there are many good structures in the culture—art, economics,
sports, vocations. Yet there are always the evil distortions of those good
structures—pornography, greed, workaholism, idolatry. The Christian
should identify with the good structures and seek their transformation
but always separate from those evil distortions.

Second, there is no simple formula for living with or resolving this
tension. Looking for *the* biblical answer to each practical question is
rarely possible. Applying the principles of Scripture to each person's situation may well produce considerably different judgments. The
believer's responsibility is to know God's Word, to know the mind of
Christ, and then choose a course of action that most faithfully represents God's revealed will.

What are some examples of this tension? In seeking to identify with
the cultural structures, while separating from their evil distortions,

should a Christian own a television set, listen to non-Christian music, darn socks or throw them away? Obviously, believers will answer these questions differently, but how each is answered represents the variety of expressions within the Christian church. How Christians personally resolve this tension should produce a healthy biblical tolerance, a thankfulness for the multiplicity of expressions of Christianity. It is not easy to resolve the tension between identifying with the culture's institutions and structures and separating from the distortions of each. Some Christians will choose not to own a television, not to listen to secular music, and to discard old socks rather than darn them. Agreeing to disagree on such matters guards against unhealthy legalism and promotes a healthy dialogue about living within a non-Christian culture.

Christians must always reconcile the tension of identifying with cultural institutions, seeking to separate from culture's evil distortions, all the while seeking culture's transformation. How we live with that tension is a mark of spiritual maturity.

FOR FURTHER DISCUSSION

1. Summarize the Bible's teaching about the world and the Christian's relation to it.
2. Define the essence of each of the following models of Christians relating to culture. Give the biblical justification for each as well.
   - The separational model
   - The identificational model
   - The transformational model
3. Summarize the strengths and weaknesses of each model.
4. Robert Webber suggests a synthesis of all three models, which he calls the incarnational model. Explain what he means.
5. What does the author mean when he discusses the tension between identifying with culture's institutions and structures and yet separating from its evil distortions? What are some of the guiding principles he offers to help resolve the tension?

Chapter Four

ABORTION

THE ABORTION CRISIS in American civilization has been called a modern holocaust. An exaggeration? Not if you maintain a biblical view of life. The purpose of this chapter is to review briefly the history of abortion in America, lay out a biblical view of life, and answer several salient questions.

THE HISTORY OF ABORTION IN AMERICA

By a seven-to-two decision in 1973 the United States Supreme Court, in the case *Roe v. Wade*, handed down one of its most radical decisions in modern history. Generally, when a case reaches the Supreme Court, the Court is asked to rule on a constitutional question. The Court decides what the Constitution says, and in this case the Court was asked whether states (in this case Texas) can restrict a woman's right to abortion. The Court could not cite any specific part of the Constitution that established the right of abortion; nor could they find such a right in the Bill of Rights (the first ten amendments to the Constitution). Therefore, the Court set a precedent that did not appeal directly to the Constitution; instead, it declared that there is an implied right of privacy in the Constitution and on that basis established the right of women to have an abortion.

In its decision, the Court stipulated that abortions could occur up to the point of "viability" (when a child could live outside the womb) but did not define when this was. The Court further stipulated that the health of the mother must play a role in defining viability but did not define the "health of the mother" concept. The result is that the United States now has one of the most liberal abortion laws in the world. For all practical purposes, it is abortion on demand—abortion as a form of birth control. Whatever the specifics of the pregnancy, if a woman can find a sympathetic doctor or clinic, abortion is guaranteed.

The Court argued that the weight of history was on the side of abortion. The idea that life begins at conception is a modern idea and must be rejected, it contended. Why? Because there is no consensus in the medical community or among theologians or philosophers as to when life begins, the Court would not decide the issue either. The weight of the Court's argument really rested on the proposition that the unviable fetus derives its meaningfulness solely from the mother's desire to give birth to her baby. In other words, the mother's rights are established absolutely to the total exclusion of the baby's.

Today American society tolerates several types of abortion:

• Therapeutic abortion—when the termination of a pregnancy is necessary for the sake of the mother's health

• Psychiatric abortion—for the sake of the mother's mental health

• Eugenic abortion—to prevent the birth of deformed, retarded children

• Social abortion—for economic reasons, especially as related to the financial needs of the family

• Ethical abortion—in the cases of rape or incest

Again, the result is a society where abortion on demand is available to anyone desiring it.

Although gruesome, it is important to review the methods of abortion practiced in America. Each method results in the death of a living human being:

• The dilation and curettage method (D and C)—Performed early in pregnancy, the surgeon cuts the fetus and the placenta into pieces, and they are removed from the womb.

• The suction method—The surgeon draws the fetus out of the womb via a powerful suction tube, killing the baby.

• The saline method—During the latter weeks of the pregnancy, the surgeon injects a salt solution through the abdomen of the mother, poisoning the baby in about an hour. Twenty-four hours later the baby is delivered stillborn.

• Chemical abortions—This is a more recent development, usually involving the administration of a drug (e.g., RU486) to the mother that in effect causes the woman's body to abort a recently fertilized egg. This is the most problematic of methods because it does not involve a medical procedure, only the administration of a pill. There are major side effects, but this approach is probably where research on abortion methodology is headed.

• Partial-birth abortion—This term "means an abortion in which the person performing the abortion partially vaginally delivers a living fetus before killing the fetus and completing the delivery."[1]

A BIBLICAL VIEW OF PRENATAL LIFE

In 1973 the Supreme Court was right: There is no consensus in the culture about when life begins. God's revelation in the Bible, however, has spoken to this issue. A thorough examination of His Word reveals that God views life in the womb as of infinite value and in need of protection. The challenge is that people in most areas of the culture—law, politics, and even religion—refuse to heed God's clear teaching on this issue.

A cluster of verses in the Bible clearly establish God's view of prenatal life:

• Exodus 21:22-24—"If men struggle with each other and strike a woman with child so that she has a miscarriage . . . he shall surely be fined as the woman's husband may demand. . . . But if there is any further injury, then you shall appoint as a penalty life for life, eye for eye, tooth for tooth, hand for hand, foot for foot."

Whatever these difficult verses mean exactly, God views life in the womb as of great value. Whether by accident or by intent, to cause a woman to miscarry demands accountability on the part of the one who caused it. The Law did not treat the fetus frivolously.

• Isaiah 49:1, 5—"The LORD called Me from the womb; from the body of My mother He named Me. . . . the LORD, who formed Me from the womb to be His Servant."

Referring to Messiah, God called Him for His mission *from the womb*. Prenatal life is precious to God.

• Jeremiah 1:5—"Before I formed you in the womb I knew you, and before you were born I consecrated you."

• Luke 1:15—"[H]e will be filled with the Holy Spirit while yet in his mother's womb." As with Isaiah, God viewed Jeremiah and John the Baptist from the womb as of infinite value. He even filled John with the Holy Spirit when he was in Elizabeth's womb.

No other passage deals with the question of prenatal life so powerfully and conclusively as Psalm 139. In this wonderful psalm, David reviews four phenomenal attributes of God—His omniscience, His omnipresence, His omnipotence, and His holiness. In reviewing God's omnipotence, David reviews God's power in creating life, which he expresses as God weaving him in his mother's womb. God made his "frame," his skeleton. Then, in verse 16, he writes, "Thine eyes have seen my unformed substance. . . ." Undoubtedly, David is referring to the embryo. If correct, then the divine perspective on life is that it begins at conception. So awesome is God's omniscience and His omnipotence that He knew all about David even when he was an embryo! This is God's view of prenatal life. Therefore, abortion brings God's judgment.

ETHICAL QUESTIONS RELATING TO ABORTION

1. *Is the fetus a human being?* At conception, all aspects of humanness, as defined by DNA, are present. Genetically, it is quite difficult to argue otherwise.

2. *Is the human fetus a person?* This is a question increasingly pressed today. The biological term *life* has been exchanged for the legal term *person.* This is a critical switch because only persons have rights, including the right to life. Paul and John Feinberg argue in their book that at conception the DNA strands of the embryo are species-specific. Furthermore, although the fetus is dependent upon the mother, he or she is an independent individual. Also, there is substantial identity between the embryo, the viable fetus, the infant, the child, the adult, and the elderly person.[2] The fetus is a person.

3. *How do the rights of the fetus relate to the rights of the mother?* American culture has so totally focused on the rights of the mother that it gives no thought to the rights of the fetus. As this chapter has shown, this is wrong. There must be a balance of rights. Somehow Christians must make the case for protecting the rights of the unborn child. Paul and John Feinberg have suggested a starting point:

> While it is difficult, and perhaps impossible, to convince a pro-abortionist of the personhood of the fetus, nevertheless from a purely ethical point of view it still makes sense to demand that human life should not be arbitrarily terminated, particularly when less dramatic solutions exist. Such solutions should be sought on the side of both the fetus and the mother. Having once been conceived, the fetus has no choice but to grow, just as it had no choice in its conception or its blond hair or blue eyes. Hence, the fetus is without recourse or remedy. The same is not true of the mother, who has at least three alternatives other than abortion. She can exercise initial will power by abstinence, which is grossly out of fashion today. She has the option to use contraceptives to prevent the unwanted child. And finally, given the birth of the child, the mother can allow the living but unwanted infant to be put up for adoption.[3]

Abortion is, therefore, an unacceptable practice from God's viewpoint. He views prenatal life as of infinite worth and value. To wantonly destroy it is to destroy what He views as precious. American society may have the legal right to enforce abortion (following *Roe v. Wade*), but it does not have the ethical right before God to do so. Is it a modern holocaust? With approximately 4,000 abortions every day of every year[4] since 1973, it is difficult to argue otherwise. Multiply it out. That's 1,460,000 human babies killed per year. By the thirty-year anniversary of *Roe v. Wade* in 2003, approximately forty-three million children had been exterminated.

FOR FURTHER DISCUSSION

1. Summarize the Supreme Court's legal argument in the 1973 *Roe v. Wade* decision. In your opinion, what did the Court ignore? How would you critique their decision?
2. What types of abortion are recognized in our culture today?
3. Why might pills like RU486 be potentially problematic for those who are against abortion? Go to your local library and find information on how safe this pill really is.
4. Using the verses cited in this chapter, write a biblical position paper on why abortion is not in God's will. Be sure to stress Psalm 139.
5. Is the fetus a human? A person? How would you present an argument that the fetus is of great value and should be protected by American law? How would you make an argument that life begins at conception?

Chapter Five

EUTHANASIA

LIKE ABORTION, euthanasia is one of the critical life issues facing American culture. With the baby boomers getting older, the pressure for widespread euthanasia will grow. In a very famous speech in the 1980s, former governor of Colorado Richard Lamb argued that the elderly must die, embracing euthanasia, to make way for the young, who simply cannot afford the medical care needed by elderly people. With the population living longer and with medical costs rising, the pressure for euthanasia as a solution over the next several decades will be relentless. How should Christians view mercy killings, doctor-assisted suicide, and "death with dignity"? One's attitude toward abortion often gives a hint of the attitude toward euthanasia because both focus on the view of human life. Whether that life is in a mother's womb or on a deathbed at age ninety, both are of infinite value to God; both bear His image.

EUTHANASIA DEFINED

The term *euthanasia* is derived from two Greek words meaning "well" or "good" death. It is today associated with language that seeks to sanitize the reality of death. "Death with dignity" focuses on constitutionally establishing the right of humans to die in a manner they choose. Usually, the reference point is old age when the bodily systems are beginning to shut down. *Mercy killing* refers to taking a person's life or allowing someone to take his or her own life to end the suffering that goes with a particular disease or a specific physical ailment or condition.

Euthanasia involves several types or methods utilized to effect the death. *Voluntary* or *involuntary euthanasia* defines whether the patient requests or has taken an active role in deciding upon the death. *Active* or *passive euthanasia* determines the method used to bring about the death. Passive euthanasia would involve, for example, allowing natural means of the body to bring death without any intervention. Not hooking a patient up to a ventilator or a heart machine would be examples because death would most certainly follow. Active euthanasia

focuses on a loved one actively taking the person's life with a weapon
or removing the life-sustaining equipment from the patient, bringing on
death. *Direct* or *indirect euthanasia* stresses the role of the patient who
dies from a specific action. Doctor-assisted suicide, where a medical
doctor gives a patient the equipment or medicine to end life, would be
an example of direct euthanasia. Dr. Jack Kevorkian of Michigan promotes this type of euthanasia. All types are currently practiced and
growing in frequency.

A CHRISTIAN VIEW OF DEATH AND LIFE

A believer in Jesus Christ views death quite differently from an unbeliever. Death in Scripture is clearly the judgment of God upon sin. God
told Adam that if he ate of the tree in the garden, he would die. When
he and Eve ate, they both experienced the separation from God that
resulted from sin and brought eventual physical death (Gen. 2 and 3).
Sin gains authority over humans, therefore, and results in separation
from God—death.

The death, burial, and resurrection of Jesus Christ dealt the death-
blow to sin and defeated death in the believer's life. Because Jesus conquered death through His resurrection, the believer need not fear death.
Although that person may die physically (the soul separated from the
body), the separation is not permanent because of the promised resurrection. Hence, Paul can write in 1 Corinthians 15:54-55, "Death is swal-
lowed up in victory. O death, where is your victory? O death, where is
your sting?"

The believer in Jesus Christ should face death with tension. Paul
gives us a window into this tension when he writes, "For to me, to live
is Christ, and to die is gain" (Phil. 1:21). Death means to be with Jesus
and to have all the daily struggles, both physical and spiritual, over.
Although inexplicable, death is the door Christians go through to be
with Christ. There is no other way, barring Christ's return for His church,
for the believer to be with Christ. There is, therefore, the constant pull
of heaven matched by the constant pull to remain and serve the Lord
on earth. Death remains in the sovereign hand of God.

At the same time, the Bible teaches that every person, believer and
unbeliever, is inherently dignified and worthy of respect. It is always
proper and ethically right to fight for life. That is because men and
women are created in the image and likeness of God (Gen. 1:26-27).
Human life is sacred (Gen. 9:1-6), and no one should be demeaned or
cursed (James 3:9-10). To treat a human, who bears God's image, as

someone without dignity, to wantonly destroy life, or to assume the position of authority over the life and death of another human is to step outside of God's revelation. The Bible affirms the intrinsic worth and equal value of every human life regardless of its stage or condition. In a word, this is the Judeo-Christian view of life.

What are some implications of this high view of life? First, it seems logical since life is so valuable that it should be terminated only under highly unusual considerations. In the Netherlands, for example, the Parliament there has empowered doctors to help individuals commit suicide if they are suffering from terminal illnesses and even if they are struggling with certain emotional/mental disorders. Dr. Jack Kevorkian, now in prison, has helped more than 100 people commit suicide, some of whom were suffering from clinical depression. Such practices violate Scripture, cheapen life, and treat a human as of little value and with no dignity. In short, to allow widespread euthanasia is to foster a culture of death.

Another implication of the Judeo-Christian view of life is that personhood is defined in biological terms. As defended in the previous chapter, a human is a person whose life begins at conception, not at birth. Personhood is not defined according to I.Q., a sense of the future, a capacity to relate to other humans, or any other such criteria (more about these criteria later). The point is that God creates the life, defines its beginning as conception, and sustains the life. Humans who believe His Word will maintain the same view and always fight for life. To end life in a premeditated manner, as does Dr. Kevorkian or as is legitimized in doctor-assisted suicide, violates the Bible's high view of life.

THE QUALITY OF LIFE ETHIC

Over the last several decades in Western civilization, especially in medicine but through the entire culture, a new ethic is replacing the Judeo-Christian ethic—the quality of life ethic. At its vital center, this new ethic places relative, rather than absolute, value on human beings. Let me cite several examples:

• Joseph Fletcher argues that infanticide (killing of infants) and euthanasia are acceptable because human beings have a moral obligation to increase well-being wherever possible. "All rights are imperfect," he claims, "and can be set aside if human need requires it." Fletcher is a utilitarian who believes that objective moral norms are irrelevant in determining right and wrong. Only what brings the greatest good to the greatest number is right. He goes on: "Human happiness and well-being are the highest good . . . and . . . therefore any ends or purposes which that ideal or standard validates are just, right, good." Suicide and mercy killing are acceptable to Fletcher because "a morally good end can justify a relatively bad means."[1]

• For Joseph Fletcher, to meet the criteria of being truly human, a person must possess minimal intelligence, a sense of the future and the past, a capacity to relate to others, and a balance between rationality and feelings. For example, a human with an I.Q. of 40 is questionably a person; one with an I.Q. of 20 or below is definitely not a person. Following Fletcher's logic, an infant, an adult, or an elderly person with a degenerative brain disease would not meet these criteria and thus would forfeit the right to life.

• Michael Tooley, a philosopher, formerly at Stanford and now at the University of Colorado, thinks it unfortunate that most people use terms like "person" and "human being" interchangeably. Persons have rights, but not every human being can properly be regarded as a person, Tooley believes. His rule: An organism has a serious right to life only if it possesses the concept of a self as a continuing subject of experiences and other mental states and believes itself to be a continuing entity. For Tooley, infanticide is allowable up to a week after birth. Presumably, an elderly person with a degenerative brain disease would also not meet his criteria and thus would forfeit the right to life.[2]

This new quality of life ethic is frightening. Rejecting any claim to ethical absolutes, this system embraces subjective criteria to define life's value and ends up justifying both euthanasia and infanticide. It violates all aspects of life's value as defined by the image of God concept and places humans in the seat of the sovereign God. Using subjective criteria, the quality of life ethic empowers other humans to decide who lives and who dies.

ANOTHER ALTERNATIVE—THE CHRISTIAN HOSPICE

This chapter has rejected the propensity of the present culture to redefine personhood and justify euthanasia. However, what does a Christian do when a loved one is diagnosed with a terminal disease? What does one do if someone dear develops Alzheimer's disease or Huntington's disease? What if extremely painful cancer develops, and the only outlook is months or years of pain to be followed by death?

There is no easy answer, but the Christian hospice movement is offering a powerful alternative for Christians today. Sometimes care is provided for dying patients within a nursing home facility or their own home. It involves managing pain with drugs, giving loving comfort, and providing daily service to meet all human needs, whatever the specific situation. The care is complemented by spiritual encouragement from God's Word, mixed with prayer and edifying opportunities as reminders of God's goodness and of eternal life. Death is not easy, but, as mentioned earlier in this chapter, the Christian approaches death differently than the unbeliever. The loving, empathetic, nail-scarred hands of Jesus are outstretched to welcome His child home to heaven. Hospice care provides the dignified alternative to honor God's creation (life) all the while preparing the dying saints for the promise that awaits them. It preserves the dignity of life that the mercy killers promise but cannot deliver.

FOR FURTHER DISCUSSION

1. What does the term *euthanasia* mean? Define its various types.
   - Voluntary versus involuntary
   - Active versus passive
   - Direct versus indirect
   - Death with dignity
   - Mercy killing
2. Summarize the Judeo-Christian view of life and describe how this view relates to the debate over euthanasia. Also summarize how a Christian views death.
3. What is the quality of life ethic? How does it differ from the Judeo-Christian view?
4. How does the Christian hospice movement provide a biblical alternative to current practices of euthanasia? Research your own community for hospice care services.

Chapter Six

BIOETHICS

NO AREA OF CULTURE is advancing faster than biotechnology and genetics technology. So serious is this development that government, in writing legislation, is screaming for guidelines and advice on how to deal with these explosive issues. For example, in 1997 Governor Ben Nelson of Nebraska asked me to serve on the Human Genetics Technology Commission for the state of Nebraska. Chartered for one year, the commission's charge was to write a report giving guidelines and recommendations in the complex area of human genetics technology. The federal government, for example, funded the Human Genome Project, which mapped the DNA strands to identify every human gene and its function. The results, announced in April 2003, mean a degree of control that the human race has never had before. What will we do with this knowledge and this control?

To further illustrate the importance of thinking biblically about this matter of biotechnology, consider the following situations and ponder how you would respond:

• Suppose a Christian couple whom you knew well came to you for some counsel. They are infertile, and they shared with you the several options their doctor offered that might solve their infertility problem. The doctor said that the wife could be artificially inseminated using someone else's sperm. No one would ever know. The doctor likewise described a process known as *in vitro* fertilization, where several of the wife's eggs would be removed from her body, and likewise sperm would be provided by the husband. In a petri dish, the eggs would be fertilized by the sperm, and the best one(s) would be implanted back into the wife's womb.

• Suppose another couple, also struggling with infertility, sought your advice about hiring a surrogate to carry a baby produced through artificial insemination with the husband's sperm. When born, the baby would, by contract, be turned over to the couple.

• Suppose a Christian couple wants to have a child but knows that

if they have a boy, he will be a hemophiliac. They know about the possibility of gender selection techniques that would insure a girl to a 95
percent probability.

• Suppose you have friends who are afflicted with dwarfism. They
would like to have children who will grow to normal height, to prevent
their children much of the pain they have suffered. They discover a
procedure where a doctor can alter the genes of the fetus *in utero* (in
the uterus) to insure more height.

Each one of these scenarios is either currently being done or could
potentially be done. The power of medical technology is awesome but
frightening, because the human race is now able to manipulate and
control areas of life unknown to all previous generations. Guidance from
God's Word is clearly needed.

MODERN VIEWS OF HUMANITY

Since the Enlightenment of the eighteenth century, the Western view of
humans has undergone radical change. Each subsequent theorist has
contributed to viewing the human being as more of a machine than an
image-bearer of God. For each of the following individuals or movements, humans are no longer the crown of God's creation; instead,
humans are products of impersonal forces beyond human control. The
last 200 years have not been good ones for those who view humans as
unique.[1]

• Charles Darwin proposed the theory of evolution in his books
Origin of Species (1859) and *The Descent of Man* (1872). For the
Darwinian hypothesis, humans are merely products of the same force
of natural selection that produced all other life forms. Nothing unique
about humans here.

• Sigmund Freud's various theories postulated that all human behavior is unconsciously or subconsciously motivated. In many cases these
forces are remarkably powerful and deep in the subconscious. The whole
discussion of sin and human accountability was changing.

• Benjamin Watson and B. F. Skinner argued that behavior is all
you can really study in humans and that human behavior is totally
explained by heredity or the environment. Divine purpose or control is
out of the behaviorist's picture.

• Today sociologists and historians emphasize the social and historical forces that inform and explain virtually all human corporate
behavior. God, theology, and human sin play little or no role in these
explanations.

• Geneticists and physiologists emphasize the genetic and chemical causes of human behavior.

The result of these various perspectives is to minimize human accountability and to discover *the* explanation that covers all aspects of human behavior. An all-inclusive understanding of the forces—internal and external—that explain human behavior is the objective of each of these disciplines. A corollary is that once these forces are understood, it is possible to control human behavior, either to improve it or to eliminate aspects most harmful to the human race.

HISTORICAL DEVELOPMENTS PRODUCING AN OPENNESS TOWARD HUMAN MANIPULATION

The new openness in Western civilization to seeking to control and manipulate humans arose from several historical developments since the Enlightenment. First is a mechanistic view of human beings. For example, with organ transplants in medicine, the maintenance of organ donor banks, sperm donor banks, discussion about the harvesting of organs from cadavers, etc., it is not an immense step to view humans as mere machines. When one part breaks down, another is ready to replace it. This is not medicine's intent, but the level of expectation is that somewhere there is a "part" for me. What naturally follows is a view of the human body as a machine that with proper maintenance and repairs can keep on functioning. This view produces an openness to accepting manipulation of conception and genetics.

Another development is the increasing human control over nearly every aspect of life. We live in climate-controlled buildings, drive climate-controlled vehicles, access voluminous amounts of information worldwide at the click of a mouse, can travel anywhere in the world in less than a day, and live longer than at any time in recent human history. The reason? Technology. Because of human dependence on technology, there is the natural expectation that all human problems can ultimately be solved by technology, including infertility problems, health problems, and emotional problems.

The concept of the scientific imperative is another cause of modern technological openness. This concept assumes that because technology has made a particular procedure, invention, or practice possible, we therefore as a civilization must go forward with it. The scientist's "can" becomes the civilization's "ought." This powerful assumption is pervasive in Western civilization. Globally, the invention of deadly weapons or procedures (even something as unthinkable as chemical and biological warfare) relentlessly presses on until someone determines these weapons must be produced. The same logic drives conception techniques and genetic procedures. Once the procedure is developed, it is nearly impossible to stop someone, somewhere from using it.

Another development producing this openness toward technological manipulation is the modern emphasis on pleasure and pain reduction as virtual moral imperatives. Think of common, everyday headaches. The typical drugstore in America is filled with dozens of headache remedies. Pain and discomfort are foreign to our lifestyle, and our expectations are that there should be a pill somewhere for each ailment. This expectation transfers as well to the "good life" that modern conveniences have produced. We expect, almost demand ease, comfort, and daily pleasure in the forms of good food, entertainment, and self-indulgence. In the words of Francis Schaeffer, "personal peace and affluence" drive Western civilization.[2] The result is an openness toward and the positive expectation about technological manipulation of human beings.

The doctrine of the autonomous self is the final development that has fostered this technological openness. *Autonomous* means "self-law." With the current view of law and with the pervasive practice of defending human behavior in terms of rights and liberties (e.g., abortion, euthanasia, homosexuality), individualism has been heightened to an extreme level. Western civilization has accepted the proposition that the individual is nearly sovereign in his or her thinking and behavior. This view is epitomized in the 1992 *Casey* case, which stated that "at the heart of liberty is the right of every individual to decide his or her own meaning of the universe. . . ."[3] Issues of control and manipulation of genes or of conception are in the hands of the individual.

TYPES OF HUMAN MANIPULATION

In the scenarios mentioned to introduce this chapter, several examples of genetic and conception manipulation were cited, namely *in vitro* fertilization, artificial insemination using donor sperm (AID), surrogate motherhood, gender selection, and genetic surgery *in utero*. In addition dozens of other technological procedures are possible or are now being discussed:

• *Cloning*—A variety of methods are currently being used in animal research, but the core idea is to remove the DNA material of a cell's nucleus from one creature (e.g., a sheep) and place that material into the nucleus of a sheep embryo's cell, eventually producing a virtual duplicate of the original. Technologically, this procedure could be done with humans, but social resistance to such a procedure remains strong. It is probable that cloning will gradually become acceptable.

• *Human/animal organ transplantation*—For decades medicine has used animal parts to cure human sickness. Cow veins have been stitched into the arms of humans needing dialysis treatment for kidney disease. Valves from pigs have been utilized to mend faulty human hearts as well. But in recent years, doctors at Loma Linda Medical Center in California have replaced a sickly child's heart with a baboon's heart. Animal livers have been used in other children's bodies. Discussion of using other animal organs to deal with children's diseases goes on.

• *A variation on the* in vitro *fertilization theme*—In vitro fertilization is producing legal challenges as, for example, in divorces where the former spouses battle over who actually has authority over the fertilized eggs.

The issue of frozen embryos grows more complex both legally and ethically as the practice grows. The United Kingdom has a law that frozen embryos cannot be kept for longer than five years. In 1997 over 3,000 frozen embryos were nearing the five-year threshold and faced destruction. The Vatican condemned the imminent destruction; couples and organizations from all over the world offered to "adopt" the embryos. They were destroyed. We do not know how to deal with these situations.

In Australia a couple had previously frozen several embryos produced through *in vitro* fertilization, but were tragically killed in a car accident. The legal authorities were struggling to determine whether the embryos would be legally able to inherit their parents' estate. Again there were no legal parameters.

• *Genetic testing*—Suppose that researchers are successful in using the data generated by the Human Genome Project to discover the relation of every human gene to all major diseases. Suppose also that widespread genetic testing occurs and the knowledge of each citizen's genetic makeup is available. Will insurance companies then refuse to insure people found to have faulty genes, under the standard of a "preexisting condition"?

Although bizarre and in some cases extreme, these scenarios represent just a sampling of the legal, medical, and ethical morass reproductive and genetic technology has produced. We not only have a crisis of moral authority, having no absolute framework for addressing these issues, but law and insurance have not caught up with medicine. There is a crying need for some guidelines.

GUIDING PRINCIPLES FOR CONCEPTION AND GENETIC PRACTICES

A list of guiding principles follows for consideration in dealing with issues of genetic and reproductive manipulation. This is probably not an exhaustive list. Its goal is to offer some guidance rooted in or inferred from God's Word. These guiding principles do not provide answers to all the issues raised in this chapter; nor do they mean that all reproductive and genetic research should be halted or outlawed. Rather, they should guide Christians into making wise decisions in these excruciatingly difficult areas of modern life.

1. *Human beings are created in God's image.* This makes humans more valuable than any other of God's creatures. We can then stipulate that humans are always more valuable (intrinsically so) than all other created things. There is an essential creation-order distinction between humans and other created things (both living and nonliving). The material in Genesis 1 and 2 establishes these guidelines.

2. *Issues and practices in both reproduction and genetics fall under the stewardship responsibility of humans.* In Genesis 1:26ff., God creates humans—male and female—in His image and then gives them the responsibility to "be fruitful and multiply, and fill the earth, and subdue it; and rule over the fish of the sea and over the birds of the sky, and over every living thing that moves on the earth" (1:28). Verse 29 extends this dominion to plants, trees, and seeds. Although colored by the reality of human sin, this dominion status is repeated for Noah in Genesis 9:1-2. Because God is sovereign and humans have dominion status, accountability of the human is a necessary corollary. This matter of accountability has powerful implications in the areas of reproductive and genetic manipulation. These technologies give humans power never realized before in history. Because humans are cursed with sin, it is difficult to be optimistic about the ultimate use of some of the genetic technologies. What must penetrate the human mind in this technology is that God is sovereign; we are stewards!

3. *The question of using these technologies is probably not so much whether to use them but how, when, and at what cost.* For example, *in vitro* fertilization involves multiple embryos produced in a petri dish. One or two embryos are implanted in the woman's womb. The remaining embryos are either destroyed or frozen. If life begins at conception (as

the Bible infers), then destruction of the embryos is the destruction of life. Gender selection of children, which is now possible, could seriously upset the gender balance of any civilization. Empowering parents to exercise this kind of control seems unwise, even foolish. The challenges of human cloning are so immense that proceeding with caution does not even seem wise; outright prohibition seems necessary. In many of these technologies, we simply do not know the effects of their widespread use.

4. *Human life itself is of higher value than the quality of human life.* With the eternal perspective that the Bible gives, many of these technologies border on the quality of human life ethic. Consider the example of the very short couple at the chapter's beginning. Exodus 4:11 contains God's response to Moses' claim that he lacked eloquence: "Who has made man's mouth? Or who makes him dumb or deaf, or seeing or blind? Is it not I, the LORD?" God's sovereignty extends to matters of stature. That God created this couple in His image establishes value—not height, or sight, or hearing. The same question can be raised about controlling the color of eyes, hair, or gender of a baby still *in utero*. Where might such practices, seemingly innocuous at first, end? What might the ungodly do with such power and control?

5. *From God's perspective, concern for the improvement of the "inner person" is always more important than concern for improvement of the "outer person."* Because of the inevitability of death, no procedure or practice will prevent it. Perhaps that is why Scripture gives focus to such issues as the fruit of the Spirit (Gal. 5:22-23) and the eight quality traits listed in the Beatitudes (Matt. 5:1-16). In the Bible's perspective these seem more important than using certain technologies with a goal that approaches human perfectibility. Carl Henry argued that there is clear biblical warrant for procedures that restore people; there is no clear biblical warrant for manipulation toward perfection, an insightful guideline in approaching some of the technologies discussed in this chapter.[4]

6. *When one views God's creation, one realizes that values like unpredictability, variety, diversity, and uniqueness are central to God's creative work.* Some of the genetic technologies seem, at least potentially, to violate His values. Control over gender selection and other human features could produce a "sameness" that God did not intend. Do people know how to exercise wisely the kind of power and control these procedures bring? With the reality of sin ever before us, it is difficult to answer in the affirmative. Caution—methodical, meticulous caution—is needed in approaching the genetic minefield. That is why the prudent biblical stance is that if a procedure

will likely and eventually violate biblical guidelines, it is best to proceed on a very selective basis or to not proceed at all.

7. *Finally, this civilization must critically examine the scientific imperative.* Simply because society can pursue a particular medical, reproductive, or genetic procedure does not mandate that it must! Especially in the area of genetics, "can" does not mandate "ought." The potential for power and control and its obvious abuse mandates an examination of this imperative. Perhaps with some of these procedures, it would be wise not to do them at all.[5]

This chapter has introduced you to issues fraught with complexity and uncertainty. We simply do not know where all of this will end. Therefore guidelines, inferred from God's Word, are imperative for analysis.

FOR FURTHER DISCUSSION

1. Review the role each of the following played in redefining humans and their uniqueness in Western civilization:
   - Darwin
   - Freud
   - Watson and Skinner
2. Summarize four or five developments in Western civilization that produced an openness toward manipulation of conception and genetics.
3. Summarizing some of the procedures discussed in the chapter, which ones would you approve or disapprove if Carl Henry's dictum (restore rather than manipulate) was followed?
4. Discuss the scientific imperative. Is it valid or not? Explain.
5. List and summarize five of the guiding principles discussed at the end of the chapter.

Chapter Seven

HUMAN SEXUALITY

THE DOCTRINE OF the autonomous self, mentioned in chapter 6, with its demand for rights and liberties, has resulted in a redefining of human sexuality in Western civilization. What only a few decades ago was unthinkable, gradually became debatable and is now becoming acceptable. The desire to legitimize the homosexual lifestyle is clearly part of a strategy to make it acceptable. That strategy is working. In politics, business, television and other entertainment, and the arts, the homosexual lifestyle is commonly presented as an alternate way of life. How should we think about this? As part of the "culture wars" ravaging society, is this an issue of moral authority? This book argues yes. Our goal is to focus on what God has said about the issue and then construct a strategy to impact culture on this matter.

THE BIBLE AND HUMAN SEXUALITY

When discussing homosexuality, evangelicals usually point to the Levitical code, to Sodom and Gomorrah, or to Paul's statements in the New Testament. I believe this is an error. The proper place to begin thinking about this issue is Genesis 2. After giving clear instructions to Adam about his stewardship of the Garden, God concludes that it is not good that Adam be alone (v. 18). To prove this to Adam, God brings all the animals before him to name (vv. 19-20). Although this act establishes his authority over the animals, it also serves as an object lesson for Adam. He is the only creature of God truly alone. So God creates the woman as his complement, his helper (vv. 21-23).

Moses then offers a theological commentary on what God did with Adam and Eve (vv. 24-25). First, God established the paradigm for marriage. The man is to leave his family with the conscious understanding that he is establishing a new family unit. Second, that means "to cleave" (like glue) to his wife. Third, in separating from his family of origin and making the unqualified commitment to his wife, the two will "become one flesh." This concept does symbolize the sexual intercourse that physically unites the two human beings, but it also symbolizes the merging of two personalities, male and female, into a complementary whole. Their personalities, their idiosyncrasies, and their uniqueness do not cease. Instead, these two totally different human beings merge into a perfect complement where both—now together—serve God in their integrity.[1]

In verse 25, Moses further comments that this couple is "naked" and not "ashamed." They were so totally centered on each other that they did not think of self. We can properly infer that their sexual oneness was characterized by no shame or discomfort either. Their physical love was beautiful and fulfilling; no selfish or carnal lust was present. The wonder of romantic love was perfectly present in this first marriage.

Theologically, what do we learn from this passage? How does this passage establish the model for a proper understanding of human sexuality and marriage? Allow me to suggest several lessons:

• When Jesus and Paul deal with questions of marriage or human sexuality, they always refer back to this creation ordinance of Genesis 2:18-25 (Matt. 19:1-12; Mark 10:1-12; 1 Cor. 7:10-11). What is stated in these verses transcends culture and time. They constitute God's ideal for sexuality and marriage.

• Marriage is to be monogamous and heterosexual—the standard, the ideal, for all marriages. From this passage it is impossible to justify polygamy or homosexuality. "Same-sex" marriages are not an option. With this standard established for marriage in the creation ordinance, the other scriptural passages dealing with human sexuality are all measured against Genesis 2. Each maintains that fornication, adultery, or homosexuality is an aberration, a radical departure from God's clear standard.

• Genesis 19:1-11 is the story of Sodom, which God utterly destroyed with fire. Homosexual commentators see the sin of the men as a violation of the ancient Near Eastern hospitality codes. But verse 5 and Lot's response in verse 8 demonstrate unequivocally that these men were intent on homosexual relations. Their behavior was a deliberate departure from God's clear revelation in Genesis 2.

• In Leviticus 18:22, 29 and 20:13, homosexual commentators often argue that we set aside most other parts of the Levitical law; so why emphasize this one so adamantly? Although Jesus' finished work on Calvary's cross did render inoperative much of the Levitical law and practices (the argument of Hebrews), issues of human sexuality transcend the law because of the creation ordinance of God in Genesis 2. What God says in Leviticus 18 and 20 is tied clearly to His standard established at creation. Homosexuality is ethically wrong.

• Paul's argument in Romans 1:26-27 about the debased sexual practices cited in the verses hangs on his use of the word *natural*. Homosexual commentators argue that Paul is condemning unfaithfulness in the homosexual relationship, not homosexuality itself. However, *natural* and *unnatural* can only be understood as departure or adherence to some standard that determines what natural and unnatural is. That standard can only be the one established in God's creation ordinance in Genesis 2.

• To motivate the Corinthians out of their spiritual complacency, Paul lists in 1 Corinthians 6:9 the various categories of sinners God will keep out of His kingdom. His goal is that they will examine themselves. Among those listed are "effeminate" and "homosexuals." Paul Feinberg argues that these two Greek words focus on both the active and the passive partner in the homosexual relationship. The emphasis of the passage is not on unfaithfulness to the homosexual partner, as the homosexual commentators contend, but on the very homosexual act itself.[2]

• In 1 Timothy 1:10, Paul also condemns homosexuality as contrary to "sound teaching." The issue is not unfaithfulness to a homosexual partner. The issue is engaging in something that violates God's clearly revealed standard. In this case, "sound teaching" is God's revelation in His creation ordinance, just as "liars," "kidnappers," "perjurers," and others would violate His standards revealed elsewhere (the Ten Commandments, for example).

In summary, the Bible resoundingly condemns the homosexual lifestyle as contrary to the ethical standard God established in His creation ordinance of marriage. Without some benchmark to settle the ethical debate on human sexuality, there will continually be heated confrontations within the culture. God's Word provides that benchmark; the human response of obedience is the only acceptable option.

CAUSATION—GENETIC OR ENVIRONMENTAL?

There is a great debate ensuing among psychologists and scholars over the causation of homosexuality. Is it genetically determined, or is it environmental? Those in the gay community argue passionately that being gay is genetically determined. Those who are in the religious gay community say that this is God's gift, claiming sexual orientation is created by God, and there is nothing anyone can do about it. Simon

LaVay, himself a homosexual, has done tests on cadavers who were homosexual and has found that the pituitary gland of these homosexual men is larger than that of non-homosexual men. Jeffrey Satinover presents compelling evidence that questions LaVay's research and the research and data of all claims that homosexuality is a genetic issue.[3]

Satinover's conclusions show that homosexuality is a learned way of life produced by circumstances that result in the choice of homosexuality. This is not a popular position today, especially in many universities and even among those of the American Psychiatric Association, which used to see homosexuality as a pathology in need of treatment. Satinover shows that the reason this organization altered its position was not due to science but to politics.[4]

At this point in time, there is no consensus on settling this question. Satinover's book is a powerful indictment of the politically correct agenda driving so many professional organizations, as well as the national gay movement itself. Gays seek legitimacy, and "fudging" evidence and research can often be a way to achieve it. Other serious researchers, some of whom are evangelical Christians, still argue for some kind of genetic role in the causation of homosexuality.[5] One important point to remember is that even if there is a genetic role in homosexuality's causation, the Bible still condemns it, and God's power is sufficient to overcome it, no matter what its cause.

HOMOSEXUALITY AND THE CHURCH

Over the last decades, the homosexual issue has deeply impacted the church of Jesus Christ. A brief review of some of the salient issues demonstrates how complex the issue has become. Let me list a few developments:

• The Metropolitan Community Church movement is spreading throughout the United States. Claiming to be evangelical, this "denomination" reads and teaches from the Bible and defends the homosexual lifestyle as completely biblical. I summarized some of its views on the human sexuality passages earlier in this chapter. A similar group is Evangelicals Concerned, centered in New York City.

• Most mainline denominations are struggling over the issue of whether to ordain practicing homosexuals into the ministry. The question is totally divisive in many of these denominations, potentially splitting some if it is not resolved. Others are struggling with the matter of same-sex marriages. Should denominational pastors perform such ceremonies? Denominations are deeply divided over this question.

• Two "evangelicals," Letha Scanzoni and Virginia Mollenkott, in 1978 published a book that shook the evangelical world, *Is the Homosexual My Neighbor?*—to which they answered yes![6]

The issues of homosexuality are massive, having tentacles that reach wide. But the bottom-line issue remains what has God said. This chapter has argued that the creation ordinance of God leaves no room for the homosexual lifestyle. It is a sin and must be faced as such.

CONFRONTING AND DISCIPLING THE HOMOSEXUAL

In 1985 Don Baker published a book, *Beyond Rejection*, which chronicles the story of Jerry, who struggled with homosexuality from his childhood, through seminary, and into marriage. It provides a needed window into the extreme difficulties of this struggle and yet the hope provided by Jesus Christ. Based on the balance brought by this book, let me suggest several action points for dealing with the reality of homosexuality in our culture:[7]

• *Remember that to the homosexual subculture, evangelicals are the enemy!* Because the Bible speaks so clearly on this issue, and evangelicals reflect that truth, there is no room for compromise or discussion. Patience, love, and compassion are needed as relationships are developed.

• *Remember that homosexuality is a sin.* That is the point of the earlier part of this chapter. But, although scandalous, it is not the "worst" sin. God's grace is completely sufficient to deal with this bondage.

• *Unconditional love is an absolute requirement in ministry to those in bondage to this sin.* Compassion, empathy, patience, and commitment for the long haul are necessary prerequisites. The reality is that many will fall back into the lifestyle, even after conversion to Jesus Christ. That is why organizations like Exodus International are so critical.[8] A ready-made support group of encouragers and accountability are central to this organization's ministry.

• *Repentance must always be the goal.* There must be a complete break with the past and with the lifestyle. No compromise or middle ground is available. Here again Exodus International insists on a crucial requirement for ministering to the homosexual.

There is no sign that the homosexual issue will subside in the culture war raging in Western civilization. Somehow the church of Jesus Christ must be able with one hand to declare that this lifestyle is morally and ethically wrong, while with the other reaching out the hand of love, acceptance, and compassion. Only God, working through His Spirit to enable the church, can accomplish this most difficult and seemingly impossible task.

FOR FURTHER DISCUSSION

1. What does the author mean by the creation ordinance on human sexuality? How do the following passages relate to it:
   - Genesis 19:1-11
   - Leviticus 18:22, 29; 20:13
   - Romans 1:26-27
   - 1 Corinthians 6:9-11
   - 1 Timothy 1:10
2. Summarize the debate between genetic versus environmental causes of homosexuality. Which do you find most compelling?
3. Summarize how this ethical issue impacts the church. Investigate your own church's official position, especially if you come from a mainline denominational church.
4. What attitude should Christians have toward homosexuals? If one of your children believed he or she is a homosexual, how would you respond? How should this issue be handled?
5. Does this issue suggest anything about the importance of both male and female role models for children from an early age?

Chapter Eight

THE CHRISTIAN
AND POLITICS

SHOULD CHRISTIANS VOTE? Should they run for political office? Is it proper for Christians to engage in civil disobedience? What exactly is the ethical obligation the believer owes to the state? Does the Bible speak to any of these questions? This chapter will argue that Scripture gives clear guidelines for all of these questions, giving the Christian a framework for making an impact in the political arena for righteousness and the kingdom of God.

CHRISTIAN OBLIGATION TOWARD
THE STATE

The New Testament teaches clearly that the Christian does have an obligation toward the state. This is the central point of Jesus' teaching in Mark 12:13-17, where, when questioned about paying taxes to Rome, He answers that we "render to Caesar the things that are Caesar's, and to God the things that are God's." We owe obligation obviously to God and His kingdom but also to the state because He created it, and it serves His purpose.[1] This passage makes clear that the obligation to the state stems from being a member of the state.

The apostle Paul expands on Jesus' argument in Romans 13:1-7 when he argues that the Christian is to submit to government because God established it. No ruler, president, prime minister, or tyrant has power that did not first come from God (Dan. 4:17-25). In verses 3 and 4 of Romans 13, Paul also argues that the state is to administer justice and thwart evil. This is the principal reason that God created government in the first place (Gen. 9:5-7). Paul seems to imply that this function of the state is actually conducive to the spread of the gospel.

The final reason for the Christian's obligation toward government is found in 1 Timothy 2:1-7. Here the believer is instructed to pray for those in authority in the state, in order that "we may lead a tranquil and quiet life in all godliness and dignity" (v. 2). As C. E. B. Cranfield argues from verses 3-7, "It is implied that God wills the state as a means to promoting peace and quiet among men, and that God desires such peace and quiet because they are in some way conducive to men's salvation."[2]

THE CHRISTIAN'S RESPONSIBILITY TO THE STATE

That Christians have a responsibility toward the state is clear, but what exactly is the content of that obligation?[3] First, the believer owes the state respect. Romans 13:7 and 1 Peter 2:17 both admonish the Christian to honor and respect government officials as ministers of God who have been ordained by Him and are accountable to Him for their solemn trust of promoting justice and thwarting evil. Respect involves treating with full seriousness even individuals who have no respect for the office or their high calling to that office. That dimension, therefore, necessitates administering rebuke and calling to account those rulers who abuse their office or treat the office itself with contempt. In the United States, respect would mean utilizing the constitutional means of impeachment to judge any federal official who has committed treason, bribery, or other "high crimes or misdemeanors."[4]

Second, the believer owes the state, its agents, and its duly enacted laws obedience (Titus 3:1; 1 Pet. 2:13-17; Rom. 13:1-7). Jesus paid the temple tax, and Paul apologized for speaking disrespectfully to a ruler. Further, Jesus' birth occurred in Bethlehem because Joseph was obedient to an oppressive government issuing a tax-assessing edict. Yet the New Testament mandate is neither slavish nor absolute; we see Peter and John defying the Sanhedrin's order to stop preaching. The issue apparently to them was clear: We obey the state until it is a sin to do so. Here civil disobedience was not merely permitted by God's Spirit; it was demanded (Acts 4:19ff.; 5:29). If the government commands something that God forbids or forbids something that God commands, we must disobey. That disobedience cannot involve violence or vandalism, actions that contradict prudence and civil order.

Thus, disobedience should never be taken lightly or with undue haste. Christians do have a higher law than that of human government. But God gives human governments in the main His seal of approval, and disobedience to them should be considered with great caution. Lynn Buzzard offers seven questions the believer should ask when facing the possibility of disobedience to the state:

1. How directly and immediately does the opposed government policy contradict an unequivocal biblical teaching?

2. What is the counsel of the Christian community about this policy? Where do godly leaders rank it among threats to the faith that must be addressed? What do they say about what the faithful person's response ought to be? To what extent have alternative legal protests been exhausted?

3. What harms to society and order are likely to result from the considered act of civil disobedience, and how do these harms compare with the desired benefits?

4. Will the form of civil disobedience evidence moral consistency and further proper respect for principled law and a moral society?

5. To what extent will the "witness" be heard and understood by the public and by government authorities?

6. To what extent are the acts central to maintaining my integrity as a person? To what extent may they reflect personal frustration and anger rather than a principled response?

7. To what extent does the idea for the act of civil disobedience issue from thought sources alien to a biblical worldview? Is it based upon biblical principles about the uses of power and coercion, the witness of the cross, and the sovereignty of God, or is it based upon purely naturalistic, humanistic principles?[5]

Third, the believer must pay taxes (Mark 12:13-17; Matt. 22:15-22; Luke 20:20-26; Rom. 13:6-7). Jesus makes the payment of taxes the fundamental mark of obligation to the state, regardless of the state's morality or ethical bankruptcy. This is clear because Jesus and Paul were both writing of tax payment to the Roman Empire, a corrupt, evil, and ethically repulsive state.

Fourth, the believer must pray for those in authority (1 Tim. 2:1ff.). Such praying is an essential part of the debt owed, whether the official is pagan or Christian, religiously indifferent or antireligious, just or unjust. I am often frustrated by Christians who relentlessly criticize governmental officials but rarely, if ever, pray for those officials. God can use praying to effect righteousness in the state's laws or to bring an unbelieving government official to Jesus Christ. Constructive criticism and calling the state to accountability need to be balanced with fervent, persevering prayer.

INFERENCES FOR A CHRISTIAN LIVING IN A DEMOCRACY

These, then, are the four ethical obligations the Christian owes to the state, but out of these obligations grow certain other inferences that are especially acute for the Christian who lives in a democracy. First, the Christian should vote. In normal circumstances, according to Cranfield, failure to vote "is to abandon one's share of responsibility for the mainte-nance of the state as a just state and therefore a dereliction of one's duty as a Christian."[6] Second, the Christian should keep as fully and reliably informed as possible concerning political, social, and economic issues. This necessitates diligent reading of newspapers and news magazines, careful watching of television news broadcasts, and reasoned, balanced discussion of such issues with friends and colleagues. Third is criticism of the government, its policies, and its agents in light of God's revelation. The Bible becomes the grid through which the Christian evaluates the state's actions and policies; the believer is willing to call the state to right-eousness in light of God's Word. Finally, the Christian should work for just and righteous laws and oppose those policies and decisions that are unjust and unrighteous. In a democracy Christians would become involved in activities such as working for candidates who support jus-tice and righteousness and supporting, through calling and writing letters, legislation that reflects genuine biblical righteousness.

CHRISTIAN INVOLVEMENT IN GOVERNMENT AND POLITICS

Increasing involvement in politics and government has grave dangers for the Christian. To provide the maximum impact for righteousness in gov-ernment, a proper and balanced perspective is needed. This necessitates rid-ding ourselves of what Chuck Colson calls a "starry-eyed view of political power."[7] Some Christians think that by marshaling a Christian voting bloc, Christ's kingdom on earth can be established. The external and lim-ited good that political power can achieve should not be confused with the internal and infinite good that God's grace produces. Further, there is danger in what Colson calls the "political illusion," the notion that all human problems can be solved by political institutions. This belief is idol-atrous because the Bible declares that the root problem of society is spiri-tual. What the Christian seeks through government is justice, not power. Our goal is, therefore, to move the culture toward the righteousness of God's revelation. The job of total spiritual transformation is the role of Christ, through the church, not the state.

How then does the Christian decide what to support and what to reject in politics? How does one decide whom to support in elections? For what kinds of laws should the believer work and fight? Robert Dugan, former director of the National Association of Evangelicals,

suggests five major principles to guide the Christian in assessing potential candidates and laws:

1. *The preeminence of religious liberty*—Any candidate or legislation
that restricts the practice of religious faith should be resisted.

2. *The protection of life as sacred*—Candidates or legislation that treat
life frivolously or that seek to destroy it (e.g., abortion, euthanasia, infanticide) should be resisted and defeated.

3. *Provision of justice for all*—Candidates and legislation must reflect
God's concern for justice and equity. The book of Amos is convincing evidence that God desires government to promote laws that protect the poor
and disadvantaged from exploitation and oppression.

4. *Preservation of the traditional family*—One of the clear teachings
of the Bible is that the family is a critical institution to God. Legislation
that negatively impacts the family should be rejected. For example, tax
legislation that promotes single-parent families or penalizes a father for
living with his family is counterproductive. The promotion of same-sex
marriages runs counter to God's revelation and should be rejected.

5. *The promotion of Judeo-Christian values in education and legislation*—For example, values of honesty, integrity, personal responsibility,
and accountability can be easily undermined by a leader who wantonly
lies and shows disrespect for the law. Fraud, bribery, and corruption
undermine public trust and confidence and are terribly destructive.
Education must reinforce the values of parents and not undermine their
authority (Deut. 6:1-10).[8]

Christians, then, as salt and light (Matt. 5:13-16), should seek to
effect righteous change in the culture through the political process, not
because the kingdom comes from Washington, but because God expects
us to be serving and waiting (1 Thess. 1:9-10).

THE ROLE OF THE CHURCH

Should the church as a local body of believers function as a political
caucus or coalition or operate at any other level of political activity?
Some Christians believe local churches should not be involved in political activities. They reason, first, that the laws of the United States are
clear concerning local churches not engaging in *direct* political activities (endorsing a particular candidate). To do so would violate (and
possibly result in the loss of) the nonprofit status for the organizations.
Secondly, the Bible gives no mandate or even logical inference for local
church political activity. Thirdly, there is no evidence of the early church
being involved in politics. Furthermore, the local church often lacks

the necessary expertise for reasoned political involvement and can even find its witness severely harmed. The local church is a spiritual body, rooted in God's revelation. Christians should individually be involved in the political arena, but the local church will do so to its peril.

On the other hand, some Christians believe the local church is not ordained as a political body; yet because individuals are charged with this responsibility, the collective group involvement can most certainly impact politics and government. Therefore, local churches *should be* involved with political issues relating to morality and justice.

Christians walk a careful balance between understanding the Christian obligation toward the state and seeking to influence that state for righteousness and justice. The two spheres of the Christian's life—the church and the state—must be kept in balance. Each has a divine job to do; neither should encroach upon the responsibility of the other.

FOR FURTHER DISCUSSION

1. Discuss why Mark 12:13-17 is foundational for the Christian's obligation toward the state.
2. What are three reasons the author suggests for the Christian's obligation to the state?
3. Summarize the specific political responsibility of each of these (when possible use Scripture references):
   - respect
   - obedience
   - payment of taxes
   - prayer
4. Should a Christian ever actively disobey the state? Is there biblical support for civil disobedience? What does Lynn Buzzard suggest as guidelines for this difficult topic?
5. What are some inferences, according to the author, for a Christian living in a democracy?
6. What is the "political illusion"? What guidelines does Robert Dugan suggest for Christian involvement in politics?
7. Should the church as a local body ever support a political candidate? Should it form a political caucus? Summarize the author's points.

Chapter Nine

THE ETHICAL
CHALLENGE OF WAR
AND CAPITAL PUNISHMENT

WAR AND CAPITAL punishment are perhaps the most excruciating ethical challenges for the Christian. As chapters 4 and 5 have shown, life is of infinite value to God and must always be respected and valued. Yet many Christians argue that it is proper and just to engage in war and kill other human beings created in God's image. Furthermore, Christians are involved in making and then deploying weapons of mass destruction. Is this justifiable in terms of God's Word? Finally, many Christians argue strongly for the right of the state to take the life of another human being who commits premeditated murder and other especially heinous crimes. How do we approach these difficult questions biblically?

A MATTER OF DEFINITION

The difference between *kill* and *murder* is critical in a discussion about war. Many Christians do not see a difference between these two terms, but the Bible does. The King James Version renders Exodus 20:13 as "Thou shalt not kill," while the New International Version renders the same verse, "You shall not murder." The Hebrew term in this case, *rasah*, does mean to kill, but it is never used in relation to animals and is always associated with murder. Furthermore, it is never used of killing an enemy in battle.[1] Therefore, not all life-taking is murder.

Two examples exist in the Old Testament. First is Genesis 9:6: "Whoever sheds man's blood, by man his blood shall be shed, for in the image of God He made man." God gave this principle to Noah before the Mosaic Law, and it was restated in Numbers 35 as part of the Mosaic Code. As Charles Ryrie states, "One can conclude that when the theocracy [of Israel] took the life of a murderer (i.e., one who violated the sixth commandment) the state (and particularly those who actually performed the execution) was not guilty of murder."[2] The second example is the conquest of Canaan. In Deuteronomy 20:10-18, God revealed His rules for war. It is clear from these regulations that Israel was not guilty of murder because they were the instruments of God's holy judgment.

Within the evangelical community there are three major positions on the problem of war. Each is defended biblically and held by committed Christians. The purpose of this part of the chapter is to review each position and offer the biblical defense of each. A short critique closes each section.

BIBLICAL PACIFISM

This position is based on God's call to be Christ's disciple. The Christian is to accept the person and teachings of Jesus and follow in His footsteps, regardless of the consequences. This includes Jesus' command to love your enemies. The goal of biblical pacifism is to lead people to a saving knowledge of Jesus Christ, bringing reconciliation with God and others and becoming ministers of the gospel of reconciliation to everyone. This goal, the pacifist argues, cannot be attained while at the same time participating in a program of ill will, retaliation, or war.

For the pacifist, the Old Testament does not justify war any more than it does polygamy or slavery. Christ came as the fulfillment of the Law, and He is God's final message. John Drescher, a defender of biblical pacifism, humorously states that the Christian cannot say, "Love your enemies [except in wartime]; Put up the sword in its place, for all that take the sword shall perish with the sword [except when the government tells me to fight]; If a man says, 'I love God,' and hates his brother, he is a liar [except when he fights in a war]; Bless those who persecute you, bless and curse not [except when my country is at war]."[3]

Killing is wrong, the pacifist categorically declares. That is the point of Exodus 20:13, buttressed with Jesus' words in Matthew 5:39: "Do not resist an evil person." The Christian is always to take the higher moral ground by protecting and securing human life. That is why war, to the pacifist, is simply mass murder, whether done within one's own society or in another. Instead, Christians are to love enemies, not kill them, which is the simple point of Matthew 5:44 and Romans 12:19-21. Myron Augsburger, a stern pacifist, declares that Jesus "never sanctioned war, never approved violence." Instead, His "every word and action repudiated man's way of hate, murder, violence and self-defense. . . ."[4]

For this reason, argues the pacifist, nonviolence is a higher form of resistance; that is, violence is not the only viable option. John Stott reviews a case from World War II to illustrate: "In his interviews with German generals after World War II, Liddell-Hart found that 'violent forms of resistance had not been very effective or troublesome to them,' for they knew how to cope with these. But they had been baffled and disconcerted by the nonviolent resistance which they encountered in Denmark, Holland and Norway."[5] War breeds more war, and it means Christians will kill other Christians, a reprehensible option for Christ's disciples.

The major New Testament support for pacifism is the Sermon on the Mount. Jesus addressed people who were under oppressive foreign occupation. He did not advocate political revolution but only spiritual revolution. Jesus demanded active peacemaking—like going the extra mile—which could change the oppression and vengeful hatred into a new relationship of willful service and reconciliation. Furthermore, His life was characterized by love and nonviolence in His relationships with people and in His death. He, therefore, demonstrated the way of peace. This is powerfully illustrated in His statement: "My kingdom is not of this world. If My kingdom were of this world, then My servants would be fighting . . . but as it is, My kingdom is not of this realm" (John 18:36).

In Romans 13, Paul declares that authorities are established by God and that the believer is to be submissive to government commands as long as these do not violate God's laws. If obedience to God conflicts with human authority, Christians must be willing to bear the consequences as Christ and His disciples did. Full allegiance must be to God first. The New Testament relationship between Christians and the state is to "pray for and honor always, to overthrow never, and to obey when not in conflict with God's will."[6]

Scripture lays out clearly the pacifist lifestyle. To kill a non-Christian in war would be taking away any further opportunity for that person to be saved from sin. Christians are to sacrifice their lives for their brother, not kill him. For Christians to be fighting Christians is to make Caesar lord, not Jesus.[7] Believers are to love their enemies. If force is necessary, it must be imposed in such a manner that reconciliation will result. The gospel forbids force that results in death. God's children put their faith to work by giving help to the needy and bearing one another's burdens. This is the opposite of militarism. The Christian is a peacemaker. Menno Simons argued:

> The regenerated do not go to war, nor engage in strife. They are the
> children of peace who have beaten their swords into plowshares and

their spears into pruning hooks and know of no war. Since we are to be conformed to the image of Christ, how can we then fight our enemies with the sword? Spears and swords of iron we leave to those who, alas, consider human blood and swine's blood of well-nigh equal value.[8]

CHRISTIAN ACTIVISM

This view represents the conviction that it is right to participate in war; it is the conviction, "my country, right or wrong." Governments are given authority to punish evil in both the Old Testament and the New Testament. Genesis 9:5-6 is the beginning of government with the authority to shed blood, presumably to deal with other nations who commit aggression and violence. Another key biblical passage is Romans 13:1-7, which for this position argues that government is established by God, and Christians must therefore submit. Verse 4 sees the ruler as a "minister" of God who "wields the sword" for justice. Since the obligation of the Christian is submission to the state, and since the state has the responsibility to use force, Christians should fight.[9] Personal feelings really play no role at all.

For the activist, government is the only guarantee of order and security. If there is no government, there will be anarchy. Thus, individuals who share the benefits of government must also share in its defense when that is necessary. It is just, according to this position, for the citizen to fulfill this obligation. Partial or total refusal to participate in defending the nation and obeying the government will further lead to anarchy and chaos. Citizens cannot, therefore, be given the freedom to choose to participate or not participate in war.

The major challenge for this view is when the state's commands contradict God's commands. When the apostles were charged by the Sanhedrin not to preach the gospel, they responded, "we must obey God rather than men" (Acts 5:29). Similarly, in the Old Testament, Shadrach, Meshach, and Abednego disobeyed an order to bow down to an idol (Dan. 3), as did Daniel when he was ordered not to pray (Dan. 6). These several biblical examples demonstrate the weakness of the activist position. The Christian obeys government until it is a sin to do so.

THE JUST WAR TRADITION

Pacifism and activism are the two extremes on the war issue. Pacifism says it is not right to participate in war; activism says it is right and necessary. Through the history of the church, a mediating view has developed called the just war tradition. This tradition sees some wars as unjust and some as just. The challenge lies in discerning which wars are just.

Since the time of the fifth-century theologian Augustine, the majority of Christians have accepted the proposition that a set of criteria exists whereby a war and its methods are deemed just. What follows is a summary of the most widely accepted criteria for the just war tradition:

1. *A just cause*—A just cause for the use of force exists whenever it is necessary either to repel an unjust attack, to retake something wrongly taken, or to punish evil. An example of this criterion is Saddam Hussein's invasion of Kuwait in 1990. Ethically speaking, just war theorists argue, Saddam's action was a flagrant case of aggression, and therefore it was justifiable for the world community to repel his unjust aggression.

2. *Right authority*—This criterion focuses on established, legitimate, and properly constituted authority using force for a "just cause." In the United States this "right authority" consists in the powers granted to the President of the United States, by the War Powers Act or by a congressional declaration of war. In international affairs today, "right authority" might involve action by the UN Security Council authorizing the use of force. The point of this criterion focuses on legitimate authority, not private individuals who wage war.

3. *Right intention*—This criterion stresses the end goal for the use of force. The aim must be, for example, to turn back or undo aggression and then to deter such aggression in the future. The end for the use of force must be peace, not aggression or continued war. Again, the Gulf War of 1991 offers an example of this just war criterion. The world community had no aggressive aims against the territory or people of Iraq. "Right intention" in this conflict meant rolling back Saddam's aggression, establishing the peace of the Middle East, and assuring that safeguards would protect that peace in the future.

4. *Proportionate means*—As a criterion, this point centers on just means in the use of force; it must be appropriate to the goal. For example, allowing aggression to stand, this view argues, is condoning an evil in itself and opening the door to yet further evil. Therefore, military force, whether land, air, or sea forces are involved, must be proportionate to the goal. Using nuclear weapons, for example, would be disproportionate in rolling back aggression of an underdeveloped nation with no air force or navy. Using chemical and biological weapons is another example of disproportionate means.

5. *Last resort*—This criterion involves the legitimate government using all diplomatic and foreign policy resources, including economic

sanctions, to force the aggressive nation to pull back. If the aggressor responds with intransigence and continued belligerence, the legitimate government has no choice but use of military force. Again, the Iraq crisis of 1990-1991 offers a classic example of this criterion: The allies used economic sanctions, diplomatic activity, and personal diplomacy to change Saddam Hussein's aggressive actions against Kuwait. He refused. Therefore, just war advocates argue, the world community was just in rolling back his aggressive actions.

6. *Reasonable chance of success*—A war cannot be just unless there is some prospect of success. Otherwise lives will be needlessly taken in pursuit of a hopeless cause.

7. *Noncombatant immunity*—This is the most difficult criterion for the just war position. The military force must not directly use noncombatants in war or intentionally target them. Of course this means going to all ends not to intentionally and indiscriminately attack civilians or bomb civilian neighborhoods.

With the advent of weapons of mass destruction, whether nuclear or chemical or biological, one sees how difficult this criterion becomes for modern warfare. Noncombatant immunity does not exist. Because entire populations are decimated, neither does proportionate means. This is why many Christians argue that nuclear warfare does not meet this just war criterion and is therefore immoral and a sin.[10]

In summary, the just war position argues that war must be fought only for a just cause and not to pursue aggrandizement, glory, or vengeance. War must be declared by a legitimate authority and have a reasonable chance of success. The resulting good must outweigh the evil of warfare and of allowing the wrongdoing that provokes the war to continue. War must be a last resort after less violent approaches have failed. Civilian populations must not be deliberately attacked, every effort must be made to minimize casualties among them, and no unnecessary force may be wielded against either troops or civilians.

Those who support this tradition give the following biblical passages as support:

1. *Genesis 9:6*—Here we find part of the Noahic covenant where God delineates the responsibility of humans to be instruments of His justice. With the killing of humans comes the responsibility of holding the murderer accountable. This, by inference, is what nations must do as well—hold aggressors and perpetrators of international violence accountable, even if it means using military force.

2. *Matthew 22:21; 1 Timothy 2:1-2; Titus 3:1; 1 Peter 2:13*—In these

passages, Christians are called upon to practice civil obedience to properly constituted authority. As stated earlier in this chapter, this is not blind obedience, for when human law conflicts with God's law, the Christian obeys God.

3. *Romans 13:4*—In this classic passage, God delegates to the state the responsibility to use the sword as an instrument of justice and to punish evil. By extension, this tradition holds that nations must use military force to promote justice and punish evil.

4. *John 18:11; Luke 22:36*—In these passages Jesus deals with the use of the sword as an instrument of self-defense. In the first He rebukes Peter for his misuse of the sword; He does not condemn the use of the sword in self-defense. In the Luke passage, Jesus seems to be allowing for a legitimate use of the sword for self-defense when, in light of His rejection, He instructs His disciples: "let him who has no sword sell his robe and buy one." Again, by inference, nations acting in self-defense are justified in using military force.

There is enormous tension in thinking about the just war tradition. Yet because we live in a sin-cursed world, it is probably the wisest choice among the three major options. But it should never soothe or bring comfort! Thinking about this tradition and then its implementation should always vex and trouble. If a nation fights what it has determined to be a just war, it must never do so with arrogance and bombastic pride; instead, it must fight with tears and with agonizing tension. War should never be easy. It remains one of the most perplexing ethical issues for the Christian.

CAPITAL PUNISHMENT

As with the issue of war, the question of capital punishment is filled with intellectual and theological tension. This section does not deal with how capital punishment is practiced in the United States or any other country. Instead, the focus is whether one can make a biblical defense of capital punishment as a responsibility of the state. If humans bear God's image (Gen. 1:26-27), then taking the life of an image-bearer in a premeditated act of murder ethically demands just punishment. Murdering a human being is an attack on the Creator God. It is a rejection of His sovereignty over human life (Deut. 32:39). But is it just to make the punishment capital? This section will argue yes.

Several key biblical passages make the case for capital punishment as a just obligation of the state:

1. *Genesis 9:6*—As Noah exits the ark, God establishes a new rela-

tionship with the human race and a new code on which to base human relationships. Because of the Flood's destruction of all life, future generations might conclude that life is cheap to God and assume that humans can destroy life also. However, the new code affirmed the sacredness of human life and held that murder is punishable by death. The text, therefore, institutes the principle of *talionic* justice, or law of like punishment. Talionic justice is not harsh, for it establishes the premise that the punishment should fit the crime. This principle is summarized elsewhere in God's Word as "eye for eye, tooth for tooth" (Exod. 21:23-25). The point of this covenant with Noah is that God removed justice from the hands of the family of the deceased and gave it to human government, eliminating the personal revenge factor and emotional anger.

2. *The Mosaic Law*—God's moral law revealed to Moses was not the first time God delegated the authority of capital punishment. This authority is central to Genesis 9:6 and is clearly implied in Genesis 4 in God's dialogue with Cain (vv. 10, 14). What God did with the Mosaic Law was to broaden the responsibility to include many other offenses: murder (Exod. 21:12; Num. 35:16-31), working on the Sabbath (Exod. 35:2), cursing father and mother (Lev. 20:9), adultery (Lev. 20:10), incest (Lev. 20:11-12), sodomy (Lev. 20:13, 15-16), false prophesying (Deut. 13:1-10; 18:20), idolatry (Exod. 20:4), rape (Deut. 22:25), keeping an ox that has killed a human being (Exod. 21:29), kidnapping (Exod. 21:16), and intrusion of an alien into a sacred place (Num. 1:51; 3:10, 38). The form of execution was normally stoning or burning.[11]

3. *Romans 13:1-7*—Verse 4 is the key verse in this critical section on the authority of the state in our lives. It gives the state the authority to wield the "sword" in its role as the punisher of evil: "it [the civil ruler] does not bear the sword for nothing; for it is a minister of God, an avenger who brings wrath on the one who practices evil." The word used for sword here is *machaira*, which refers not only to a sword used in battle, but also to a sword used in executions, as when Herod killed James, the brother of John, in Acts 12:1-2.[12] Paul's use of this word gives strong support to the idea that the state receives from God the authority to execute. It gives no help in deciding which crimes are capital offenses.

In summary, the principle of talionic justice, implied in Genesis 4:10, 14, was clearly instituted in Genesis 9:6 and reaffirmed quite broadly in the Mosaic Law. It is likewise power delegated to the state according to Romans 13:4. The New Testament did not negate the Old Testament standard of capital punishment. The continuity of the Testaments is affirmed.

IS CAPITAL PUNISHMENT A DETERRENT?

Both the criminal justice system and theologians are divided as to whether capital punishment deters criminal behavior. When comparing crime rates of states that use capital punishment to those that do not, it is impossible to argue that capital punishment is a deterrent. Statistics can be stated to posit whatever you want them to say. But from the perspective of Scripture, this is beside the point.

The view of capital punishment defended in this chapter gives focus to the fundamental biblical reason for capital punishment. Specifically, killing another human (an image-bearer of God) demands taking the murderer's life based on the principle of talionic justice. Whether this form of justice deters further murders is almost irrelevant to the issue. Justice demands payment. The universal and binding principle that God instituted in Genesis 9:6 is as applicable today as it was in Noah's day.

In conclusion, whether one is thinking about war or about capital punishment, enormous tension exists. Neither issue is simple. This chapter has suggested the just war tradition as a possible way of reducing some of the tension on the issue of war. It has also defended the matter of capital punishment as an issue of justice. Both war and capital punishment are carried out with remorse and tears, looking to God for wisdom and discernment.

FOR FURTHER DISCUSSION

1. Explain the use of the term *kill* in Exodus 20:13.
2. Summarize in one sentence the three views of war:
   - pacifism
   - activism
   - just war
3. Summarize in detail the biblical passages used to defend pacifism and activism.
4. List and explain the criteria used to defend the just war tradition.
5. Summarize in detail the biblical defense of the just war tradition.
6. Explain how each of the following was used in the defense of the biblical principle of capital punishment:
   - Genesis 4:10, 14   • Talionic justice
   - Genesis 9:6   • Romans 13:4
7. In the author's opinion how important is the issue of deterrence to the question of capital punishment?

Chapter Ten

THE ETHICS OF
WORK AND RACE

SOME PEOPLE HATE to do it. Some love to do it. Some go to great lengths to avoid doing it. Some do it too much. While there are many different attitudes toward work, one thing remains constant: Work must be done. Since the Garden of Eden everyone has worked or depended on someone else's work for their survival. Furthermore, work sets a person's lifestyle—where to live, when to sleep and eat, time with family, and even dress. If a person is not content with work, the rest of life is in turmoil. What should be the Christian's attitude toward work? Is it a blessing or a curse? Is work a means to justify the ends of leisure and entertainment? This chapter focuses on developing a Christian work ethic and discussing the proper perspective on work relationships.

A BIBLICAL VIEW OF WORK

Work is ordained by God. It was His creative invention from the beginning. While we do not usually think of God as working, and while we do not know all the details, the Bible declares that God worked (Gen. 1—2). By working, we resemble God. Like God, humans have the ability to work, make plans, implement them, and be creative. In addition, Genesis 1:28 and 2:15 proclaim that God gave humans the task of ruling over and taking care of His creation. Theologian Carl Henry writes:

> Through his work, man shares the creation purpose of God in subduing nature, whether he is a miner with dirty hands, a mechanic with a greasy face, or a stenographer with stencil smudged fingers. Work is permeated by purpose; it is intended to serve God, benefit mankind, make nature subservient to the moral program for creation. Man must therefore apply his whole being—heart and mind, as well as hand—to the daily job. As God's fellow worker he is to reflect God's creative ability on Monday in the factory no less than on Sunday when commemorating the day of rest and worship.[1]

Apparently Adam and Eve's pre-Fall work had both a physical and spiritual dimension. With respect to the Garden of Eden, God told them "to cultivate it and keep it" (Gen. 2:15). The Hebrew word translated "keep" is used in 3:24, referring to the angel who was "to guard the way to the tree of life." Adam and Eve had that same responsibility, an immense spiritual stewardship, before their rebellion against God. Therefore, work has both a physical and a spiritual dimension.

Work is not only toilsome, due to sin, but it is for a lifetime. Genesis 3:19 says, "By the sweat of your face you shall eat bread, till *you return to the ground*" (emphasis added). Apparently God intends that humans are to work as long as they live. Meaningful activity plays a critical role in what we are as human beings. Retirement does not end work; rather it must include work—for a person's overall well-being. This proposition speaks volumes about the manner in which Western civilization views the retirement years. The magical age of sixty-five should not end meaningful, purposeful work.

When interpreting Genesis 3:17-19, some argue that work is a curse resulting from the Fall. While God's curse in these verses has an enormous effect on work, work itself is not a punishment. God's point is that pain and toil are involved when humans seek productive results. In addition, counteracting forces tend to restrict those results. Until death, humans are always faced with painful, laborious toil. God did not create work as drudgery; that is the result of sin. Therefore, we speak today of "getting back to the grind" or to the "salt mine." Work today is tedious, difficult, and often frustrating.

Despite the "painful toil," work has three basic purposes: to meet human needs, to provide for a quality of life, and to serve (and worship) God. First, work provides money (or resources) to supply the necessities of life. Jesus said that it is proper to pray for our "daily bread" (Matt. 6:11), and a way that prayer is answered is through work. Second, work enhances the quality of life. Work enhances the satisfaction of life and is the strongest predictor of life span, even above general happiness and other physical factors.[2]

Furthermore, psychological and mental health are related to work. A person receives a sense of personal dignity and worth from work. Most Americans, when introducing themselves, share their name and occupation. People who are without work often suffer from depression, poor self-image, and mental illnesses.[3] God gave work as a gift of fulfillment in life. The worker is to enjoy it for more than simply its economic benefits. Ecclesiastes 2:24-25 (NIV) argues that a human being "can do nothing better than . . . find satisfaction in his work. This too, I see, is from the hand of God, for without him, who can eat or find enjoyment?"

The final purpose of work is to serve God. Colossians 3:22—4:1 is the major biblical passage on the proper ethical attitude for work. Here Paul writes to slaves and masters. However, remember that the vast majority of workers in the Roman Empire were slaves, working usually for life with limited rights. In many ways, the slave's relationship to his master is similar to the employee/employer relationship of today.

In this passage, the apostle Paul details three principles on the ethic of work. First is the principle of obedience, consistency, and sincerity (Col. 3:22). The Christian is to approach work as a matter of obedience to God; it is a stewardship from Him that demands a commitment of obedience and a consistency even when the boss is not looking. Christian workers likewise approach the job sincerely, in a conscientious manner. The second principle is the lordship of Jesus Christ; Christian workers serve "the Lord Christ" (Col. 3:23-24). One could easily argue that our real boss is Jesus Christ. We work for Him, and we are to see our work as service to Him, not simply to our employer. Finally, verse 24 states that the reason Christians maintain such a high work ethic is because we know God will reward us. In other words, there is eternal significance to work. Part of God's reward system involves reward for our work. What would happen to the quality of products and to productivity if all workers viewed work according to the standards of Colossians 3?

From this chapter so far, it would seem that people should be excited about the idea of going to work. Yet the opposite is true. Strikes, low productivity, union demands, absenteeism, and high turnover rates are symptoms of dissatisfied workers. Due to sin, the meaning of work has become distorted and twisted. The goal of work today is to enjoy the end product and work only because it is a means to that end—leisure. Even Christians fall into this mind-set. Leisure is not *the end*. Work, as this chapter has shown, is the end in itself. It is a stewardship from God, and how we approach it has eternal implications.

IMPLICATIONS OF A CHRISTIAN WORK ETHIC

From the argument presented in this chapter, it is possible to deduce several implications for a Christian work ethic:

1. Everyone should work. Since God ordained work, humans will only find fulfillment in working. It is the key to finding purpose in life.

2. Excellence is the worker's standard. Ephesians 6:6-7 exhorts the

Christian to "render service, as to the Lord, and not to men," not to be men-pleasers but God-pleasers. God's standard of excellence needs to be the human standard.

3. Respect and obedience are to characterize workers. Both Colossians and Ephesians challenge the slave (employee) to show respect to the master (employer). The master (employer) is likewise to show respect and treat kindly the slave (employee). Love, mutual respect, and justice must characterize the employer/employee relationship.

4. All professions and all kinds of work, assuming they are legal and biblically ethical, are honorable before the Lord. There simply is no dichotomy between sacred and secular work. All work brings glory to God and fulfillment to the human if it is done to God's glory (1 Cor. 10:31).

5. Work provides an opportunity for a witness. As the disciple of Christ follows a Christian work ethic, he or she manifests a powerful message, both verbal and nonverbal, of a supernatural approach to work. The world today needs this powerful witness.

6. Work is actually a form of worship. Such an attitude cultivates honesty, integrity, and excellence.

In conclusion, the gospel of Jesus Christ brings total transformation to the human being. It brings personal responsibility, dignity, and purpose—core values for a productive, God-centered work ethic. The Christian's daily job is a daily offering to God. This is a transformational, supernatural, eternally significant perspective on the mundane chore called work.

THE ETHICS OF RACE

America has a history littered with ugly manifestations of the sin of racism. Principally, the United States institutionalized chattel slavery, which was fundamentally racist in its orientation; it centered on the enslavement of Africans. It took the bitter and costly Civil War (1861-1865) to destroy this monstrous evil. Many years have passed since the Civil Rights Acts of 1964 and 1965, which freed African-Americans from legalized segregation, denial of voting rights, and blanket discrimination in the labor market. Racial identification of any kind no longer presents a hindrance to voting privileges. The African-American representation in the House of Representatives is now approaching its proportion to the total population. Although minorities (particularly African-American) are far from economic parity with Caucasians, high positions in government, the military, business, and education are attainable for them.

Nevertheless, almost everyone agrees that something remains wrong, and the dream of Martin Luther King, Jr., for an integrated society where people would be judged by character rather than color has not been fully realized. Racism, in all its ugliness, remains a part of American society. What does God's Word say about race? How should we view people of a different color? What is the biblical solution to the ongoing remnants of racism toward all minorities in America?

There are several biblical passages critical to forming Christ-mindedness on the subject of race:

1 Corinthians 1:18—The apostle Paul establishes that from God's viewpoint there are only two groups of human beings: those who are with Christ and those who are without Christ—in other words, those who have trusted Jesus Christ as Savior and those who have not. The Bible does not allow for racial differences as a basis for discrimination or ranking of humans. Jesus' death on Calvary's cross was for *all* of humanity—red, black, brown, yellow, and white.

Genesis 9:20-27—Historically, this passage has been used to justify the enslavement of the black race that occurred in the United States after 1619. Since some of Ham's descendants populated Africa, Noah's curse (some conclude) must therefore apply to all those who are from Africa. Many in the southern part of the United States prior to the Civil War used this argument to justify racial slavery. Unfortunately this perception about Noah's curse remains today.

The behavior of Noah after the Flood provided the occasion for Ham's sin. There is a remarkable contrast between Noah's conduct before the Flood and after. Noah, who walked in righteousness with God, planted a vineyard, became drunk, and lay naked in his tent. Unfortunately, since the Fall, drunkenness or nakedness can lead to personal slavery or decadence!

Noah's actions induce Ham's sin. Verse 22 states that Ham "saw the nakedness of his father, and told his two brothers." Despite many interpretations, there is no clear evidence that Ham did anything other than see his father's nakedness. As Allen Ross makes clear, "Nakedness in the Old Testament was from the beginning a thing of shame for fallen humankind. For Adam and Eve as sinners, the state of nakedness was both undignified and vulnerable. . . .To be exposed meant to be unprotected; to see someone uncovered was to bring dishonor and to gain advantage for potential exploitation."[4] By stressing that Ham entered and saw Noah's nakedness, Genesis depicts Ham's looking as a moral flaw, a first step in the abandonment of a moral code. In the words of Ross, "Ham desecrated a natural and sacred barrier. His going to tell his brothers about it without covering the old man aggravated the act."[5]

But Noah's curse in verses 25-27 was on Ham's youngest son, Canaan, that Canaan would be a "servant of servants" (i.e., slavery). Noah's curse anticipated in Canaan the evil traits that marked his father Ham and so judged him. The text prepares the reader by twice mentioning that Ham was Canaan's father, signifying more than lineage. To the Hebrew mind, the Canaanites were the most natural embodiment of Ham. "Everything the Canaanites did in their pagan existence was symbolized by the attitude of Ham. From the moment the patriarchs entered the land, these tribes were their corrupting influence."[6] The constant references to "nakedness" and "uncovering" in Leviticus 18 designate a people enslaved sexually, reminding Israel of the sin of Ham. These descendants of Ham were not cursed because of what Ham did; they were cursed because they acted as their ancestor did.[7]

In conclusion, it is simply impossible to see any justification for slavery or any type of inferiority from the curse on Canaan. It is a gross distortion of God's Word to do so. Furthermore, as Charles Ryrie affirms, "it is [also] irrelevant today since it would be difficult, if not impossible, to identify a Canaanite."[8]

Acts 10:34-35—The point of this extraordinary passage is that the salvation God offers is to all humans everywhere, regardless of racial background or characteristics. Peter learns that ". . . God does not show favoritism but accepts men from every nation who fear him and do what is right" (NIV). Racial hatred or discrimination is impossible when one sees people the way God does.

James 2:1-9—The story is told of Mahatma Gandhi's search for truth and harmony for his people of India. Raised a Hindu, Gandhi did not believe that Hinduism offered the solution to the horrendous discrimination and rigid caste system of India. As he studied law in South Africa, he believed that Christianity might have the answer. Hoping to find in Christianity what Hinduism lacked, he attended a church in South Africa. Because the South African church embraced the system of racial segregation called apartheid, the usher offered him a seat on the floor. Gandhi decided that he might as well remain a Hindu, for Christianity has its own caste system as well. What a tragedy!

James 2 will have none of this. James decries the typical situation of the early church where the wealthy were given a place of privilege and honor in worship, while the poor were only permitted to sit on the floor. Such discriminatory practices violate God's royal law: "Love your neighbor as yourself." To show favoritism is sin; it desecrates God's standard of love.

The church of Jesus Christ should therefore model the supernatural impartiality that refuses to discriminate. The church should model reconciliation of all races and ethnic groups. It should cut the radical path for all of society, for it alone sees people the way God sees them: Whatever race or ethnic background, all need Jesus Christ, and all bear His image. The church has the radical solution to society's struggle with racial and ethnic differences. It is a supernatural solution—disciples of Jesus Christ who have experienced His salvation and who love one another with the supernatural love of their Savior. All the world needs to see this radical solution lived out.

FOR FURTHER DISCUSSION

1. Show from Scripture that work predated the Fall of Adam and Eve into sin.
2. In what sense does work have a spiritual dimension? Explain.
3. What does the author argue are the three purposes for work?
4. From Colossians 3:21—4:1, summarize the apostle Paul's three principles for work.
5. List and describe the author's six implications of a Christian work ethic.
6. Using the following Scripture passages, show that racism is a sin:
   - 1 Corinthians 1:18
   - Acts 10:34-35
   - James 2:1-9
7. How would you respond to someone who says the "curse of Ham" mentioned in Genesis 9 proves that black enslavement was part of God's plan? Be sure to focus on a proper understanding of Genesis 9:20-27.

Chapter Eleven

THE CHRISTIAN, THE ARTS, AND ENTERTAINMENT

TODAY THE ARTS—both performing and visual—are often ignored by the church of Jesus Christ. Rarely do evangelical Christians attend art museums, classical music concerts, or ballet. Such enterprises are often considered secular and unworthy of Christian involvement. The result is that the arts are almost exclusively in the domain of the world; very few Christians are in leadership positions in the arts; nor do they participate in the visual or performing arts. This is a tragedy, for God is a God of beauty, and He desires that His creatures reflect His commitment to beauty as well. That is certainly part of being in the image of God.

Franky Schaeffer, in a highly provocative book, *Addicted to Mediocrity*, argues that Christians have sacrificed the artistic prominence they enjoyed for centuries and have settled for mediocrity. Today "Christian" doodads, trinkets, clothing, and bumper stickers are the major contribution Christians make to creative expression. This is a sad state of affairs. Christians need to be involved in the arts. To neglect this area is to surrender a pivotal opportunity for influence (e.g., the medieval cathedrals).

CREATIVITY—A CHRISTIAN CONCEPT

When the Christian thinks of creativity, it is usually in the context of the arts. Those with artistic ability are said to be "creative types," while the untalented look on with envy. But this attitude is totally unbiblical. Creativity is basic to life. God is a God of beauty, creativity, and variety; one need only look at His physical creation for proof. We bear His image (Gen. 1:26), and creativity is a part of being in the image of God.

Definition of Creativity

Peter Angeles defines *creation* as "bringing something new into existence out of something previously existing."[1] *Creation*, the noun, refers to the act of creation or the product of the act. *Creative*, the adjective, refers to the quality one possesses to create. The verb form is transitive, meaning "to produce, to give rise to something." Several conclusions flow from this definition:

1. Creativity is not quantitative but qualitative.

2. Creativity is a process that involves movement, progression, and change. There is no single creative act, only creative action. Painting a picture involves many acts; taken as a whole, painting is a process.

3. Because creativity is a quality and a process, it cannot be measured. The only way to "see" creativity is through its effects (e.g., paintings, compositions, sculptures, etc.).

4. Because *create* is a transitive verb, it always has an object. Thus, the creative process always has a product. The composer produces a composition, the painter a painting, and the sculptor a sculpture. The product of Genesis 1:1 is the universe.

5. Finally, creativity is an actualizing of potential. Things that exist have the potential to be rearranged, put together, or simply become different.

Biblical Principles of Creativity

Rooted in the proposition that God is the Creator and we are His creatures, the following principles provide the basis for thinking and acting biblically when it comes to creativity. Such a foundation, then, enables the Christian to gain an appreciation for and an involvement in the arts.

1. Human creativity derives its value from God's creativity. In Genesis 1:26-30, after God had finished His creative work, He detailed His creation mandate for humanity. Humans are to subdue and have dominion over His creation.

2. Human creativity manifests God's image. Bearing God's image means that we carry His creativity into our human capacity for sensory, intellectual, and emotional delight.

3. Creativity is to be developed in all persons, not just a creative elite. Since all bear His image, all have some dimension of creativity.

4. Creativity extends to all cultural activities, including art, science, work, play, thought, and action. One of the clear teachings of God's Word is the lordship of Jesus Christ. If He is Lord of all, then that lordship extends to all dimensions of life.

5. Human creativity exists for the glory of God. First Corinthians 10:31 makes clear that we are to do all to the glory of God. Each time

we exercise our creative potential, we are giving glory to the one who created and gifted us. All praise to Him![2]

Characteristics of the Creative Christian

What follows is a list of characteristics that foster creativity. It is not exhaustive, merely suggestive. The list is rooted in the proposition that God is creative, and so are His creatures.

1. The creative person is well rounded. This means that creativity is exercised in all areas of life—social, intellectual, spiritual, and psychological. The growing Christian is a balanced person developing all of life's aspects.

2. The creative person is curious. Curiosity is eager to learn and grow. When we realize that all aspects of creation are God's, then our goal is to understand *all* of God's creation. Our propensity to inquire and to learn produces creativity.

3. The creative person is courageous. It takes courage to learn a new subject, to explore a new area of knowledge, or to do a new activity (e.g., painting, music, ballet). To be bold and courageous goes hand in hand with creativity.

4. The creative person is humble. The realization of absolute dependence on God is the beginning of creativity. All gifts or talents come from God, and we exercise them for His glory. Humility and a proper understanding of self are the keys to the proper exercise of God's gifts.

CHRISTIANITY AND THE ARTS

Many evangelicals have a vague discomfort about the arts. They are uncertain whether or not art has any meaningful value. They are confused about where it fits into God's priorities.

This confusion and misunderstanding further results in one of two attitudes about art: either antagonism or neglect. Gordon Jackson observes, "Whether by the activism of hostility and antagonism . . . or by the passivity of inaction and neglect, the outcome is the same: there is within evangelical circles minimal patronage of the arts, and even less interest in integrating that segment of culture with the Christian faith." Cultural illiteracy, Jackson argues, is one result; little production of quality art by evangelical Christians is another. For example, he noted that out of an estimated thirty-three million church-going evangelicals in the United States, "not even one outstanding novelist has emerged."[3]

The Value of Art

Novelist and playwright Dorothy Sayers notes that the very first thing we learn about God is that He *creates*.[4] Indeed, as the Creator of the universe, God is the ultimate example of creative expression: "If from this world around us we can learn anything about God's character, surely it is that we have a creative God, a God of diversity, a God whose interest in beauty and detail must be unquestioned when one looks at the world which he has made around us, and people themselves as the result of his craftsmanship."[5]

God creates for usefulness, enjoyment, and even as a means of revealing His character. Some aspects of His creation are beautiful exhibitions of His creativity and yet are never seen by humans. Philip Yancey asks the question: "Why is it that the most beautiful animals on earth are hidden away from all humans except those wearing scuba equipment? Who are they beautiful for?"[6] Evidently, their beauty is for God alone. Schaeffer remarks, "we live in a world full of 'useless' beauty."[7] Therefore, art and beauty have intrinsic value.

As this chapter has already noted, because we are God's image-bearers, we are taken "deep into the nature of our human creative ability. For one of the marks of the image of God that we bear is that we, too, in our creaturely way, are makers. And in no human activity is this aspect of God's image more evident than in our making art."[8] Just as God's artwork needs no utilitarian justification, neither does ours; it has inherent value because it is given by God as part of His image. It is inherently good in His eyes.

A basic function of art is that it both expresses and shapes people's values and their worldview.[9] This is obvious because art usually deals with major issues: life and death, love and hate, etc. The worldview expressed in a culture's art reflects the worldview of that culture's people. Witness the impact of modern music and entertainment. That is why withdrawal from the arts is so potentially devastating for Christianity.

Schaeffer contends, "Any group that willingly or unconsciously sidesteps creativity and human expression gives up their effective role in the society in which they live. In Christian terms, their ability to be the salt of that society is greatly diminished."[10]

A related but slightly different value for artistic expression is that it offers insight into reality. Art communicates the familiar in a fresh, enlightening way. Art enables one to experience newfound insights into ourselves, others, and the world around him or her. For example, reading a well-written story about someone grieving over the death of one's father enables one to know what it is like to lose a father. A good painting of poverty enriches understanding of what it means to be poor.

Art likewise has emotional power. It is able to communicate one perspective of truth as nothing else can. For example, one of the best expressions of God's glory is Handel's *Messiah*. This work communicates that subjective element of truth like few other musical compositions.

The Value of Specific Art

Artists create works of art, and the diversity of literature, music, dance, cinema, and graphic arts is the result. Within these widely different fields each piece of art is unique and demands its own critique. If art in general is inherently valuable, is every work of art inherently valuable? Are all works of art equally valuable, or should their value be determined relative to certain standards?

Although human creative ability is part of bearing God's image, this image was marred through the Fall. Gaebelein reminds us, "No biblical thinker, whether in aesthetics or in any other field, can afford to slight the fact that, because of the fall, man has an innate bent toward sin, and that bent is reflected in what he does."[11]

Can such art really have inherent value, really be of inherent good in God's sight? If art has a great potential for good, it also has a great potential for evil. As products of fallen humanity, art is tainted by the human sin nature. As products of finite beings, art is an imperfect expression of the creative nature of God. What then should we do? What criteria should Christians use in evaluating art?

Allow me to suggest three basic criteria for evaluating art and beauty. First, is the artist skilled (achieving mastery in the medium)? Second, what is the content of the artwork (conveying truth, morals, or specific worldview)? Finally, how creative is the artwork (providing a fresh perspective)?

In each of the three criteria, God has an ideal for artistic beauty. In skill, He is pleased with excellence; in content, He is pleased with truth; in creativity, He is pleased with quality and depth. Each of these criteria is a reflection of His character—excellence, truth, and creativity. Without trying to oversimplify this complex issue, it seems that the closer a piece of art is to these ideals, the more pleasing it is to God. But beauty remains nebulous, argues Gaebelein:

> . . . to justify beauty exclusively with harmony and orderliness does
> scant justice to the power and truth the arts are capable of. . . .
> Dissonance in music, stark realism in literature, and the "ugly" in

visual art all have an indispensable relation to beauty. The concept of beauty in art must be large enough to include the aesthetic astringencies. For beauty wears different faces.[12]

To be a Christian is not to be taken out of the world and made a purely spiritual being. Rather, it is to be transformed into the image God had for humans at creation. Sanctification is the making of real humans. (See 1 Thess. 5:23, where the whole "spirit, soul, and body" are spoken of in relation to sanctification.) Rookmaaker argues that ". . . God is the God of life and . . . the Bible teaches people how to live, how to deal with our world, God's creation."[13] This certainly gives focus to the need for a biblical view of art. Such a focus is reflected in Calvin Seerveld's call for the church to recognize the value and necessity of art:

> This is my argument to you Christians: Given the contemporary situation of clenched despair and practical madness . . . how can you live openly in this world, God's cosmic theater of wonder, while the (common) graciously preserved unbelievers revel in music and drama, paintings, poetry and dance, with a riot of color, a deafening sound raised in praise to themselves and their false gods, how can you live openly and be silent? . . . That men of darkened understanding can make merry under God's nose and curse him with desperately, damnable forceful art should hurt you . . . only different art, not censorship, will take this antithesis earnestly and meet it.[14]

CHRISTIANITY AND ENTERTAINMENT

One of the greatest inhibitors of creative potential is television. According to Richard Zoglin, "except for school and family, no institution plays a bigger role in shaping the American child" than television.[15] The average American child will watch 5,000 hours of television before first grade and will have watched a total of 19,000 hours by the time of high school graduation. The lifetime total for television viewing is nine years by the age of sixty-five.[16] The average home today has the television on six hours and seventeen minutes a day!

The effect on the brain of watching television is staggering. Clement Walchshauser observes that "watching television produces highly altered brain wave states when people watch for a mere twenty minutes." It puts the brain into a totally passive condition unaware of its surroundings and lessening the attention span.[17] Obsessive television watching has further negative effects:

• *It demands our time.* It is nearly addictive as it draws the viewer in, resulting in less time spent serving God, family, or others.

• *It determines behavior.* A national report entitled *Television and Behavior* was issued by the National Institute of Health in 1982. The report, a summary of more than 2,500 studies conducted since 1972, demonstrated "overwhelming evidence of a causal link between children's watching television violence and their performance of violent acts."[18]

• *It distorts the perception of reality.* Children especially confuse real life with television life and values. A recent study discovered that 90 percent of boys surveyed would rather watch their favorite television program than spend time with their fathers. Quentin Schultze reports that ". . . the lure of the television is strong for young boys, who especially like the aggressive characters and automobile violence of the action shows."[19]

• *It dulls moral sensitivity.* A steady diet of soap operas, situation comedies, or movies desensitizes, enabling acceptance of what earlier would have been rejected (e.g., adultery, premarital sex, homosexuality, murder, violent rage). Obsessive viewing of such activities produces an acceptance and toleration of acts repugnant to God.

• *It destroys meaningful family life.* Time in front of the television set diminishes time for games, reading, music, etc. Watching television can be lethal to cultivating creativity.

Obsessive viewing of television, then, not only affects creative potential, but it may also produce significant negative behavior. Guidelines rooted in Scripture help us develop wise principles:

1. *The principle of stewardship of time* (Eph. 5:15-16)—Time is like any other commodity. We are accountable to God for what we do with it. This includes entertainment choices and the amount of time those choices require.

2. *The principle of control* (1 Cor. 6:12; Gal 5:23)—Self-control is a fruit of the Spirit. There is no greater test of this virtue than personal discipline in television and/or movie viewing.

3. *The principle of moral purity* (Phil. 4:8)— We must make the choice as to "whatever is true, . . . honorable, . . . right, . . . pure, . . . lovely, . . . of good repute, if there is any excellence and if anything worthy of praise, let your mind dwell on these things." These virtues form the grid to making wise entertainment choices.

4. *The principle of edification* (1 Cor. 10:23)—The believer in Jesus Christ has great freedom, but with that freedom comes immense responsibility. Although we may have the freedom to participate in many forms

of entertainment, most of those forms may not build us up in the Christian faith. In fact, a regular diet of poor entertainment may actually tear down our faith.

5. *The principle of God's glory* (1 Cor. 10:31)—There are no exceptions on the overarching theme of this book that we do all for God's glory, including entertainment choices.

What then should Christians do? Entertainment choices are never easy. Yet in light of these principles several practical suggestions follow for wise decision-making:

• *Participate actively in entertainment choices.* Be a critical thinker. Always ask yourself, "How is this affecting me?" when it comes to entertainment. Passivity is unacceptable.

• *Be selective in choosing family entertainment.* The television or the movie theater are not the only choices. Consider visiting an art museum, a concert, or historical location. Also, consider reading a book out loud together as a family.

• *Read program descriptions for television and movies carefully and critically.* Prepare your children for what they will see and then discuss the entertainment content, themes, and worldview presented in the program or movie.

• *Log how much money is spent by the family on entertainment.* Periodically evaluate with the children whether too much is being spent.

• *Do not stare passively at commercials.* Discuss the product or persuasive content of the advertisement with one another.

• *Practice turning off the television.* Explain to your children that when a program offends or behavior is addictive, it is wise to exercise such self-control.

Psalm 101:2-3 seems most appropriate:

I will give heed to the blameless way . . .
I will walk within my house in the integrity of my heart.
I will set no worthless thing before my eyes;
I hate the work of those who fall away;
It shall not fasten its grip on me.

FOR FURTHER DISCUSSION

1. How does the author define creativity? Do you agree? Offer your own definition.
2. List and elaborate upon the biblical principles of creativity. Cite some examples of each.

3. Comment on the author's contention that television is an enemy of creativity. Is he calling for the banning of television from Christian homes? Do you agree with his analysis?

4. List and summarize the biblical principles for making wise entertainment choices. How could you apply these in your own home?

5. List the practical guidelines for making wise entertainment decisions. Do you agree? Can you add any of your own?

6. The author argues that Christians are often confused about the role of art in their lives, which causes them to either treat art with antagonism or neglect. Explain what he means.

7. What does the author mean when he argues that art has intrinsic value and worth, not only utilitarian value?

8. Summarize the meaning of these purposes that art serves:
   - Art reflects a people's worldview.
   - Art reflects reality.
   - Art has emotional power.

9. List and explain the three criteria for art that pleases God.

10. What is your response to Seerveld's quote issuing a challenge to Christians?

Chapter Twelve

THE CHRISTIAN
AND THE ENVIRONMENT

IN TODAY'S WORLD many Christians are confused about environmental issues. Disciplined but unchastened Catholic theologian Matthew Fox says we should turn from a theology centered on sin and redemption to develop a creation spirituality, with nature as our primary revelation and sin as a distant memory. In 1967 historian Lynn White, Jr., argued that it is precisely the Christian view of persons and nature that created the whole ecological mess. Meanwhile, many evangelicals come close to celebrating the demise of planet Earth, enthusiastically citing the decay as proof of Christ's return.[1]

Complicating things further is the emergence of the doctrine of Gaia, most famously represented in Rosemary Ruether's book.[2] Ruether, a Catholic feminist theologian, argues that male domination of women and male domination of nature are interconnected. She defines *sin* as wrong relationships among people and between humans and the rest of nature. These distorted relationships foster not just economic and political injustice, racism, and sexism, but also threaten the destruction of the entire created order. The Gaia hypothesis holds that our planet is a living creature. The theory, in fact, imputes a kind of divine power to earth. Respect for the planet is the key to restoring the right relationships destroyed by male dominion.

What are we to think about all of this? Is Christianity to blame for the environmental crisis? As Christians, how are we to treat the physical world? What is the value of nonhuman life? How much responsibility do we as Christians have for nature? How does God look at nonhuman creation?

When my daughter, at about age six, was found outside systematically killing ants on the sidewalk, I asked her what she was doing. She responded, "Daddy, Mommy does not like ants; so I am killing them."

Sensing this was a teachable moment, I asked her, "Joanna, do you think God is pleased with killing ants like this? Are they in Mommy's cupboards? Are they hurting us here on the walk?" She did not know how to respond at first. Our subsequent talk focused on treating God's creatures with respect because God holds us accountable for managing His creation well. I doubt she understood all we discussed, but it began a process of teaching stewardship of God's creation.

In 1970 Francis Schaeffer published *Pollution and the Death of Man: The Christian View of Ecology*.[3] Much of the material in this chapter echoes his argument. Schaeffer's pioneering work continues to influence my thinking on the environment and my responsibility to God in this area.

INADEQUATE VIEWS ON HUMAN RESPONSIBILITY TOWARD CREATION

Theology is the major issue in the current debate about how to view the physical environment. There are at least three inadequate theological perspectives in the culture today. First is the equality view, often associated with St. Francis of Assisi, declaring all aspects of God's physical creation equal; there is no difference between the birds and humans. Legends about Francis depict him preaching to the birds and giving counsel to a wolf that threatens a small town in Italy. Biblically, the particulars of God's creation are not equal. Genesis 1 and 2 make it clear that humans are the crown of God's creation. Humans are the only ones who bear His image. Jesus did not die for birds; He died for human beings.

Second is pantheism, the view that all reality is one; all is God, and God is all. Pantheists reason that California redwoods should not be cut down because the trees are god. They also reason that whales should be saved because animals are god. Such is the pantheistic position reflected by many celebrities, the Gaia hypothesis, and the entire New Age worldview. The Bible does teach the presence of God everywhere (e.g., Ps. 139), but rejects the idea that *all* is God. He created all things and is above and beyond His physical creation. Pantheism is an unacceptable, unbiblical position.

Third is a commitment to platonic dichotomy, i.e., the idea that the spiritual world is all that is important, and the material world has no value to God or to us as His disciples. This philosophy views the world as passing away, and so it does not matter whether we treat it well or abuse it. Again, Scripture will not support this idea. The Bible details the goodness of God's creation (e.g., Gen. 1—2; 1 Tim. 4:4). It is wrong to view God's physical creation as unimportant. Furthermore, the physical body is of such importance to God that He will one day resurrect it (Rev. 20:5; 1 Thess. 4:16).

BIBLICAL PRINCIPLES FOR A PROPER VIEW OF THE ENVIRONMENT

A proper biblical view of the physical creation begins with a proper view of God. The challenge is to keep in balance God's transcendence and His immanence. God's transcendence focuses on His radical separateness from creation; He is both above and beyond His physical world. God's immanence focuses on His presence in His physical world. To stress His immanence at the expense of His transcendence is to land in pantheism where everything is god. To stress His transcendence at the expense of His immanence could lead to viewing the physical world as insignificant and a tool for exploitation. Neither is satisfactory nor God-honoring. We need to strike a balance between God's transcendence and His immanence, between His intimate involvement in all aspects of His physical creation (Ps. 139) and His radical distinction from creation. While creation is finite, limited, and dependent, He is infinite, unlimited, and self-sufficient.[4]

Second, to view the physical creation rightly, we need a proper view of humans. The Bible declares human uniqueness. This book has made much of humans as image-bearers of God with communion status. No other physical part of God's world can claim this status (Gen. 1:26-30). As argued in chapter 10, Genesis 2:15 is the corrective to dominion exploitation. Humans are to serve and watch lovingly over God's creation. We are God's stewards of His creation. He has the sovereignty; we have the dominion.

Human beings are both interdependent with the rest of creation and unique within it because we alone bear His image and have stewardship over the earth. Christians frequently forget our interdependence with the rest of God's world. Our daily existence depends on water, sun, and air. There is indeed a global ecosystem.[5] It matters how we treat the water, the trees, and the animals. If they are harmed, so are we.

Francis Schaeffer also argued that humans have two relationships—one upward and one downward. The upward is the personal relationship with God, a relationship not enjoyed by the rest of the created order. Downward is the "creaturely" relationship with the rest of the created order (Gen. 2:7; Job 34:14-15). As with most issues, the struggle is to maintain a balance. We tend to highlight the upward relationship to the virtual exclusion of the downward, resulting in horrific neglect or ruthless exploitation of the physical world. Or we tend to highlight the downward to the virtual exclusion of the upward. The gross error of the evolutionary hypothesis sees humans as the product of the impersonal force of natural selection, not of God's purposeful design.[6]

Third, the nonhuman creation is of great significance to God. He created the physical world as a deliberate act and takes pleasure in it. Note 1 Timothy 4:4: "For everything created by God is good, and nothing is to be rejected if it is received with gratitude." Psalm 104:31 also records God rejoicing in His works. The point is, if the physical world is of importance to God, then it must also be to us—His creatures (Job 39:1-2; Col. 1:16; Ps. 19:1-4).

As Ron Sider points out, it is likewise imperative to note that God has a covenant, not only with humans but also with the nonhuman creation. After the Flood, God made a covenant with the physical creation: "Behold, I Myself do establish My covenant with you, and with your descendants after you; and with every living creature that is with you, the birds, the cattle, and every beast of the earth with you; of all that comes out of the ark" (Gen. 9:9-10).[7] The physical world has dignity, worth, and value quite apart from its service to humanity.

Incredibly, God's plan for redemption has a cosmic quality to it. As Sider states, "This fact provides a crucial foundation for building a Christian theology for an environmental age."[8] The biblical hope that the whole created order, including the material world of bodies and rivers and trees, will be part of the kingdom confirms that the created order is good and important. Romans 8:19-23 demonstrates that at Christ's return the groaning of creation will cease, for the creation will be transformed: "The creation itself will be liberated from its bondage to decay and brought into the glorious freedom of the children of God" (v. 21 NIV).

THE MOTIVATION FOR GOOD STEWARDSHIP

Since we are God's stewards over His creation, what should be our motivation? Are we good stewards for *pragmatic* reasons or for *moral* reasons? The pragmatic view posits that we should be good stewards over God's world because our very survival depends on it. For example, if we farm the hills irresponsibly, we will lose topsoil and harm our ability to produce food. If we wantonly kill snakes, eventually we will be overrun by rodents. If we mine copper irresponsibly, we will cause horrendous erosion. If we burn the rainforests, we pollute the air and destroy oxygen-producing trees, which in turn will threaten our supply of oxygen. But the Bible rejects this motive for good stewardship.

Instead, Scripture implores humans to exercise good stewardship over the physical world because to do so demonstrates honor and respect for God's created order. The physical creation should not be exploited because it is morally wrong to misuse God's created order. Having God's perspective, we responsibly farm, we do not wantonly destroy animal life, we responsibly mine copper, and we cease burning the rainforests because we respect and honor what God has honored and respected. We show honor to the physical world with which God has a covenant relationship. Christians should, therefore, be the leaders in responsible environmentalism. As God's theocratic stewards, we represent Him when we honor His physical world.

THE ENVIRONMENTAL SOLUTION

Francis Schaeffer argues that the church needs to be a "pilot plant" where the proper relationships between human beings and the physical world are modeled.[9] The church, he states, must be a place "where men can see in our congregations and missions a substantial healing of all divisions, the alienations, man's rebellion has produced."[10] A macro-plan for reconciliation would involve five dimensions.

Humans Properly Related to God

For any type of reconciliation to occur, humans must trust Jesus Christ for salvation. The apostle Paul referred to his ministry as one of "reconciliation" (2 Cor. 5:18)—reconciling God and humanity through the finished work of Jesus Christ. Humans will never exercise proper God-honoring stewardship without first being reconciled to Him through Christ.

Humans Properly Related to Self

Humans must see themselves as God sees them—of infinite value as creatures and, in Christ, as redeemed. Because we have God's view of ourselves, we have proper respect for the body as eternally significant. A mark of the redeemed Christian is a commitment to care for and respect one's body. It belongs to God, and to allow it to be an instrument of sin or to treat it with disrespect is to say something about God, for He created and redeemed it. The Christian is no longer independent but forever dependent on the Lord who purchased him (Rom. 12:1-2; 1 Cor. 6:19-20).

Humans Properly Related to Other Humans

Because we now have Christ's mind, Christians view other humans through God's eyes. Christians treat all humans with respect, realizing shared creatureliness and shared value as image-bearers of God. This behavior is at the heart of Jesus' command to love God with heart, soul, mind, and strength and our neighbors as ourselves. The Good Samaritan story powerfully illustrates *how* one loves one's neighbor (Luke 10:30-37). All humans, redeemed and unredeemed, are of value and worth to God.

Humans Properly Related to Nature

Humans are to treat all aspects of God's physical creation with respect and honor. If all of God's creation is "good," then His disciples must have the same regard He has. It is ethically wrong to destroy wantonly what God has created. The nonhuman creation serves humans; that is the point of having dominion status. But humans are God's stewards representing Him. Stewardship also implies accountability—to Him.

Nature Properly Related to Nature

Romans 8:20-23 clarifies the phrase in verse 22, "the whole creation groans"; it awaits the return of Jesus when it will be restored. Then nature will be properly related to nature, and the horrific consequences of human sin that wreak havoc on the physical creation (Gen. 3) will end.

Christians must be at the forefront of the ecology movement so that God's glory is not preempted by a narrow humanistic agenda or an "antihuman" value system endemic to modern pantheism. We must not conclude that the earth is good and humanity evil. Also, we must not conclude that being concerned about the environment makes one an advocate of some form of pantheism or the Gaia hypothesis. The beauty and complexity of the earth are God's good gifts. We must cultivate respect and honor for God's physical creation. We are His stewards, and He is watching!

FOR FURTHER DISCUSSION

1. In the chapter's introduction, the author cites several wrong views of the relationship between humans and the physical environment. What is the Gaia hypothesis?
2. Explain each of the following inadequate views of the environment:
   - St. Francis of Assisi's view
   - Pantheism
   - Platonic dichotomy
3. Explain the three biblical principles for understanding God's perspective on the environment:
   - A proper view of God

- A proper view of humans
- A proper view of nature
4. Motivation for proper stewardship of the environment is critical. Explain the difference between pragmatic motivation and moral motivation.
5. Relying on Francis Schaeffer, the author proposes an "environmental solution" that consists of five levels. Explain each level:
   - Humans properly related to God
   - Humans having a proper view of self
   - Humans properly related to other humans
   - Humans properly related to nature
   - Nature properly related to nature

NOTES

CHAPTER 1: ETHICS: AN INTRODUCTION

1. R. C. Sproul, *Ethics and the Christian* (Wheaton, Ill.: Tyndale House, 1986), 9-22.
2. The Kinsey report was a massive human sexual behavior study conducted by Alfred Kinsey and first published in 1948. The report remains very controversial, and Kinsey's data collection methods have been called into question many times.
3. Erwin Lutzer, *The Necessity of Ethical Absolutes* (Dallas, Tex.: Probe, 1981), 14.

CHAPTER 2: ETHICAL OPTIONS FOR THE CHRISTIAN

1. James P. Eckman, "Preparing for the Postmodern Challenge," *Grace Tidings* (November 1997), 1.
2. Erwin Lutzer, *The Necessity of Ethical Absolutes* (Dallas, Tex.: Probe, 1981), 24.
3. Louis P. Pojman, *Ethics: Discovering Right and Wrong* (Belmont, Calif.: Wadsworth, 1995), 35.
4. Joseph Fletcher, *Situation Ethics* (Philadelphia: Westminster, 1966). This book was revised in 1997. Controversial at its first printing, the work remains debatable for its thesis that some acts (lying, murder) may be morally right depending on the circumstances.
5. Lutzer, *The Necessity of Ethical Absolutes*, 24-39.
6. B. F. Skinner, *Beyond Freedom and Dignity* (New York: Knopf, 1971), 231.
7. Lutzer, *The Necessity of Ethical Absolutes*, 70.
8. Bill Crouse, *Abortion and Human Value* (Dallas, Tex.: Probe, 1979), 1-4.
9. Anthony Hoekema, *Created in God's Image* (Grand Rapids: Eerdmans, 1986).
10. Francis Schaeffer and C. Everett Koop, *Whatever Happened to the Human Race?* (Old Tappan, N.J.: Revell, 1979), 153.

CHAPTER 3: HOW SHOULD A CHRISTIAN RELATE TO CULTURE?

1. Robert E. Webber, *The Secular Saint: A Case for Evangelical Social Responsibility* (Grand Rapids: Zondervan, 1979).
2. Ibid.

CHAPTER 4: ABORTION

1. Section 1531 (b), *The Partial-Birth Abortion Ban Act* (HR 1833) as vetoed by President William Clinton on April 10, 1996.
2. Paul and John Feinberg, *Ethics for a Brave New World* (Wheaton, Ill.: Crossway Books, 1993), 58.
3. Ibid., 71-72.
4. Marvin Olasky and Joel Belz, *Whirled Views* (Wheaton, Ill.: Crossway Books, 1997), 27.

CHAPTER 5: EUTHANASIA

1. Joseph Fletcher, *Situation Ethics* (Philadelphia: Westminster, 1966), 156-157.

2. James Manney and John C. Blattner, "Infanticide: Murder or Mercy," *Journal of Christian Nursing* (Summer 1985), 10-14.

CHAPTER 6: BIOETHICS

1. See the discussion on human development in Paul and John Feinberg, *Ethics for a Brave New World* (Wheaton, Ill.: Crossway Books, 1993).
2. Francis Schaeffer, *How Should We Then Live?* (Old Tappan, N.J.: Revell, 1976), chapter 12.
3. Russell Hittinger, "A Crisis of Legitimacy," *First Things* (November 1996), 26.
4. Carl Henry, *Christian Personal Ethics* (Grand Rapids: Eerdmans, 1957), 210.
5. Wray Herbert, "The Politics of Biology," *US News and World Report* (April 21, 1997), 72-80.

CHAPTER 7: HUMAN SEXUALITY

1. See Allen P. Ross, *Creation and Blessing: A Guide to the Study and Exposition of Genesis* (Grand Rapids: Baker, 1988), 117-129; Raymond C. Ortlund, Jr., "Male-Female Equality and Male Headship," in John Piper and Wayne Grudem, general editors, *Recovering Biblical Manhood and Womanhood* (Wheaton, Ill.: Crossway Books, 1991), 95-112.
2. Paul and John Feinberg, *Ethics for a Brave New World* (Wheaton, Ill.: Crossway Books, 1993), 199-201.
3. Jeffrey Satinover, *Homosexuality and the Politics of Truth* (Grand Rapids: Baker, 1996), 78-81.
4. Ibid., 16-17.
5. See the helpful article by Wray Herbert, "The Politics of Biology," *US News and World Report* (April 21, 1997), 72-80.
6. Letha Scanzoni and Virginia Mollenkott, *Is the Homosexual My Neighbor?* (New York: Harper, 1978). The book is actually a pro-gay theology text.
7. Don Baker, *Beyond Rejection* (Portland, Ore.: Multnomah, 1985). This book is must reading for the church, providing the balance of truth and compassion so needed on this issue.
8. Exodus is a worldwide interdenominational Christian organization focused on helping Christians minister to those affected by homosexuality. For more information, visit their web site at www.exodus-international.org or call 888-264-0877.

CHAPTER 8: THE CHRISTIAN AND POLITICS

1. Charles Colson, *Kingdoms in Conflict* (Grand Rapids: Zondervan, 1987), 109-121.
2. C. E. B. Cranfield, "The Christian's Political Responsibility According to the New Testament," *Scottish Journal of Theology* 15 (1962), 179.
3. Ibid., 176-192.
4. See the United States Constitution, Article 2, Section 4.
5. Lynn Buzzard, "Civil Disobedience," *Eternity* (January 1987), 19-25.
6. Cranfield, "The Christian's Political Responsibility," 185.
7. Charles Colson, "The Political Illusion," *Moody Monthly* (October 1994), 22-25.
8. Quoted in Bob Reynold, "Onward Christian Voters," *Moody Monthly* (September/October 1996), 23-25.

CHAPTER 9: THE ETHICAL CHALLENGE OF WAR AND CAPITAL PUNISHMENT

1. Peter Craigie, *The Problem of War in the Old Testament* (Grand Rapids: Zondervan, 1978), 58.
2. Charles Ryrie, *You Mean the Bible Teaches That . . .* (Chicago: Moody, 1974), 30.
3. John Drescher, "Why Christians Shouldn't Carry Swords," *Christianity Today* (November 7, 1984), 17.
4. Norman Geisler, *Christian Ethics* (Grand Rapids: Baker, 1989), 223.
5. John Stott, *Involvements* (Grand Rapids: Zondervan, 1985), 44.
6. Drescher, "Why Christians Shouldn't Carry Swords," *Christianity Today*, 23.
7. Ibid., 21-22.
8. *The Complete Writings of Menno Simons, Circa 1496-1561,* ed. John C. Wenger, trans. Leonard Verduin (Scottsdale, Pa.: Herald Press, 1956), 42-43.
9. Geisler, *Christian Ethics*, 225.
10. Ibid., 220-228.
11. Ryrie, *You Mean the Bible Teaches That . . . ,* 26-27.
12. John Eidsmoe, *God and Caesar* (Wheaton, Ill.: Crossway Books, 1989), 200.

CHAPTER 10: THE ETHICS OF WORK AND RACE

1. John A. Bernbaum and Simon A. Steer, *Why Work?* (Grand Rapids: Baker, 1986), 6-7.
2. See Arthur Holmes, *Contours of a World View* (Grand Rapids: Eerdmans, 1983), 219; Stanley Cramer and Edwin L. Herr, *Career Guidance and Counseling Through the Life Span* (Boston: Little Brown, 1979), 387.
3. Holmes, *Contours of a World View*, 216.
4. Allen P. Ross, *Creation and Blessing: A Guide to the Study and Exposition of Genesis* (Grand Rapids: Baker, 1988), 215.
5. Ibid.
6. Ibid., 217.
7. Ibid., 218.
8. Charles Ryrie, *You Mean the Bible Teaches That . . .* (Chicago: Moody, 1974), 60.

CHAPTER 11: THE CHRISTIAN, THE ARTS, AND ENTERTAINMENT

1. Peter Angeles, *Dictionary of Philosophy* (New York: Harper and Row, 1981), 51.
2. These principles are deduced from a seminar presented on the campus of Grace University by Dr. Howard Hendricks of Dallas Theological Seminary entitled "Creativity in Ministry," in the summer of 1992. Also see Arthur Holmes, *Contours of a World View* (Grand Rapids: Eerdmans, 1983), 206-210.
3. Gordon Jackson, "Evangelicals and the Arts: Divorce or Reconciliation?" *Spectrum* (Summer 1976), 17-19.
4. Quoted in Frank E. Gaebelein, "Toward a Biblical View of Aesthetics," *Christianity Today* (August 30, 1968), 5.
5. Francis Schaeffer, *Art and the Bible* (Downers Grove, Ill.: InterVarsity, 1974), 17.
6. Philip Yancey, *I Was Just Wondering* (Grand Rapids: Eerdmans, 1989), 3.
7. Schaeffer, *Art and the Bible*, 17.
8. Gaebelein, "Toward a Biblical View of Aesthetics," *Christianity Today*, 5.

9. H. R. Rookmaaker, *Art Needs No Justification* (Downers Grove, Ill.: InterVarsity, 1978), 31.
10. Schaeffer, *Art and the Bible*, 24.
11. Gaebelein, "Toward a Biblical View of Aesthetics," *Christianity Today*, 5.
12. Ibid., 13.
13. Rookmaaker, *Art Needs No Justification*, 18.
14. Calvin Seerveld, *A Christian Critique of Art and Literature* (Toronto: Association for the Advancement of Christian Scholarship, 1968), 28-29.
15. Richard Zoglin, "Is TV Ruining Our Children?" *Time* (June 19, 1989), 75.
16. Ibid.
17. Clement Walchshauser, *Fundamentalist Journal* (October 1984), 12.
18. Linda Winder, "TV: What It's Doing to Your Children," *Living Today* (March-May 1987), 5.
19. Quentin Schultze, *Television: Manna from Hollywood?* (Grand Rapids: Zondervan, 1986), 150.

CHAPTER 12: THE CHRISTIAN AND THE ENVIRONMENT

1. Ronald J. Sider, "Redeeming the Environmentalists," *Christianity Today* (June 21, 1993), 26.
2. Rosemary Ruether, *Gaia and God: An Ecofeminist Theology of Earth Healing* (New York: Harper, 1993).
3. Francis Schaeffer, *Pollution and the Death of Man: The Christian View of Ecology* (Wheaton: Tyndale, 1970).
4. Sider, "Redeeming the Environmentalists," *Christianity Today*, 28.
5. Ibid.
6. Schaeffer, *Pollution and the Death of Man*, 47-61.
7. Sider, "Redeeming the Environmentalists," 29.
8. Ibid.
9. Schaeffer, *Pollution and the Death of Man*, 81-93.
10. Ibid., 82.

BIBLIOGRAPHY

CHAPTER 1

Lutzer, Erwin. *The Necessity of Ethical Absolutes*. Dallas: Probe, 1981.

Sproul, R. C. *Ethics and the Christian*. Wheaton: Tyndale, 1986.

CHAPTER 2

Berkouwer, G. C. *Man: Image of God*. Grand Rapids: Eerdmans, 1962.

Crouse, Bill. *Abortion and Human Value*. Dallas: Probe, 1979.

Hoekema, Anthony. *Created in God's Image*. Grand Rapids: Eerdmans, 1986.

Pojman, Louis P. *Ethics: Discovering Right and Wrong*. Belmont, Calif.: Wadsworth, 1995.

Schaeffer, Francis, and Koop, C. Everett. *Whatever Happened to the Human Race?* Old Tappan, N.J.: Revell, 1979.

Skinner, B. F. *Beyond Freedom and Dignity*. New York: Knopf, 1971.

CHAPTER 3

Niebuhr, H. Richard. *Christ and Culture*. New York: Harper, 1951.

Webber, Robert E. *The Secular Saint: A Case for Evangelical Social Responsibility*. Grand Rapids: Zondervan, 1979.

CHAPTER 4

Feinberg, Paul and Feinberg, John. *Ethics for a Brave New World*. Wheaton, Ill.: Crossway Books, 1993.

Wilkie, John. *Handbook on Abortion*. Cincinnati: Hiltz, 1971.

CHAPTER 5

Fletcher, Joseph. *Situation Ethics*. Philadelphia: Westminster, 1966.

CHAPTER 6

Henry, Carl. *Christian Personal Ethics*. Grand Rapids: Eerdmans, 1957.

Schaeffer, Francis. *How Should We Then Live?* Old Tappan, N.J.: Revell, 1976.

CHAPTER 7

Baker, Don. *Beyond Rejection*. Portland, Ore.: Multnomah, 1985.

Piper, John, and Grudem, Wayne. *Recovering Biblical Manhood and Womanhood*. Wheaton, Ill.: Crossway Books, 1991.

Ross, Allen P. *Creation and Blessing: A Guide to the Study and Exposition of Genesis*. Grand Rapids: Baker, 1988.

Satinover, Jeffrey. *Homosexuality and the Politics of Truth*. Grand Rapids: Baker, 1996.

Scanzoni, Letha, and Mollenkott, Virginia. *Is the Homosexual My Neighbor?* New York: Harper, 1978.

CHAPTER 8

Colson, Charles. *Kingdoms in Conflict*. Grand Rapids: Zondervan, 1987.

CHAPTER 9

Clouse, Robert G., ed. *War: Four Christian Views.* Downers Grove, Ill.: InterVarsity, 1981.

Craigie, Peter. *The Problem of War in the Old Testament.* Grand Rapids: Zondervan, 1978.

Eidsmoe, John. *God and Caesar.* Wheaton, Ill.: Crossway Books, 1989.

Geisler, Norman. *Christian Ethics.* Grand Rapids: Baker, 1989.

Ryrie, Charles. *You Mean the Bible Teaches That . . .* Chicago: Moody, 1974.

Stott, John. *Involvements.* Grand Rapids: Zondervan, 1985.

Wells, Ronald, ed. *The Wars of America: Christian Views.* Grand Rapids: Eerdmans, 1981.

CHAPTER 10

Bernbaum, John A., and Steer, Simon. *Why Work?* Grand Rapids: Baker, 1986.

Cramer, Stanley H., and Herr, Edwin L. *Career Guidance and Counseling Through the Life Span.* Boston: Little, Brown, 1979.

Engstrom, Ted W., and Juroe, David J. *The Work Trap.* Old Tappan, N.J.: Revell, 1979.

Holmes, Arthur F. *Contours of a World View.* Grand Rapids: Eerdmans, 1983.

CHAPTER 11

Rookmaaker, H. R. *Art Needs No Justification.* Downers Grove, Ill.: InterVarsity, 1978.

Schaeffer, Francis. *Art and the Bible.* Downers Grove, Ill.: InterVarsity, 1974.

Schaeffer, Franky. *Addicted to Mediocrity: 20th-Century Christians and the Arts.* Westchester, Ill.: Cornerstone, 1981.

Schultze, Quentin. *Television: Manna from Hollywood?* Grand Rapids: Zondervan, 1986.

Seerveld, Calvin. *A Christian Critique of Art and Literature.* Toronto: The Association for the Advancement of Christian Scholarship, 1968.

Yancey, Philip. *I Was Just Wondering.* Grand Rapids: Eerdmans, 1989.

CHAPTER 12

Ruether, Rosemary. *Gaia and God: An Ecofeminist Theology of Earth Healing.* New York: Harper, 1993.

Schaeffer, Francis. *Pollution and the Death of Man: The Christian View of Ecology.* Wheaton, Ill.: Tyndale, 1970.

Since 1930
Evangelical Training Association

THE MINISTRIES OF EVANGELICAL TRAINING ASSOCIATION (ETA)

Experienced – Founded in 1930.
Doctrinally Dependable – Conservative and evangelical theology.
Educationally Sound – Engaging all adult learning styles.
Thoroughly Field-Tested – Used by a global constituency.
Recommended – Officially endorsed·by denominations and schools.
Ministry Driven – Committed to quality training resources for equipping lay volunteers to serve Christ more effectively in the church.
Affordable – Attractive and reasonably priced.

For many local ministries, the most important step to an effective lay leadership training program is locating and implementing an inspiring, motivational system of instruction. ETA curriculum is available as traditional classroom courses, audio and video seminars, audio and video CD-ROM packages, and other resources for your classroom teaching or personal study.

Contact ETA today for free information and a 20-minute video presentation. Request Information Packet: Crossway Partner.

EVANGELICAL TRAINING ASSOCIATION
110 Bridge Street • PO Box 327 • Wheaton, IL 60189
800-369-8291 • FAX 630-668-8437 • www.etaworld.org